AUGUSTINE ON EVIL

AUGUSTINE ON EVIL

G.R. EVANS

Sidney Sussex College
Cambridge

CAMBRIDGE UNIVERSITY PRESS

Cambridge

London   New York   New Rochelle

Melbourne   Sydney

Published by the Press Syndicate of the University of Cambridge
The Pitt Building, Trumpington Street, Cambridge CB2 1RP
32 East 57th Street, New York, NY 10022, USA
296 Beaconsfield Parade, Middle Park, Melbourne 3206, Australia

First published 1982

Printed in Great Britain at the University Press Cambridge

Library of Congress catalogue card number: 81-21793

British Library cataloguing in publication data
Evans, G.R.
Augustine on evil.
1. Augustine, Saint, Bishop of Hippo
2. Good and evil
I. Title
231'.8   B655.27
ISBN 0 521 24526 5

CONTENTS

De Mendacio (394–5) *De Mend.*

Ad Simplicianum De Diversis Quaestionibus (396) *De Div. Quaest. Simp.*

Contra Epistolam quam vocant Fundamenti (396) *Fund. Ep.*

De Doctrina Christiana (396–426) *De Doct. Chr.*

Quaestiones Evangeliorum (397–400) *Quaest. Ev.*

Contra Faustum Manichaeum (397–8) *C. Faust.*

Confessiones (397–401) *Conf.*

Contra Felicem Manichaeum (398) *C. Fel.*

De Natura Boni contra Manichaeos (399) *De Nat. Bon.*

Contra Secundinum Manichaeum (399) *Secund.*

Adnotationes in Job (399) *In Job*

De Catechizandis Rudibus (399–40) *De Cat. Rud.*

De Trinitate (399–419) *De Trin.*

De Fide Rerum quae non videntur (400) *De Fid. Rerum*

De Consensu Evangelistarum (400) *De Cons. Ev.*

De Bono Conjugali (400–1) *De Bon Conj.*

De Sancta Virginitate (401) *De Sanct. Virg.*

De Genesi ad Litteram (401–414) *De Gen. ad Lit.*

De Peccatorum Meritis et Remissione (411–12) *De Pec. Mer.*

De Spiritu et Littera (412) *De Sp. et Lit.*

De Videndo Deo ad Paulinam (413) *De Vid. Deo.* (= Letter 147)

De Civitate Dei (413–27) *De Civ. Dei*

De Natura et Gratia (413–15) *De Nat. et Grat.*

Tractatus in Joannis Evangelium (?408/414–7) *In John*

De Origine Animae (415) *De Or. An.* (= Letter 166)

De Perfectione Justitiae Hominis (415–6) *De Per. Just. Hom.*

De Gratia Christi et de Peccato Originali (418) *De Grat. Chr.*

Locutiones in Heptateuchon (419) *Loc. in Hept.*

Quaestiones in Heptateuchon (419) *Quaest. in Hept.*

Quaestiones VIII ex Vetero Testamento (419) *Vet. Test.*

De Anima et eius Origine (419–21) *De An. et Or.*

Contra Mendacium (420) *Contra Mendacium*

De Nuptiis et Concupiscentia (420) *De Nupt.*

Contra Duas Epistolas Pelagianorum (420–1) *Against Two Letters*

Contra Julianum (421–2) *C. Jul.*

Enchiridion ad Laurentium (421–3) *Enchiridion*

De Gratia et Libero Arbitrio (426–7) *De Grat. et Lib. Arb.*

Retractationes (426–7) *Retr.*

De Praedestinatione Sanctorum (428–9) *De Praed. Sanct.*
De Dono Perseverantiae (428–9) *De Don. Pers.*
Contra Secundam Juliani Responsionem Opus
    Imperfectum (429–30) *Op. Imp.*

ACKNOWLEDGEMENTS

I should like to thank Dr D. Turner and Dr R. Williams, who kindly read drafts of this book, and the Rev. Professor H. Chadwick, Mr John Ferguson, Professor R. Markus and Sir Richard Southern, with whom I have talked over various parts of it, for their kindness and for their advice.

PREFACE

Again and again, over a period of nearly half a century, Augustine returned to the problem of evil in his writings. The solution he puts before us as he works it out stage by painful stage, is the result of his own struggle with a problem he urgently wanted to solve from the moment when, as a boy, he first understood what it meant. Even when he thought he saw the way to an answer it proved to be full of unforeseen difficulties. One modern critic has complained that his solution suffers from 'a radical incoherence'. It was an incoherence which he himself undoubtedly felt, and that is why he continued to work at the matter; but his very bafflement, the very open-ended quality of his thought, helped him to perform what was arguably the greatest service he did for his contemporaries and successors: he set the problem out in all its complexity.

This study attempts to follow him in his progress towards a solution. It is a challenging task to master Augustine's views on any subject, not because his arguments are difficult to follow, or because he does not make himself clear, but because he raises in passing almost as many questions as he answers. It seemed so to his contemporaries, too. His readers often wrote to him to ask him to develop a point or settle a question he had left untouched. We cannot do so now; but in one respect we are better placed than those who knew him personally: we can stand back and look at the unfolding of his solution as a whole, at its strengths and weaknesses. We can try to distinguish the elements of permanent value and those strands of Augustine's thought which will no longer bear the weight he puts upon them.

Above all, we can watch a mind at work. That capacity for making connections which was perhaps the most distinctive feature of Augustine's thought, enables him to draw the threads together, weaving a fabric of great richness and subtlety out of the assumptions and habits of thought of the day. Augustine's solution to the problem of evil is a *tour de force*. Whether we regard it as still helpful, or as interesting principally because of the influence it has had upon

Western thought for fifteen hundred years, it cannot but be striking in its scale and magnificence, its essential boldness and simplicity and in the patient working out of its details.

Augustine believed that truth is absolute and never changes. If we abandon his view of truth we cut ourselves loose from the fixed points of reference which seemed so sure to Augustine and to many generations after him. This is the criterion by which we must judge the value of his solution of the problem of evil for today, if only because if we adopt any other measure we shall not be considering Augustine's solution at all.

Nevertheless, it is important to distinguish between the notion that the truth itself does not change, and the view that statements which were held to be true by those who formulated them must remain true for all time in the same terms. No technical terminology changes more subtly and elusively in meaning from generation to generation than that of the theologian. Augustine himself was aware of this; he is full of concern for differences between common usage and the special usages of Scripture, and he is alert to novelties of usage. He framed his definitions in the terms of contemporary philosophy, but with caveats and provisos. In the same spirit of caution, he took as axiomatic a number of principles whose self-evidency would now be open to question: among them much of the apparatus of Neoplatonic thought. Was the *res* which underlay his *verba*, the 'reality' of which he was struggling to speak accurately, a lastingly valid solution to the problem of evil?

Whether or not we regard his monumental achievement as a satisfactory answer to the problem depends on where we believe the real problem of evil lies. Does it consist in the intolerability of the idea that something may be contrary to the good, in a universe created by a Being who is entirely good and all-powerful – as Augustine thought at first? Or does it lie in the damage evil does to rational beings – those beings most like God and intended to live in loving unity with him; the beings most like God, for whom, arguably, the rest of the world was made? Is the existence of sin the real problem of evil? That is the view to which Augustine came gradually after his conversion. Everything else – animal pain, disruptions to the natural order such as earthquakes, traffic accidents – can be referred to one or the other of these. The problem of evil must be either God-centred or man-centred. We may regard Hell as an estrangement of man from God for all eternity because sin stands between them, or as a region of darkness, a metaphysical anomaly, the dwelling-place of spirits who have no kinship with God at all, as the Manichees envisaged it. The alternative to the view that man is the source of evil (and that it is man that we must examine if we are to understand what evil is and what it does) is the view that God is helpless in the face of an evil which threatens him – or else himself the source of an evil which would seem to contradict his very nature.

The four types of argument about the problem of evil which, at different times and in different forms, have been put forward since Augustine's day can all be reduced to these two alternatives. The explanation that evil is nothing, a mere contrast which makes the goodness of the good more striking, an illusion, is tantamount to saying that metaphysically speaking there is no problem of evil. God is good, and everything that exists is good, and there is no such thing as evil. The God who is the Supreme Good of Neoplatonism remains intact. This is a God-centred view of evil, in which the fact of God's divine nature thrusts out the possibility that evil may exist.

A second 'God-centred' view admits the existence of evil as an independent principle. A latter-day Christian dualism sees God as engaged in a battle with evil. Christ's death upon the Cross and his Resurrection was a victory over an evil which had to be fought and defeated. 'Process' theology sees God himself as a limited being, struggling against evil, gradually bringing the universe to order, involved in a conflict in which, metaphysically, evil is very real indeed.

A third 'God-centred' view says that God cannot do wrong, and that everything he does is therefore good. The problem of evil disappears if we take the view that nothing that happens can be evil. By definition, everything must be included in the sphere of the good, and what appears to be evil is not an absence of good at all, but itself a good. There are elements of all these explanations (rejected or accepted) in Augustine's writings. There have perhaps been no fundamentally new insights about the problem of evil, but merely a shifting of emphasis, a moving of the pillars of the discussion.

The same might be said of the fourth possibility, a man-centred view of the problem, and that is the notion that goodness would be less valuable if it were an inalienable part of man's nature. Man must become perfect by freely co-operating with God. Here, too, we are on familiar ground, although Augustine came to doubt more and more that man could earn his goodness in any way at all by his own efforts.

This explanation assumes that 'Man is so made that on any hypothesis to fulfil his destiny he has need of God's external help.'[1] Whether man had ever sinned or not, he would have needed God's assistance through grace to become perfect. Augustine is sure of that. Ultimately, evil is irrelevant. God takes it into his plan for the universe and makes it work for him. It is the 'creation' of a creature, sprung from man's misuse of his will, and the misuse of the wills of the fallen angels. It is no more than a gnat-bite – certainly not a hideous disease deforming the universe. A man-centred view of the problem of evil makes evil of far less account than a God-centred view. It is an optimistic explanation. Augustine's confidence grew as he saw more clearly the implications of the idea that evil springs from the will alone. He ceased to feel the deep anxiety which had troubled him when he believed that evil was something which threatened or limited God. Without for a moment under-estimating the damage evil may do in the individual human soul, he saw evil diminish before him.

Augustine came to see the world, then, as a 'vale of soul-making',[2] and evil of no more importance in a man's life than he consents (with the aid of divine grace) to allow it to be. There is a magnificent calm about the Augustinian conception in its final working-out; it gives the believer that tranquillity of mind which he and the philosophers alike believed to be the mark of a good man. Whether we find it an acceptable view now depends, not on the lasting validity of the forms of words Augustine used, but on our willingness to accept his premises: that God is good and the author of all things; that all things are good; that man is the cause of his own troubles; that those troubles are an illusion – that evil is, in other words, no more than a deceiving appearance.

ABBREVIATIONS

CCCM   Corpus Christianorum Continuatio Medievalis
CCSL   Corpus Christianorum Series Latina
PG   J.P. Migne, Patrologia Graeca
PL   J.P. Migne, Patrologia Latina

ABBREVIATIONS USED IN THE TEXT FOR THE WORKS OF AUGUSTINE

Contra Academicos (386) *C. Acad.*

De Beata Vita (386) *De Beata Vita*

De Ordine (386) *De Ord.*

Soliloquia (386) *Sol.*

De Immortalitate Animae (387) *De Im. An.*

De Musica (387) *De Mus.*

De Quantitate Animae (388) *De Quant. An.*

De Libero Arbitrio (Book I, 388; Books II–III, 391–5) *De Lib. Arb.*

De Moribus Ecclesiae Catholicae (388) *De Mor. Ecc. Cath.*

De Moribus Manichaeorum (388) *De Mor. Man.*

De Genesi contra Manichaeos (388–90) *De Gen. c. Man.*

De Diversis Quaestionibus lxxxiii (388–96) *De Div. Quaest.*

De Magistro (389) *De Mag.*

De Vera Religione (389–91) *De Ver. Rel.*

De Utilitate Credendi (391–2) *De Ut. Cred.*

De Duabus Animabus contra Manichaeos (391–2) *De Duab. An.*

Ennarrationes in Psalmos (392–420) *En. Ps.*

De Fide et Symbolo (393) *De Fid. et Symb.*

De Genesi ad Litteram Imperfectus Liber (393–4) *De Gen. ad Lit. Imp.*

De Sermone Domini in Monte (394) *Sermon on the Mount*

Expositio 84 Propositionum Epistolae ad Romanos (394–5) *Exp. ad Rom.*

Epistolae ad Romanos Inchoata Expositio (394–5) *Ad Rom.*

Expositio Epistolae ad Galatas (394–5) *Ad Gal.*

I · THE EXPERIENCE OF EVIL

At the age of forty-three, Augustine, Bishop of Hippo Regius, a popular and respected North African churchman whose books were already widely read, began to write his autobiography. It was an entirely personal account of his own spiritual progress, and yet it had an instant appeal to a readership in distant parts of the Empire, as well as to the friends for whom he wrote it. Augustine's story had something in it for everyone; he had been a philosopher and a Manichee; he had gone to the circus and the theatre; he had been to astrologers and magicians; he could recount tales of his childhood, experiences of family life like those which everyone remembered for himself.

He addressed himself to the God who, he had come to believe, had been guiding him throughout his search. (Among his friends he was usually the leader; here he follows humbly at a distance.) Yet there is nothing private about the *Confessions*. The dramatic monologue (we hear only one side of the conversation) was intended to be overheard. God already knows all, and more than all, that Augustine can tell him. It is for the sake of others that he has written down his experience.

That is not quite all. He had always been in the habit of talking his ideas over with his friends, and he knew well enough how to make himself clear to his readers, but in writing the *Confessions* he hoped to clarify his own ideas, too. He wanted to take stock, to review his progression through his intellectual difficulties.

He gives an account of his life and spiritual development up to a point eleven years before when he had become a Christian, and then he looks at the difference his conversion has made to him. The story has its climax in a famous moment of recognition and commitment in a garden in Milan. 'In an instant, it was as if my heart was flooded with the light of confidence, and all the shadows of uncertainty disappeared' (*Conf*. VIII.xii.29). He might have omitted 'as if'. The condition of his mind seemed to him to have changed not metaphorically but literally from darkness to light. In a sentence he gives us the principle which solved for him the problem of evil.

Where light shines there cannot be darkness. When light comes, darkness proves to have been simply the absence of light. Where there is good, evil is driven out; it proves to have been simply an absence of good. The notion was grasped in an instant; Augustine says twice in the same chapter that it was presented to him outright (*Conf.* VII.xii).

It was not a new idea. A century before, Plotinus, the philosopher Augustine admired as a Plato reborn, had discussed the possibility that evil is nothing (*Ennead* I.viii.3). Epictetus, the Stoic philosopher who died about 130 A.D., says in his *Manual* that 'As a mark is not set up for men to miss, so neither does the nature of evil exist in the world', but as Augustine explored it, he discovered that, looked at in the light of Christian faith, it was an idea with a surprising capacity for development. It enabled him to solve a great many of the problems which had long troubled him. He spent the rest of his working life as a Christian writer exploring its implications. In the end it became something quite new in his hands, as fresh in its fully developed form as it had seemed to him when he first perceived its possibilities.

In the first Book of the *Confessions*, Augustine looks back upon his childhood self and exclaims to find himself 'Such a little boy and so great a sinner!' (*Conf.* I.xii.19). In what can he have sinned as a small child (*Conf.* I.vii.11)? He remembers that it is common to see infants crying greedily for food, or screwing up their faces with jealousy to see other children being fed, even when they are not themselves hungry (*Conf.* I.vii.11). Too young to have learned to control or hide their urges, children reveal transparently the evil that is in them. Augustine is in no doubt of the seriousness of the matter. Jealousy is, he believes, as strong in the infant as it would be in the adult. It is merely that infants are physically weak and undeveloped, and cannot act upon their wicked impulses as effectively as an adult would. It is the weakness of his body that makes an infant harmless (*innocens*), not any harmlessness or innocency of mind. Indeed, evil is so strong in the child that it seems to provide the very motive for his learning to speak. He strives to equip himself with language so that he can express his desires effectively (*Conf.* I.viii.13). Augustine's observations of other children confirm what he remembers of his own feelings at the same age. The problem of evil is not merely academic; Augustine has felt the fearsomeness of evil in his own experience. (Even though he did not at first perceive that this was so, evil was always primarily a human problem for him.)

2

Yet this powerful force seems to spend itself in emptiness. The distinguishing mark of an evil action, as Augustine has observed it even in small children, is its unprofitableness. He sinned as a boy by acting against the wishes of his parents and teachers and refusing to work hard at school. This was wrong, not necessarily because they were right in their advice. (In fact their intention was that he should gain a skill which would advance him in the world. The learning he might have had could have been put to a higher use, certainly, but that was not the reason why his parents wanted him to have it.) Augustine disobeyed them, not because he wanted to do something better with his time, but out of sheer frivolity and a competitiveness which was directed at winning empty victories (*Conf.* I.x.16). The sheer inanity of evil is fully brought out in Augustine's description of the occasion when he and some friends stole pears from a tree in a neighbour's orchard. (This was an episode which, for Augustine, had the classic features of an evil action. Everyone knows, he says, that stealing is wrong; even a thief will not let others steal from him without protest.) When Augustine and his friends stole the pears they did so, not because they wanted to eat them, but from sheer love of evil. Augustine was wicked for a purpose so trivial that he can only say he was wicked for nothing (*gratis malus*). The cause of his wickedness was nothing but wickedness itself (*Conf.* II.iv.9). His pleasure lay, not in eating the pears, which were of poor quality, but in the wickedness of the act of theft, which was a *condimentum* greatly improving their flavour (*Conf.* II.vi.12).

Here lay the apparent paradox which perplexed him for so long. Evil is a powerful force, fully formed and fully effective in the smallest child, and yet evil is utterly trivial. To love evil is to love nothing (*Conf.* II.viii.16). If Augustine got pleasure from nothing but the theft itself in the pear-tree episode, then he got pleasure from nothing at all, for that was nothing. This remained the fundamental paradox of evil for him. *Deprivatio* is one thing – a mere absence; but *depravatio* is something altogether more fearsome in its positive potential for doing damage.

Looking back, Augustine recognises the effect of evil upon him as one of obfuscation. He could not see the object of his enquiry clearly. He struggled to brush away the encircling fog of uncleanness, which was darkening his mind (*Conf.* VII.i.1). At every point he found a cloud cutting him off from the divine truth (*Conf.* II.xvi.8). From the other side of the cloud, he is aware, the light was trying to break through, to illuminate his heart and penetrate its shadows. To change the image, we may say that evil is dirt and its presence makes it difficult for the understanding to operate by clogging the mind with filth. Out of that filth God was waiting to pluck him and wipe him clean (*Conf*. VI.xvi.8). While he was stuck fast in it, he could not make sense of the paradox of evil. Or we may say that the sinful soul is like a ruined house (*Conf*. I.v.6), which only God can rebuild. It is narrow and confined (*Conf*. I.v.6), and only God can enlarge it. The inhabitant of this 'house of the soul' cannot understand the problem of evil while he lives in disorder in so confined a space.

No image of evil seemed so apt to Augustine as that of the knot or entanglement. He describes how the cloud of evil tried to entangle him by rolling him over and over (*Conf*. III.xi.19); how Alypius was caught up in the entertainments of Carthage: (*volveretur*) (*Conf*. VI.vii.12). He speaks of the 'knots of cunning calumnies' (*Conf*. VI.iii.4), and asks, 'who can untie that most twisted and entangled knottiness?' (*Conf*. II.x.18). The paths he treads in his sinfulness are twisted ones (*Conf*. II.ii.3; V.xii.22), but God straightens out his actions and turns him back into the path which leads straight to himself (*Conf*. IV.iv.7). He now realises that the question of the cause or origin of evil was itself a knotty and entangled problem (*explicita et enodata*) (*Conf*. VII.iii.4–5); it proved to be full of contradictions when he came to investigate it.

'Knots' form because when the good has been abandoned and the will has moved off course by a falling-away (a *defectus*) or a turning away (an *aversio*) it will career crazily about, lost, without a sense of direction, and tie itself in knots. The knots are the inevitable ultimate result of the first *defectus* of the will. The curve in things which is initiated by a divergence from the straight becomes a twist and then a kink and then a knot, and finally a hopeless tangle, as it moves further and further away from the straightness of the good. The degree to which evil has affected the good can be measured by the extent of the knottiness it has produced.

These images were not new ones. Augustine takes over for his own use several notions which are to be found in contemporary writings. The images he employs have a literalness for him which makes them an exact description of evil's effect and operation as he has experienced it. They are presented in the *Confessions* as though they came freshly to Augustine's mind; no doubt it seemed to him that they did. They almost cease to be images in his hands; like the experience of illumination at the moment of his conversion, they seemed to him to describe not metaphorically but literally the nature and operation of evil.

He sees now that the very attempt to search for the cause of evil in the way that he did was itself an evil thing. He observes that the Manichees were full of wickedness themselves, although they pretended to be searching for evil from the highest motives (*Conf.* VII.iii.4). Augustine himself, when he sought the cause of evil, sought it wickedly (*male quaerebam*), because he followed a distorted route. He should have sought God first and then looked about him to see where evil was (*Conf.* VII.v.7). That would have led him by the straight and proper road to the conclusion that evil could be nowhere at all, because it could have no existence in God's universe. In that way, the attempt to search for the cause of evil would have been a good thing, and everything would have fallen into place. The apparent paradox would have been seen to be an illusion. Now, in the *Confessions*, he is able to write of his search for evil in a good and proper way, because he is beginning from the right place, from God himself.

At first, he had been readier to believe that God could be affected by evil than to accept that man could do evil (*Conf.* VII.iii.4). Before he could make any headway with a solution to the problem of evil, Augustine had to shift his ground and see that the root of the trouble lay with man. If God had anything to do with evil, its presence in the world would be intolerable to the minds of his rational creatures, for it would make him either himself evil, or a weak and feeble God who could not resist evil. Only on the hypothesis that he gave his intelligent creatures so supreme a freedom that they could choose to turn away from him could God's good creation be seen to be capable of evil. And given Augustine's strong sense of the powerfulness of evil's effect, it was a short step from there to an understanding of the way in which one man's act, Adam's sin of disobedience and greed for the fruit of the tree of knowledge, could infect all his posterity and require divine intervention of a kind astounding in its generosity to repair the damage. By becoming man and dying, God demonstrated in a grand paradox a strength in weakness which reversed the effect of evil on human nature. The logical entailment of these steps was irresistible to Augustine when once he was a Christian and understood their implications.

But for the moment, as he reflects on his thinking before his

5

conversion, he sees that again he was approaching the problem from the wrong end, and discovering contradiction and paradox as a result. If he had begun from the assumption that the divine substance could not be affected in any way by evil, he would have found himself looking for the source of a *corruptio* which was powerless against the good, and he would have come much sooner to the conclusion that evil was nothing (*Conf*. VII.iii.4–iv.6). In the same way, he would have understood at once how it was that he himself could both will evil and not-will good, for he would have known that evil was the absence of good (*Conf*. VII.iii.4). He would have seen why it was that of his own will he could do only evil. For if God is the source of all that is good, and all that exists is good, Augustine himself can be the source only of what does not exist: that is, of evil. Only by the grace of God can he do good (*Conf*. II.vii.15). He would have realised that the fear of evil is itself evil, indeed that the more the thing feared is nothing, the more evil is the fear of it, because evil itself is a nothing (*Conf*. VII.v.7). He would have seen the absurdity of being afraid of something which is not there (*Conf*. VII.v.7). All the problems which seemed insoluble for so many years would have vanished at a stroke. Above all, he would have found his central problem solved: how can there be room for evil in the universe, since God made everything, and everything he made is good? (*Conf*. VII.v.7). The question 'Where is evil?' can have only one answer which makes sense of all Augustine's difficulties. Evil is nowhere because evil is a nothing.

It might be objected that this solution resolves one set of apparent paradoxes, only to give rise to another, as indeed Augustine found, but for Augustine it had one substantial recommendation – a conceptual elegance which made it seem self-evidently true when he hit upon it. He had found himself disappointed over and over again by explanations which seemed satisfactory for a time and then left him caught in paradox again. He came in the end to a point where nothing but a 'mathematical' degree of certainty would satisfy him. He wanted to be as sure of the solution to the problem of evil as he was that seven and three make ten (*Conf*. VI.iv.6), as sure, in other words, as reason could make him (for he borrows his arithmetical example from Aristotle).

II · THE PROBLEM PRESENTS ITSELF

1 A Changed Man

When he was twenty, newly arrived in Carthage from his home town of Thagaste to study rhetoric, Christianity seemed to Augustine merely one of a dozen religious and philosophical systems he might choose between, and far from the most attractive. He had been brought up by a Christian mother; Christianity was familiar to him through her example, but he understood it as yet only superficially. It was customary to keep the deep things of the faith from catechumens and to allow only the baptised to be present at certain acts of worship. Augustine came to see this *disciplina arcani* as a desirable thing. He emphasises in his commentaries on John's Gospel (xcvi.3) how helpful it is in making the Christian value these secret things when at last they are revealed to him. But the effect on the young Augustine was to encourage him to reject Christianity because he found its façade unimposing.

By the time he was forty he was burning with enthusiasm for the Christian faith. It seemed to him to outshine all other faiths and philosophies so brightly that no other choice made any sense at all. The change came dramatically in the end, but, looking back, Augustine could see how he had progressed stage by stage through all the alternatives, until he understood the unique rightness of the Christian view of things. What was the driving force behind all this striving? It was in some respects unremarkable: the search for enlightenment and a way to a higher life was something on which many of Augustine's friends were also engaged. He did not make his intellectual and spiritual odyssey alone. He took his friends with him – often literally – and there were always talks and discussions on the way. Augustine's friend Alypius was converted first to philosophy and then to Manicheism; he was a young man given to excesses, but Nebridius, another friend and a man of naturally puritan inclination, followed a similar path. It was the natural thing for an able young man to do in the society in which Augustine grew up; an interest in religion was rather like the interest a modern counterpart of Augustine might be expected to take in politics while he was at university.

For Augustine the search had a particular point. Side by side with his desire to discover where the truth lay and how best to arrive at it, was his need to find an answer to the problem of evil in the universe. This troubled him more than any other single question. At first it seemed to him that Christians left the difficulty unresolved. It was weariness with the effort of making sense of their apparent failure to grapple with the problem which drove him to those heretics the Manichees for an explanation, he claims (*De Lib. Arb.* I.ii.4); when the Manichees disappointed him too he turned to the philosophers.

Serious in his quest he certainly was, but he enjoyed the chase. He speaks of the *scholae dissentientes* of which he had read among the philosophers, the 'diverse' beliefs about the nature of the gods, the ascent of the soul to its true state as a spiritual creature, the role of fate and of providence in men's lives, the place of the created world in the scheme of things, which gave such variety to contemporary religious debate (*De Ver. Rel.* I.i). 'They all disagree!' he exclaims (*De Ver. Rel.* v.xi). This is an expression of exasperation, but there can be no doubt of his own delight in the rousing debate (which had now come more or less to a consensus among the philosophers themselves). The late fourth century was a stimulating time for such a mind as the young Augustine's, serious and passionate, cultured, not scholarly perhaps, but full of life and curiosity.

Many of the systems of the philosophers would have offered him the satisfaction of achieving a high purpose by effort and self-discipline. They provided answers to great questions and a sense of direction. Philosophy demanded as much of a change in the philosopher as Christianity did in the Christian. Seneca, Stoic of the first century A.D., describes the alteration it had brought about in him. 'I realise, Lucilius', he says, 'that I am not only being made a better man; I am being transformed.' (*Letter* 6.1). In this way philosophy met many of the needs Christianity also met. We may speak of a philosophical 'conversion'; Augustine himself experienced one, as we shall see, more than a decade before his conversion to Christianity. The Pythagoreans abstained from meat so as to purify their souls for the contemplation of things beyond carnal imagination. The Cynics taught detachment from the business of the world, as a way to free the soul for higher preoccupations. The Stoics encouraged a piety in which there was a hope of moral improvement for the individual. The Epicureans wanted to teach men how to be happy. Each offered a way of life.

Although he had as yet only an inkling of all this, it is easy to see how, from the vantage-point of his early twenties, it seemed to Augustine a poor-spirited thing to adopt his mother's religion, which appeared merely a simple piety, and become a Christian. He did not reject Christianity altogether, but his education had taught him to think of the spiritual as something lodged in the realm of abstract thought – to which it was generally agreed that philosophy gave the best means of access. Both the elegance of expression and the tightness of argument he had been taught to admire were more apparent to him in the systems of the philosophers than in the book on which his mother Monica's quiet faith rested. She was, as Augustine describes her, full of good works, devout with the simple piety of a countrywoman, which showed itself in a devotion to the shrines of the martyrs for which St Ambrose later chastised her (*Conf.* VI.ii.2). It is unlikely that she had education or wit enough to match her son in argument, or impress him with an intellectual Christianity.

Augustine first lived away from home at Carthage, where he went to study in 374. Like any undergraduate, he felt free to choose for himself how he would live and what he would believe, and he sampled all the religious spectacle Carthage had to offer. He describes, with a profound distaste in retrospect, how as a young man he used sometimes to watch the 'sacrilegious entertainments' the pagans put on for their gods. He used to enjoy the games, 'shameful' though they were, and the performances before the mother of the gods, Berecynthia (Cybele, Rhea), which, with 'lewd actions and filthy words' made a mockery of the purification which was the pretext of the festival held in her honour each spring. 'If these are sacred rites, what is sacrilege?' asks Augustine (*De Civ. Dei* II.4). In later years the theatre often came into his mind when he was looking for an image of all that is false and deceitful. But in Carthage he did not feel constrained by his Christian upbringing. He went to the theatre and enjoyed it.

It would not be true to say that his upbringing in a Christian household left no mark on him. He was attracted by the theatre because he found in the plays stimulus for his own fantasies ('fuel for my own fire', as he puts it), and a vicarious pleasure in the events enacted before him ('images of my own miseries'), not because he wanted to worship the gods in whose honour the plays were performed (*Conf.* III.ii.3–4). He kept up a nominal Christian observance, going to church more with an eye to the girls who might be seen there than out of piety. His mother had strengthened in him a naturally powerful spiritual need and a habit of religion.

In his *Confessions* (III.iv.8) he describes the 'conversion' he experienced when – in the ordinary course of study at Carthage – he came to read Cicero's *Hortensius*. The book showed him the height above his present petty concerns to which he might rise by taking up philosophy. 'That book contains an exhortation to philosophy' which, he says, 'changed my outlook'. He saw that only wisdom was worth pursuing, and with all the singlemindedness of his nature he bent a fervent desire on the attainment of wisdom. This first insight which fired him with a love of ideas was to sustain him through many disappointments.

How far his conception of this 'wisdom' was coloured by Christian habits of thought it is difficult to say. In his description of the episode he sees in it the first occasion when God firmly took hold of him and turned his face towards him, but he was writing many years later, and as a Christian. It would be surprising if there had been no admixture of Christianity in his response, for the idea of Christ which was strongest in the minds of contemporary Christians envisaged him as the Wisdom of God. In fourth-century pictures and reliefs Christ is not represented on the cross but teaching his wisdom to a group of disciples, much as a philosopher would teach in the schoolrooms with which Augustine was familiar.

It is striking evidence that this was indeed a natural association of ideas that Augustine turned, not to the writings of the philosophers, but to the Bible for help in his quest (*Conf.* III.v.9). He found Scripture too crude for his tastes. His orator's education made it seem philosophically and stylistically *indigna* in comparison with the *Tulliana dignitas*, the Ciceronian elegance of the book which had inspired him. Why did he not simply read the philosophers, which would have seemed the obvious course? The principal impediment probably lay in the difficulty he had in learning Greek (*Conf.* I.xiii and xiv). In Latin he was fluent at an early age, but it seems unlikely that he ever succeeded in reading Greek with ease. If he wanted to read philosophical authors, and especially those whom Cicero had in mind in the *Hortensius*, he had to make use of translations, or else puzzle out the text with a dictionary. Shortly before he became a Christian in 386, someone presented him with some books of the 'Platonists' (*Conf.* VII.xx.26), but these books seem to have been new to him then. Whether because he did not have access to translations in Africa, or because his discovery of 'philosophy' in the *Hortensius* was largely an emotional and perhaps a spiritual experience, rather than an intellectual one, when he sought for Wisdom in the pages of the Bible and did not find it, his enthusiasm was easily dashed. Later, he put down the failure of this conversion experience to the fact that the *Hortensius* 'did not contain the name of Christ'. Cicero had misdirected him, to a purely philosophical Wisdom, and although at the time he had looked, unwittingly, in the right place, he had not then been able to see the Truth because his intellectual vision had been clouded by sin.

2 The Manichees

Augustine's greatest difficulty in reading the Bible lay in accepting the content of the Old Testament as worthy of serious study. Not only in language, but in its portrayal of the conduct of Abraham, Isaac, Jacob and Moses and those who came after them, it seemed crude stuff in comparison with the rarefied concept of Wisdom with which the *Hortensius* had excited and uplifted him. Even when he wrote the *Confessions* he had some difficulty in justifying the conduct of the patriarchs, although he now had a solid respect for Scripture (*Conf.* III.vii.12). One contemporary sect of self-styled Christians promised to resolve the problem for him, by their rejection of the Old Testament and their emphasis upon the New.

The Manichees were founded in the third century by the Persian prophet Mani. He believed that he had been granted a direct revelation of the nature of God and the universe. So strongly did his teaching appeal to his contemporaries in many parts of the Empire and beyond, so convincingly did it draw together the threads of the existing Gnostic tradition, so lasting was its influence, that by the eighth century it had a hold as far East as China. The Manichees held that God spoke to the soul directly, through his Word, illuminating it so that the enlightened could see him. Augustine's idea of the

11

intellectual character of spiritual discernment, his distaste for the historical books of the Old Testament, his urgent need for answers which would satisfy him, all made him receptive to these teachings. Besides, the Manichean missionaries were evidently a spectacular attraction. From their arrival in North Africa in 297 they had drawn crowds to hear them and see the Elect in person.[1]

We can learn something of what Augustine himself later believed to be his reasons for becoming a Manichee from a letter *On The Profit of Believing*; he wrote it in 391, a few years after his conversion, to a friend of his, Honoratus, whom he had introduced to the Manichean school of thought, and whom he was now anxious to rescue from his errors.

He begins by recalling the reasons why he and Honoratus began to follow the Manichees. The *De Utilitate Credendi* cannot have been an easy letter to write. He had to unsay all that he had once said, lead his friend back from the positions into which he had once led him, and he had to do it without loss of face on either side.

He sees the principal attraction the Manichees had for him clearly enough. They appealed to his intellectual vanity. An austere, rather obscurantist sect, they offered him a means of showing that he was different from the common run; and they offered him a path to God by the exercise of his reason, a way which did not require him to allow authority to anyone; they gave him the satisfaction of feeling that he had found and held the solution by his own wits (*De Ut. Cred.* 2). Looking back, Augustine is aware of this youthful pride in his reason: 'Who would not be attracted by such promises, especially the mind of a young man who wanted to discover the Truth, and, moreover, a proud and loquacious mind?' Augustine was disdainful of 'fables'; few texts had authority for him, as yet. He had, in his youthful puritanism, a desire for a clean, sharply-defined 'Truth', 'open and pure' (*De Ut. Cred.* 2). The Manichees flattered this intellectual preference for higher things by mocking the Old Testament. Inexperienced as they were, intelligent, impatient to make the great discoveries of maturity at once, Augustine and Honoratus and their friends dismissed the Scriptures almost unread (*De Ut. Cred.* 13). The very arrogance of the Manichean claim appealed to them. The Manichee believes his soul to be not merely spiritual but divine, his body a mere encumbrance, perfection within his grasp.

It was his preoccupation with the problem of evil above all which held him in thrall to the Manichees for nine years. The Manichees did not attempt to avoid the problem of evil; indeed, by finding a place for evil in the universe they made it a fundamental principle in their system. More, they appealed to a deep sense of something at war within himself in Augustine; they recognised what he had himself felt about his soul and his body, 'That they have been enemies since the creation of the worlds' (*Manichean Psalm-Book* ccxlviii). The philosophers did no less, but the Manichees made the matter something cosmic in its scale; they took from Augustine the private responsibility for his own soul's health on which the philosophers insisted, and allowed him to cast his burden into the cosmic maelstrom. When he was young, he notes wrily, he was readier to believe that the universe was out of joint than that there was something wrong within himself (*Conf*. VII.iii.4). He came close to believing that God could be affected by evil, rather than admit that he himself was the agent of evil. He tried every way his wit could devise to avoid the conclusion that he himself might be the source of the evil he was seeking, ensnarer of his own soul, gaoler of the prison.

For a long time Augustine had great hopes of the Manichees. Their scheme seemed to combine the advantages of the Christian explanation with those of the philosopher's explanation. The data of their system were familiar at many points to a young man who had been brought up in a Christian household. God is held to be entirely and supremely good, incapable of any evil; good is seen to be opposed to evil; man is recognised as a compound creature, made up of body and soul. Man's task is to seek the good; he can see his way only by divine illumination: 'This is the way of Truth, this is the stairway that leads to the height, that will lead us up to the Light', says the *Manichean Psalm-Book* (ccxxvii). The truth is sometimes revealed suddenly in a flash of light: 'Come to me, O living Christ; come to me, O Light of day. The evil body of the Enemy I have cast away from me, the abode of Darkness that is full of fear', has the *Manichean Psalm-Book* (ccxlvii). There are echoes of the Christian Scriptures everywhere in the Manichean writings: 'Light your lamp, for lo, the Saviour has come' (*Psalmoi Saratoton*, p. 165); God's light shines on them 'that are evil and them that are good equally, spreading his light upon every man' (*Ps*. ccxxxix); 'I am thy sheep: thou art my good shepherd', says the disciple (*Ps*. ccli); 'Let us worship the Spirit of the Paraclete.

Let us bless our Lord Jesus, who has sent to us the Spirit of Truth' (*Ps.* ccxxiii). There was no reason why Augustine should judge these false coin; at this time he would have known no more of the Bible perhaps than he had picked up from his mother and in his rather casual encounters with Scripture. The Manichean system had all the ingredients he had learned to look for, and he seems to have felt at home in it.

The Manichees made their own deductions from these principles. When the 'Hearer' who sought to follow the Manichees was 'filled with light' the illumination showed him that he must distinguish between the good in him, which was his soul, and the perturbations of mind, the passions and bodily lusts, which were brought about by evil. The line which divided the good from the bad was also held to divide the spiritual from the material. So clear did it seem to the Manichee that nothing but good could come from God that he was forced to concede the existence of some opposing principle, independent of the good, not created, but a First Principle like God himself. This evil force he held to be eternally pressing upon the good and trying to push the dividing line further by surrounding and restricting the good. 'When the Holy Spirit came', says the *Manichean Psalm-Book*, 'He revealed to us the way of Truth and taught us that there are two Natures, that of Light and that of Darkness, separate one from the other from the Beginning' (ccxxiii). Evil cannot alter the good, but it can crowd it in on every side and impede its movement, for the good is not naturally warlike and it does not seek to meet evil with active opposition unless it recognises its danger.

The human soul is perfectly good, a very fragment of the divine substance (*Conf.* iv.xvi.31), but it is trapped by the body and its lusts. 'Do not be at ease in thy body and pay the penalty with thy soul', warns the *Manichean Psalm-Book*. 'The fire that dwells in the body, its affair is eating and drinking; but the soul thirsts for the word of God always' (cccxxxix). 'Bestir thyself, O soul that watchest in the chains that have long endured, and remember the ascent into the air of joy; for a deadly lure is the sweetness of this flesh' (ccxlv).

This is a crude enough explanation, as Augustine later came to think, but it has the forcefulness of simplicity. The Darkness must itself be confined to prevent it confining the Light (*Manichean Psalm-Book* ccxxiii). Manicheism even offered something of the same scientific respectability Augustine thought at one time that he had found in the work of the Astrologers (who proceeded by calculation and analysis and despised prayers and sacrifices) (*Conf.* IV.iii.4). One of the Manichean Psalms describes how God set the Sun and Moon on high, 'to purify the soul. Daily they take up the refined part to the height, but the dregs however they erase' (*Ps.* ccxxiii). The Manichean explanation took away the need to search his heart and to avert his eyes from the troubled state of his own conscience, and allowed him to turn his attention to the world, to argue grand issues concerning the structure of the universe. It allowed him to make compartments in his thinking, and to shut off from his gaze those things within him which were to trouble him all his life when once he began to think about them clearly.

In writing the *De Utilitate Credendi* for Honoratus, Augustine tried to trace out a path back to common-sense for him. If we see our souls, not as fragments of God, but as lesser, created spiritual beings, and able to err, the spiritual odyssey takes on another appearance, he points out. Augustine asks Honoratus to take this as a working hypothesis, and to imagine that he is now for the first time seeking for a religion to which to entrust his soul (*De Ut. Cred.* 19).

Where should he begin? If Honoratus will accept that the Christian religion has now become the obvious place to start (for it is winning so many converts that there are now more Christians than Jews and pagans together), Augustine will try to demonstrate its superiority to the Manichean system by taking Honoratus through the process he himself experienced when he abandoned the Manichees. Augustine found that he was looking deeper and more frequently into his own soul, and discovering subtleties and complexities which were not explained by the bold primary colours of the Manichean explanation. He began to find, by experience, that his own reason was not enough to enable him to solve the problems of the universe. He discovered that he needed help. He wept and sorrowed and asked the aid of a divine providence which had been weak in the teaching of some sects, but which he now found to be abundantly strong. He listened to the preaching of Bishop Ambrose and was moved. His soul had been tossed about, in a way the Manichean system could not help him to control, and he wanted a settled goal (*De Ut. Cred.* 20). If Honoratus will be honest with himself, he will see the shortcomings of the Manichean explanation too.

Augustine came to perceive them even before he lost faith in the sect. His reading of the philosophers (*Conf.* v.iii.3) over the last decade had raised a number of questions in his mind, which he hoped would be answered by the great Manichean leader Faustus, when he had an opportunity to meet him. 'For almost nine years, during which I had been a Hearer (or disciple) of the Manichees with an unquiet mind (*animo vagabundus*), I had waited on tenterhooks for this Faustus to come', he says (*Conf.* v.vi.10). The meeting when it came at last was a grave disappointment; in fact, Augustine found that he was better-educated than the master, and he was able to suggest a programme of reading to him, so that he could prepare himself to converse with the *intelligentsia* of the region. Although the meeting with Faustus was the precipitating factor, Augustine was driven from within to abandon the Manichees by the very conflict from which he hoped the Manichees had rescued him. The problem of evil remained unsolved for him.

3 Italy

Disillusioned with the Manichees, Augustine was now thoroughly unsettled and began to want to leave Carthage. He was becoming irritated by the way in which the students there behaved, coming in and out of his school whether they were his own pupils or not, bursting into the classroom as they pleased, without apology (*inrumpunt impudenter*) so that the quiet of the classroom was shattered and it was impossible to maintain discipline. He had heard that in Rome things were better ordered; and his friends assured him that he could advance himself in his profession by going to Italy (*Conf.* v.viii.14).

In 383 he set out for Rome, against his mother's wishes; she pleaded with him to stay; she declared she would come with him if he left; and at last he evaded her only by a trick, and left her behind weeping (*Conf.* v.viii.15).

In Italy, he fell seriously ill with fever, and when he had recovered enough to begin to teach he found that the students in Rome had bad habits of their own. They were not unruly and disruptive, but they cheated their master of his fee by not paying their bills.

Augustine continued to associate with the Manichees, rather listlessly, dabbling a little in philosophy and beginning to compare Christian and Manichean answers to the questions which troubled him. He was looking for a new direction, but he found his mind *captum et offocatum*, 'closed in and stifled', and he could not free himself of the *corporalia*, the 'bodily images' which restricted his thinking about the divine (*Conf.* v.xi).

Enquiries had been sent to Rome for a suitable candidate for the post of master of rhetoric in the city of Milan, to Symmachus, Prefect of the City. Augustine's Manichean friends proposed that he should try for the place: he had no reason to wish to stay in Rome. His oration, performed as a public audition, impressed the Prefect and he won the post (*Conf.* v.xiii.23). Within a year he was in Milan, pleased at this opportunity to better himself. He hoped that by delivering the annual panegyric there before the Emperor he might win the notice he sought and achieve his ambition one day to be a provincial governor. His mother joined him (*Conf.* vi.i.1).

In Milan Augustine came into contact with a circle of philosophers, Zenobius, Hermogenianus, Manlius Theodorus,[2] who met from time to time as a society. These were 'renaissance' men, adherents of a platonism reborn, who thought of themselves not as 'Neo'-Platonists but as *Platonici*. Platonism had been brought alive again in Italy by the work of two Greek Academicians of the third century: Plotinus and his pupil Porphyry. Plotinus (204/5 – 268/70) was a pioneer, a teacher, an original thinker, but no organiser of his material. It was his pupil Porphyry who produced a systematic philosophy out of his teaching, editing the *Enneads*, in six books of nine essays each. Porphyry himself (232/3 – c. 305) was a prolific writer, and was thought of in Augustine's day as more an original philosopher than Plotinus. Plotinus appeared an interpreter of Plato, and one so close to the master that he was like Plato reborn.[3] The work of Plotinus and some other Neoplatonic writings made their impact on the intellectual life of the capital of the Empire in the translations which Marius Victorinus made in the middle of the fourth century. Victorinus was, like Augustine, a teacher of rhetoric from north Africa who had become a Christian. He had, *ipso facto*, effected a rapprochement between philosophy and Christianity which is explored in his own writings on the Trinity;[4] but, more importantly for our immediate purposes, he had made Academic philosophy accessible to cultured but not necessarily scholarly Latin-speakers like Augustine, whose education fitted them to be orators rather than philosophers.

It was now, in Milan, that Augustine was able to obtain a few books by the 'Platonists' (*Conf.* VII.ix.13), and read some philosophy for himself, beyond what was to be found in Cicero, and the *multa philosophorum* he had picked up elsewhere, during his Manichean years (*Conf.* v.iii.3): and he was able to talk. Augustine's thinking always progressed best when he had friends about him with whom he could discuss his developing ideas, or mentors prepared to give him time and answer his questions. No doubt the helpfulness of the Manichees in this respect had been one of the factors which kept him so long among them.

In Milan Augustine found Bishop Ambrose, who received him with fatherly kindness (*Conf.* v.xiii.23), and in whom he saw another mentor. Augustine went to hear him preach. Uppermost in his mind was the desire to judge him as a public speaker, as a performer in his own line. He listened for technical points: for delivery and form and structure, rather than for content. But something of what Ambrose was saying lodged in his mind, and he began gradually to see more clearly what he had begun to suspect in Carthage, not only that the Manichees were wrong, but also that there were strong arguments for the Catholic faith: indeed that the ridicule the Manichees poured on it could be turned back upon themselves. Ambrose had not yet brought him to embrace Christianity, but he freed him from his last lingering adherence to the Manichees (*Conf.* v.xiv.24).

Augustine now found himself in sympathy with the weary sophistication which made it impossible for a latter-day philosopher of the Academic persuasion to arrive at an opinion on anything of significance (*Conf.* v.x.19).[5]

Augustine's account of the Academy's beliefs is given most fully in the *Contra Academicos* which he wrote soon after his conversion. The circumstances in which it was composed mean that it must be more representative of his views as a Christian philosopher than of his state of mind in the early days in Milan. Nevertheless, it may not be out of place to say something of the Academic position here, because it illustrates what was Augustine's own dilemma at this time. Augustine explains that the Academics laid emphasis upon two points:

> Firstly, man cannot have knowledge of philosophical truth, and anything less is not worth considering.
> Secondly, it is, nevertheless, possible for man to be wise, and his wisdom will consist in his not giving his assent to anything

at all, since he cannot have certain knowledge of the truth (*C. Acad*. II.i.1).

The first is a view which Augustine attributes to Zeno, who held that truth could be perceived only by signs about which there could be no doubt, for they would be such as could not be present in that which was not true. The Academics held that there could be no such signs; they pointed to the disagreements among philosophers, the erroneous impressions of the senses, dreams, delirium, sophistries and fallacies which deceive men in argument, as clear evidence that none of the signs men go by are certain. They concluded that therefore truth cannot be known, and that is why the wise man will never assent to anything. The Academics had thus arrived at a point where the only course open to a wise man was to cease from activity altogether; but in order to avoid living lives of total inactivity, some of them proposed a middle way, by which a wise man might act according to what seemed probable, what looked like truth, *faute de mieux*. That was not a state of mind with which such a decided and energetic thinker as Augustine could long remain content, but it had an appeal for him as a *modus vivendi* during this time of casting about for a direction.

Ambrose captured Augustine for Christianity at last by providing him with the unifying principle he needed to bring together everything he had held in respect in all the systems he had explored. Ambrose was delivering a series of sermons on the six days of creation when Augustine heard him. He found that Ambrose had explained for him one or two of the passages in Genesis which had seemed to him particularly difficult, and which had been one of the stumbling blocks the Manichees had appeared to remove until he saw through their arguments (*Conf*. v.xiv.24). When he heard Ambrose's 'spiritual' exposition of the Law and the Prophets he was humbled; he saw how arrogant he had been in thinking them crude. More, Ambrose was able to draw Augustine's knowledge of the philosophers together with the teaching of Scripture; Ambrose made use of the work of the Greek Fathers who had pioneered the work of reconciling Christianity and Neoplatonism: the Jew Philo of Alexandria and Origen in particular. He offered Augustine an account of the creation of the world in which philosophy and Christianity are united. Origen takes up the matter, for example, in *Contra Celsum* v.59, where he comments on the pagan Celsus' view of the Bible's description. Celsus thought 'the cosmogony' of Scripture 'very silly' (*C. Cels*. VI.49) and Origen was anxious to put him right (*C. Cels*. VI.49 and VI.60ff). Celsus objected to the notion that God rested on the seventh day, because that would seem to imply that he was tired, and it would be a poor God who would be wearied by his labours. Origen patiently shows that Celsus has misread this and other passages.

In the light of what Ambrose was able to say about these matters, Christianity no longer seemed to Augustine a creed for the simpleton. It became the system of systems for him. Although after nine years Augustine had exhausted the Manichean system, to the point where it seemed to him a thin tissue, he never exhausted Christianity. On the contrary, its fabric seemed to him ever more richly embroidered and substantial as he studied it. It gave him what he had once thought to find in philosophy, and later in the teachings of the Manichees – that experience of discovery, of learning more of the truth, which was his greatest intellectual pleasure, and it helped him to a solution of the problem of evil.

All this lay in the future. For the moment, as Augustine grew more interested in what Ambrose was saying in his sermons, he wanted urgently to discuss with him his own difficulties in reading the Bible, but Ambrose was a busy man. He was always surrounded by people; and when sometimes he sat down to read in silence, although he sent no-one away, those who were waiting to see him were afraid to interrupt him, so intense was his concentration. Augustine had difficult questions, requiring long discussion, and although it was easy enough to find an opportunity to ask a brief question, Ambrose could not give him the leisurely attention he needed (*Conf*. VI.iii.3). Augustine was obliged to wait. 'All this time I held back, and did not allow my heart to commit itself to anything, fearing to fall over a precipice', he says, but in his state of suspense he was in greater pain than if he had allowed himself to rush into a fresh commitment. 'For I longed to be as sure of the invisible truths as I was that three and seven make ten', he remembers (*Conf*. VI.iv.6).

In the meantime he talked his difficulties over 'intimately' with his friends, especially with Alypius and Nebridius (*Conf*. VI.vii.11). Alypius was a fellow-townsman and an old friend, a former pupil of Augustine's both in Thagaste and at Carthage, who had come to Rome ahead of Augustine and was now with him in Milan. He had always loved the circus and the games and Augustine had persuaded him to give them up and practise the austerity of life the Manichees enjoined. In Rome he was again drawn to the games and the gladiatorial contests and Augustine now busied himself with the task of winning him back to more serious interests (*Conf*. VI.vii.11–viii.13). Together, he and Alypius journeyed in their conversations towards the point where Augustine was almost ready to accept that the Christian faith held the answers he sought.

An old attachment was broken during his time of preparation. His parents had discouraged him from marrying when he was young (*Conf*. II.iii.8), and so he had taken a mistress, with whom he had lived faithfully, in Africa and in Italy. A son, Adeodatus, had been born to them. Now that his prospects of advancement were good, his mother became ambitious for him to make a good marriage. A young girl was fixed upon, who was still two years too young to be married. While he waited for her, his mother dictated that Augustine must send his mistress back to Africa (*Conf*. VI.xiii.23, xv.25). We may measure the depth of his pain by his almost total silence about her. He tells us nothing of their years together. He found the separation intensely distressing and he fell into a depression, brooding upon death and judgment and the question of immortality and discussing 'the nature of good and evil' with his friends (*Conf*. VI.xvi.26).

(Much has been made of the connection between this abrupt ending of a long and presumably happy common law marriage and Augustine's subsequent writing on the uncontrollable force of sexual desire in fallen man. It may be that he suffered frustrations in what was to be henceforth a celibate life. But there is no evidence that he became obsessed with the matter. He came to think that the damage to Adam's human nature was transmitted to his progeny by a physical act of begetting them which had become nothing more than an act of ungoverned will or lust. He could not condone the pleasure of sexual intercourse because he believed that it was a tainted pleasure. But he accepted that it had a proper place in the procreative act within marriage. His treatises on marriage are full of common-sense, and it is not without significance that he emphasises the importance of the opportunity it provides for the lasting companionship of two souls seeking God.)

At last Augustine thought of going to see Simplicianus. Simplicianus was to be Ambrose's successor as Bishop of Milan, but he had been Ambrose's 'father in receiving' God's 'grace' and Ambrose loved him as a father, Augustine comments (*Conf.* VIII.ii.3). He had also been much involved with the philosophical circles in which Augustine had recently been moving. He told Simplicianus his story and the old man was pleased to hear that he had been reading the *platonici* in Victorinus' translations (*Conf.* VIII.ii.3). Not only had Augustine done well to prefer the Platonists to those other philosophers who were worldly and would have misled him, but in reading Victorinus he had placed himself in the hands of a Christian philosopher. Simplicianus had known Victorinus well while he was in Rome, and he was able to describe to Augustine how Victorinus had impressed him with his learning, and his profound understanding of the works of the philosophers. This great orator who had 'with resounding eloquence' for so many years upheld the worship of the Roman gods, felt it no shame, no humiliation 'to be the child of Christ' and an 'infant' at the fountain of the Christian God, bowing his head beneath the reproach of the Cross (*Conf.* VIII.ii.3).

Simplicianus' words struck deep into the sediment of intellectual pride in Augustine's mind. He could see himself in Victorinus. Their histories were similar, his own position close to that of Victorinus at the point of his commitment.

Augustine's moment of illumination and certainty was still slow in coming. There was more talk, more disturbance of mind; there were tears; but at length in the garden of his lodging-house, racked by painful emotions, he heard a child in a nearby house chanting '*Tolle, lege*', 'Take and read'; 'Take and read', over and over again. Augustine had had Paul's Epistle to the Romans with him when he came into the garden. He had left it with Alypius, who was now sitting nearby. He remembered the story of St Anthony who, coming in during a reading of Matthew's Gospel, heard the words 'Go and sell what you have and give it to the poor, and you shall have treasure in heaven; and come and follow me.'[6] Augustine went back to the place where he had left his book, picked it up and opened it. His eye fell on the passage (Romans 13.13–14) 'Not in rioting and drunkenness, not in chambering and wantonness, not in strife and envying; but put ye on the Lord Jesus Christ, and make not provision for the flesh, to fulfil the lusts thereof.' Closing the book, he looked at Alypius, with a face full of peace (*Conf.* VIII.xii.30).

4 A New Life

At about the time of his conversion Augustine had been obliged by
chest trouble, which no doubt affected his voice, to give up his career
as a teacher of rhetoric (*Conf*. IX.iv.7). He was now free from both
professional pressures and the spiritual stress under which he had
been living until recently. He went into philosophical retirement at
Cassiciacum near Lake Como. His friends were about him, his mother
with him, delighted beyond measure that at last he was a Christian
(*gaudet . . . exultat et triumphat*) (*Conf*. VIII.xii.30).

The early dialogues, written there in the autumn of 386, breathe a
relaxed and yet purposeful air. Augustine and his companions had
withdrawn from the world so as to employ their leisure in
constructive discussion (*De Ord*. I.ii.4). Augustine had work for his
mind, and problems to solve in their company which were important
and interesting to him. These problems were difficult enough to keep
him awake at night, but he had no anxiety about the outcome. He did
not fear that the answers he would find would overturn his new-
found certainty. He saw himself as a man recovering from a long and
desperate illness, physically, mentally, spiritually, entitled to enjoy
his *otium* with no immediate thought of the morrow's responsibi-
lities. He was happy, as he records in the *Confessions* (IX.v.13–vi.14).
The days did not seem long enough to hold his glad thoughts of God
and his reflections on the working of the universe.

The group was an assorted one. Alypius was there. He was
baptised with Augustine after they left Cassiciacum, and was perhaps
the closest to Augustine of them all. Romanianus' son Licentius was
with them, an impulsive, lively-minded young man, just beginning
his philosophical education. Romanianus, a wealthy and generous
citizen of Thagaste who had taken Augustine up as a boy, made him
free of his house, helped him in innumerable practical ways when his
father died, encouraged him in his ambitions and first created for him
the ambience in which he had sufficient freedom from petty anxieties
and money worries to address himself to the search for the Truth (*C.
Acad*. II.ii.3). Of Trygetius, another of Augustine's pupils from
Tagaste, and another young member of the group, little is known,
except that it appears from the dialogues that he had been bored by
student life and had gone into the army for a time. Navigius,

Augustine's brother, first makes his appearance at Cassiciacum.

Augustine sent the first product of their discussions and his first book, the *Contra Academicos*, to Romanianus. He tells him that it is he who has brought him to his present confidence that he will find the Truth in Christianity. Romanianus had offered to relieve Augustine of the duty to support his dependents by teaching and set him free to 'live in philosophy' (*C. Acad.* II.ii.4–5) as soon as he could put his affairs in order (he was involved in a number of lawsuits). Augustine's desire now is that Romanianus should join him in the pursuit of Truth.

Augustine did not put philosophy from him, then, when he became a Christian. 'Do you doubt at all that we ought to know truth?' he asks in the *Contra Academicos*. 'Certainly not', says Trygetius (*C. Acad.* I.ii.5). He puts his mature attitude to philosophy like this: the very name of 'philosopher', if we translate it into Latin, means a 'lover of wisdom'. If wisdom is God himself, then the philosopher is a lover of God, but not all philosophers are lovers of true wisdom, and so we must seek out those whose understanding of that which they seek is closest to Christian truth. Of all the schools of the philosophers he knows, the Christian Augustine singled out that of the Platonists as the nearest to Christian teaching in their understanding. Plato had an idea of God which saw him as the cause of all that exists, the ultimate Reason of which human reason is a shadow and image, the end and purpose of all things (*De Civ. Dei* VIII.1–4). He defined the wise man as one who imitates, knows and loves this God (*De Civ. Dei* VIII.5).

It was not clear to Augustine all at once how Platonism was to be transformed into Christianity. The main purpose of the group of friends at Cassiciacum was to work out the implications of their adoption of the Christian faith. 'God is as yet conceived by me in faith rather than understood by reason', he says as he outlines his plan of action in the *Contra Academicos* (II.ii.4). His most urgent need – and we may suppose that his friends were of the same mind – was to establish where he now stood on a number of matters which had long troubled him as Manichee and as philosopher. The records that the group kept of their discussions of November 386 were published by Augustine in the form of the three dialogues, *Contra Academicos*, *De Beata Vita* and *De Ordine*. The discussions covered the subject-matter of all three books, and Augustine arranged the material later under three heads.

The dialogues are full of the intellectual excitement of the Cassiciacum days. In the *De Ordine* Licentius pulls himself up suddenly beside Trygetius' bed and says: 'I am asking you now; is God just?', and Trygetius realises that he has been struck by an inspired thought and makes no answer, waiting to see what he will say next (*De Ord.* I.vii.19). A little earlier Licentius had asked not to be distracted from something which he could not yet see clearly, but which was beginning to be revealed to him, and which he was concentrating on with all his might (*De Ord.* I.iv.10). During their discussions there would be moments when everyone was rigid with attention, intent with desire to hear what was to be said next (*De Ord.* I.x.28). The conversations were recorded on tablets, so conscientiously that when Augustine's mother Monica came into the room and made a comment, it was solemnly written down, even though she pleaded that she had intended to make no contribution to the discussion; when the group had used up all the tablets they had to hand, they made a break in the discussion (*De Ord.* I.xi.32). Something was being freshly captured in these talks, which it was felt might not come again if any part of it was allowed to slip from their grasp.

Early in 387, Augustine returned to Milan to prepare for baptism. His son Adeodatus was now fifteen, and old enough to join the party. Alypius accompanied Augustine, too. This was a step of momentous importance, not only because it involved a public commitment, but because baptism gave a once-only opportunity for 'rebirth'. Augustine's description of its effect upon him echoes his words about his moment of conversion. It seemed to him that his sin vanished like the darkness of his mind, at the entry of divine grace into his soul. 'We were baptised', he says, 'and there vanished from us the anxiety of our past life': *baptizati sumus et fugit a nobis sollicitudo vitae praeteritae*. He was profoundly moved by the experience. 'How I wept', he remembers, recalling the emotions he felt as the psalm-chant poured into his ears and an understanding of the truth flooded his heart (*Conf.* IX.vi.14).

Enlarged by the addition of Evodius, a fellow-countryman of Augustine's, later to be bishop of Uzalis, the party of friends now set off for the south, intending to return to Africa. They were forced to pause in Ostia because of the civil war of 387–8 between the Gallic usurper Maximus and Theodosius I and the blockade of the ports of Rome. There, two events brought about an abrupt change in the tranquillity of Augustine's mood, and encouraged him to look beyond the gentle satisfactions and the tender emotions of the last months. Although he felt himself changed he still found his mind imperfectly clear and his sinfulness active in him. In the second and perhaps the greater climax of the *Confessions* he describes how at Ostia, only two weeks, as it proved, before his mother's death, he and Monica were standing at a window overlooking the garden courtyard of the house where they were staying. They talked of God, in a mood of profound joy, and of how, if a man were to be free from the sense impressions and images which surround him and crowd upon him; and if he were to lose his sense of his own identity, so that he could rise above himself, then he would hear God speaking to him directly, not through the medium of created things. It seemed to them both that, for an instant, as they strove for the experience with all their hearts, it was granted to them: *attingimus eam modice ictu cordis (Conf.* IX.x.25). This *ictu cordis*[7] was a 'thrust' of both understanding and feeling, involving the whole 'inner man' of the soul. It was an experience which convinced Augustine at a stroke of the rightness of the direction his thinking had been taking.

It was followed abruptly by the loss of the companion whose quiet spiritual confidence had borne him up all his life. Within a few days Monica caught a fever and died. This, and the temporary stay on his plan to return to Africa which interrupted the steady progress of his plans, jolted him out of the complacent happiness of the Cassiciacum mood.

Augustine describes his grief for his mother briefly and with restraint. He tried to keep uppermost in his mind the knowledge that she died content that he was a Christian, and that she was not lost to him for ever (*Conf.* IX.xii.29). The funeral was conducted without tears, but in secret Augustine wept as he lay awake at night (*Conf.* IX.xii.32), and he is frank about his 'childish' pain at the loss of her company (*Conf.* IX.xii.31). Nothing could have brought the idyll of Cassiciacum so decisively to an end.

The companions returned to Rome to wait until the blockade was lifted, and then they left for Africa.

5 Africa, Priesthood and a Bishopric

In Africa, Augustine was to change the pattern of life he had had in mind when he retired to Cassiciacum for another, less philosophical retirement. In late 388 Augustine and Alypius were back in Carthage. They were given lodgings by Innocentius, an ex-advocate of the deputy prefecture, a pious man, who took them in as an act of charity, understanding that they were perhaps to be ordained (*De Civ. Dei* XXII.8). Now that they were baptised, they wanted to live a life of public commitment, to mix with other Christians. Augustine summed up their new design in a famous passage in a letter to Nebridius, who had come back to Africa and was now living with his mother near Carthage. They were 'to grow like God in their retirement' (*deificari in otio*) (*Letters* 9.1 and 10.1).

The retirement was short-lived. Some attempt was made to take up the old community life again on Augustine's family estates at Thagaste, but the community's number was soon depleted by the death of Augustine's son Adeodatus. Nebridius died, too. Alypius was soon made Bishop of Tagaste, for men capable of leading the Christian community were few and valuable. Left without his familiar circle, uncertain of his future plans, Augustine began to be wary lest the same thing should happen to him.

In the spring of 391 he was in Hippo, looking for a suitable site to found a monastery (*Serm.* 355.2); he had arranged to meet someone there who had expressed an interest in joining such a community. He tells the story in a sermon given many years later to his flock at Hippo. 'I would not go to any place where there was no bishop', he says. Hippo seemed safe enough, because he knew it had a bishop. What he had not bargained for was that he should be seized and made a priest, in a forced ceremony (as was common enough practice in the late Roman world). The local people knew him to be an able man, and they wanted to keep him. The bishop himself, Valerius, an old man and a Greek-speaker from Sicily, was anxious not to let the opportunity slip. He gave him what he had come to Hippo to seek: permission to set up a monastery and the use of a garden.

Augustine's reputation as an orator had preceded him. Here was a preacher of power and natural authority, who was badly needed in Valerius' troubled diocese. It was not usual for anyone but the bishop to preach. If Augustine was to be useful to him, it was necessary for Valerius to endeavour to get him consecrated as a fellow-bishop; and so Augustine found himself in 395 in the position he was to occupy for the rest of his life, all thought of retirement over, and urgent work to be done to suppress the Donatist schismatics of the area.

Augustine's writings against the Donatists are the works in which he is perhaps least concerned with the problem of evil. The Donatists were fanatically ascetic Christians. The schism had arisen early in the fourth century, when Mensurius, bishop of Carthage, had attempted to discourage the excesses of Christians bent on martyrdom. Mensurius' archdeacon Caecilianus was made Bishop of Carthage after him in 311, but those hostile to Mensurius' campaign contested the validity of his consecration. They set up a rival candidate, Majorinus – whose successor, in 315, was Donatus. A series of appeals, to the Emperor Constantine and to Melchiades, Bishop of Rome in 313, and to the Council of Arles in 314, resulted in a decision against the party which was to be known throughout the century as the Donatists. A further appeal to the Emperor resulted only in further condemnation. Nevertheless, the schismatics flourished throughout the fourth century, attracting Christians of an ascetic persuasion.

Augustine's concern was, then, with a local problem of long-standing and of more than local importance. He approached his task confidently, sure that if only the Donatists could be brought to see their error, they would be reconciled with the Catholics. His engagement with the problem was practical rather than intellectual perhaps, but it gave him employment for his mind and a period of comparative detachment from his old pre-occupations.

When he returns to them, we shall see that he had been making progress with them unawares.

III · EVIL IN THE MIND

1 The Christian Philosopher

Everything Augustine has to say about evil must be read in the light of one central principle: that the effect of evil upon the mind is to make it impossible for the sinner to think clearly, and especially to understand higher, spiritual truths and abstract ideas. We have already seen something of the Augustinian epistemology of evil at work in his reflections throughout the *Confessions* upon the difficulty he had in understanding the nature of the good in any but the most crude and concrete terms.

If we are to see how Augustine overcame this difficulty and evolved his epistemology of evil, we must look first at the development of his philosophical ideas – in particular the Neoplatonic principles he wove into his Christian philosophy. Thomas Aquinas saw with great clarity the way in which he went about making his synthesis: 'Augustine knew the doctrines of the Platonists well; whenever he discovered in their teaching something which was consistent with Christian faith, he adopted it; and those things which he found to be inconsistent with faith, he amended' (*Summa Theologiae* I Q. 84 a. 5., *Resp.*). But Aquinas imputes to Augustine a clear-headedness in these matters which he acquired only gradually, as he reflected upon the ideas of the Platonists after his conversion.

It is not easy to trace the process by which those ideas became Augustine's own – as they undoubtedly did. His is not an eclectic system of thought but an attempt to build upon truths which seemed to him to be self-evident, truths he recognised perhaps in other men's writings, but which he took, not on their authority, but on the grounds of the reasonableness of the ideas themselves.

The Greek Neoplatonist Proclus, a younger contemporary of Augustine (he was born about 412), composed an *Elements of Theology* in which he tried to imitate the method of Euclid's *Elements* and demonstrate from first principles a series of theological pro-

29

positions which would stand on their self-evident reasonableness. There are sufficient parallels with Augustine's ideas to show that he was drawing upon a living contemporary tradition as well as upon the writings of previous generations in making Christian use of Neoplatonism. *Propositions* 26–7 of the *Elements*, for example, deal with the idea that the Highest Good overflows in creation. In *Confessions* I.iii.3 Augustine describes God as pouring himself out over us (*cum effunderis super nos*). In *Proposition* 28, Proclus advances the principle that what is nearer to God is more like God than what is farther from him. Augustine has the same idea in *De Civitate Dei* XI.7. 'The more like God someone is, the closer to God he is.' *Proposition* 52 puts it that what is eternal is wholly present at every time. This is a common notion in Augustine (*Conf*. XI.xi.13, for example has: *Totum esse praesens*). *Proposition* 98 deals with the paradox of the divine immanence in all creation from which, because he is divine, God is infinitely distant. Augustine puts it like this (*Conf*. VI.iii.4): 'You are wholly everywhere, and You are in no place.' To Augustine, as to Proclus, these notions are ultimately incapable of demonstration. They are axioms. We recognise them to be true because we are reasonable beings.

In the *Contra Academicos* Augustine makes a claim for the reasonableness of his new faith. Christianity is 'the one most true philosophical discipline', he claims (*C. Acad*. III.xix.42). It is not like the philosophy of this world, in which human minds, their reason blinded by the darkness of their manifold errors, fail to raise themselves to the highest good. Augustine asks what manner of understanding this is (*Conf*. X.i.1). He concludes, in accordance with Proclus' 28th *Proposition*, that if he is to come near to God it must be with the most Godlike part of him, that is, with his rational soul, for understanding is an intellectual activity, not an activity of the bodily senses. To be a Christian is to be, in the true sense, a philosopher.

His reading of the Neoplatonists enabled Augustine to order his thoughts. It brought into focus certain points of doctrine with which he was able, in some cases to match, in others to contrast, the fundamental principles of the Christian faith as he came to understand it better.

Augustine sees God as Being (who is also the One). Plotinus thinks of God as One who is above Being. Despite the fundamental difference this implies at the heart of the two systems,[1] Plotinus helped

Augustine to perceive the transcendancy of God more clearly by his emphasis upon the awful remoteness of the One. The *Hortensius* had excited him by making him realise the existence of higher things. Here was the ultimate height.

Porphyry describes the philosopher's search in his treatise on abstinence from animal food (1.29). His purpose, says Porphyry, is to arrive at the contemplation of true Being. The soul is a fallen being, which must make an ascent towards the true Being. This can only be done by the intellect, because the intellect is that part of man which is 'truly-existent being'.[2] To help the soul return to itself, we must try to detach ourselves from the objects of the bodily senses and from the passions which they stir, and raise ourselves to a state in which the intellect operates, free of images of material things, and without perturbation (1.30). Anything which smacks of these things is to be rejected. Once, before the Fall, we were intellectual beings; we are still rational, but our reason is impeded from its proper operation by the senses. It follows (1.31) that we must try to return to our former condition by living in the intellect, and not through our bodily senses; and 'conjunction' with things allied to the body (such as thinking in 'bodily images') is false. The senses can manage their own work without the aid of the intellect (III.22). There is no excuse for living a life of the mind in which there is any admixture of bodily life, and concession to the fact that our souls dwell in mortal bodies. This is the very stuff of Augustine's own enquiry, and, with some modifications, it was his own response as a Christian thinker to the perception of the existence of the Supreme Being to try to return to him by helping his soul rise free of his body, towards the heights for which it was made.

Augustine's Trinitarian doctrine is not that of Plotinus; Plotinus emphasises the hierarchical arrangement which places the One above Being or Nous (which is not the Logos in Plotinus), and the World Soul beneath Being. Augustine insists, with the Council of Nicaea, on the equality of the Persons of the Trinity. Nevertheless, Augustine found in the Neoplatonists a philosophically satisfying account of the notion of threeness in God. They gave him the intellectual assurance that there was no crude polytheism here, but real philosophy.

Again, there is a significant difference between Plotinus' view of the nature of God's relation to his creation and that of Augustine: Plotinus seeks to understand how the multitudinousness of the world is related to the One; Augustine how an eternal and immutable God can create, and work in, a world which is in a continuous state of change. The relationship of Becoming and Being; and that of the manifold and the One: the two problems are not identical, but they are of the same order. In each case, the fixed and transcendent divine nature is contrasted with the shifting and evanescent creation which appears to have some point of articulation with it. Once more, by his reading of the Neoplatonists, Augustine is given a framework within which to explore.

The point of juncture between the Supreme Being and the world (for the One is too high in Plotinus' view to have direct dealings with the world) is a gateway through which divine care may flow. Ancient philosophers had given a good deal of thought to the question of the way in which the Creator might act upon the world, to the nature of Providence, and to the notions of fate and fortune. Augustine found it necessary to emphasise that the cause of the greatness of the Roman Empire was a matter neither of fortune nor of fate, but of Providence (*De Civ. Dei* v.1).

His Christian Platonism is optimistic: it gives an account of an orderly world, where God is always in benevolent control of his creation, watching over its welfare, unchanging and kind, but it is also a system designed to accommodate the problem of evil, to show how, by the exercise of Providence, God contains evil and makes it impossible for it, in the last analysis, to do harm. Indeed, he foresaw evil and planned to make the best of it.

The problem which evil posed for Augustine at the time of his conversion lay, not so much here, for he had supreme confidence in his God, but in the metaphysical question of the relation between matter and evil. Up to the time when Ambrose's sermons had prepared his mind for his conversion, but before he had finally committed himself, Augustine admits that he had the utmost difficulty in envisaging God except in terms of something corporeal, perhaps infused into the world in some way, or diffused beyond it (*Conf.* VII.i.1).

Augustine, as he himself points out, was much influenced here by reading Aristotle's *Categories* when he was barely twenty (*Conf.* IV.xvi.28). The *Categories* were just becoming available in Latin, and although no contemporary translations survive, we know that Victorinus had made one (Cassiodorus, *Institutiones* II.18) and, apart from the mysterious *Categoriae Decem*, attributed to Augustine himself by the Carolingians, a large part of the *Categories* was available in Martianus Capella's *De Nuptiis Philologiae et Mercurii*. There was something of an 'Aristotelian revival' among Augustine's contemporaries. The impact of the *Categories* would have been the greater, perhaps, because of the novelty of the work. Augustine was reading something newly-fashionable,[3] at an age when his mind was being formed.

In these circumstances he found Aristotle's account of 'being' so satisfactory that he thought whatever existed, even God himself, must be capable of being described in terms of the ten categories: 'illus decem praedicamentis putans quidquid esset omnino comprehensum' (*Conf.* IV.xvi.28). At the very least we must say that God is 'like' a substance. Accordingly, he tried to visualise the divine and spiritual 'substance', and evil too, in the same corporeal terms as Aristotle had shown to be appropriate to the description of created things in the material world. Above all it was the teaching of the Manichees which led him to believe that evil was a certain substance (*Conf.* V.x.18) and had a mass like matter. Even if it were something more tenuous and diffuse yet it could still be described in bodily terms; it was still a body, if a 'subtle body', like the 'body' of the air (*Conf.* V.x.18).

Augustine accordingly envisaged good and evil as two masses (*moles*) set in opposition to one another, both infinite, but the evil mass in some way more confined or limited than the good. This evil mass is not God's creation. Indeed, at the point where he confronts evil, God is finite, although he is infinite in every other respect. This compromise, which he saw to be unsatisfactory, was the best Augustine could manage, given his self-confessed inability to think in any terms but those of images drawn from sense-experience. As he writes the *Confessions* it is clear to him what he did not then realise: namely, that he was using the wrong instrument of perception and so he could not rise above the conceptual limitations imposed by his bodily state. It is not that he was thinking so crudely that he envisaged God in the likeness of a human body; but he certainly thought of him as some sort of body (*corporeum aliquid*) (*Conf.* VII.i.1), somehow penetrating the whole mass of the world, which is a huge lump (*Conf.* VII.iii.5).

If he had recently been reading Plotinus' fifth *Ennead* he might be excused a certain confusion over the matter. Plotinus describes the mode of God's presence everywhere like this: God cannot be in the world in the way that something may be contained in a container. If he were, he would have to be 'where' the world is, and there is no 'where' where God may be said to be. But God is not nowhere; he is everywhere. 'Imagine a place where [he] is not', says Plotinus, 'and it will be clear that he is in another place'; 'at once he is contained, and there is an end of his placelessness'. God must somehow be instantaneously present everywhere, 'nothing containing and nothing left void'; for 'we cannot think of something of God here and something else there, nor of all God gathered at some one spot' (*Ennead* v.v.9). Plotinus has exploited his conceptual resources to the limit and yet he has been obliged to talk in the language of physical location. Augustine's own words reflect the same difficulty. He says that when he tried to banish the idea of physical space from his mind he could put nothing in its place. Even when he tried to conceive of 'nothing', Augustine could describe it to himself only in corporeal terms, as the 'space' from which something had been removed (*Conf.* VII.i.1): 'If a body is removed from a place, and the place remains empty of every body', then we have 'nothing'. 'Nothing' is an 'empty space (*locus inanis*)', a 'spacious nothing (*spatiosum nihil*)', and it is conceivable only in terms of the bodily substance which surrounds it, and which defines it.

The only way out which presented itself involved abandoning the 'corporeal' view of things which had seemed such safe ground – indeed the only possible ground. 'Nothingness' must be something rather different from the *spatiosum nihil*, the empty space Augustine had already rejected as a possibility.

If he read Plotinus' first *Ennead* Augustine would have found a discussion of the nature of substance and the possibility of there being a contrary to substance which may have helped him. Plotinus demonstrates that in the unique case of the Highest Being 'it is not true that an Essence (or Substance) can have no contrary', because 'things utterly sundered, having nothing in common, standing at the remotest poles, are opposites in nature: the contrariety does not depend upon quality or upon any other generic type, but upon the utmost difference' (*Ennead* I.viii.6).

If there can be a contrary to substance, or essence, perhaps it is here that we shall find 'nothing', non-substance, non-being. If all that exists is good, it follows that what is deprived of goodness is deprived of existence (*Conf.* VII.xii.18). Even corrupt things are good, for if there were nothing good in them, there would be nothing there to be corrupted. If it were possible to deprive things of all goodness, they would no longer exist. Evil begins to look like a taking away, a privation, a tendency to nothingness, rather than a *locus inanis*, a pocket of nothingness in a good world. Once Augustine perceived this possibility he saw that he need no longer try to understand how evil can have a bodily place in the universe, 'where' it is, 'whence' it comes, or how it 'enters into' a universe that is filled with the divine Being.

This did not entirely resolve for him the question of the relationship between evil and matter, however. Plotinus shows how matter differs from the Highest in all its attributes. It is utterly different from and alien to the Good, indeed from all existing things (*Ennead* II.iv.13). 'The distinctive character of Matter, then, is simply its manner of being – not something definite inserted in it but rather a relation towards other things, the relation of being distinct from them', but that is true of evil too. Matter is that which absolutely lacks all good things 'and so is in destitution'; thus it 'must be evil in its own kind', says Plotinus (*Ennead* II.iv.16). To Augustine, too, it seemed that the non-spiritual or material must at least be on a par with evil in being Not-God.

Augustine's difficulty in thinking out his position lay partly in the crude state of contemporary technical terminology in Latin. He and the Manichees had been in the habit of speaking of *natura* in the same 'bodily' terms as *substantia*, for in common usage they were synonymous. In his *Reply to the Fundamental Epistle of the Manichees*, Augustine insists that the 'nature' of wisdom and truth or the 'nature' of the soul cannot be seen as something extended in space (*Fund. Ep.* xvi.20). The Manicheans had been making the mistake of thinking of all nature and all substance as if they were bodily things. Augustine is now careful to qualify 'substance' with 'bodily' where he means material substance, because he can see that there are substances and natures which do not behave like bodies. Not only did this misconception prevent him and the Manichees from forming abstract ideas, he says, but it also encouraged them to regard physical substance or matter (*Hyle*) as something which might possess a mind, and be capable of imposing forms, instead of merely receiving them

(*C. Faust.* xx.14). It had led them to make a god of matter, albeit an evil god.

There persisted, however, a lingering association between matter and evil which Augustine never quite severed. The result of his failure to do so is most apparent in the theory of knowledge he worked out in the first years after his conversion, and in which we can see clearly how he believed evil to be at work in his own mind, clouding his vision of God. Everything Augustine has to say about evil in his maturity rests upon the epistemological foundations he laid at this time.

2 The Clouded Mind

(a) BODILY IMAGININGS

Augustine believed that evil has the effect of obscuring the understanding and impeding the working of the mind. That is why heretics cannot argue correctly. Faustus the Manichee was suffering from such a handicap when he argued in fallacious syllogisms (*C. Faust.* xxv.1). Before there can be any degree of 'spirituality' in Faustus' thinking, so that he can move beyond the physical notion of a *finis* or actual boundary lying at the edge of the good and making it finite, he must be freed from the habit of thinking in terms of 'carnal and material ideas' (*C. Faust.* xxv.2). The Manichees recognise only the light their eyes can see, not the inaccessible light of God's dwelling. They can form no idea of evil but as a material substance (*In John* xcviii.4). His heretical creed prevents the Manichee from proceeding beyond these limits, by leading him to think of the soul (and God himself) as well as the body, as if they all occupied space alike, when in reality only the body does so (*C. Faust.* xxv.2). He whose mind is not yet illuminated by the ray of truth is easily deceived by such material images (*De Mor. Man.* xvi.38). The Manichee's fundamental misconception about the existence of evil is, then, impeding his understanding (*De Mor. Man.* ii.4), because it is encouraging him to think in bodily terms about matters which require an altogether different approach. The 'light of wisdom' (*De Ver. Rel.* II.xxxix) is needed to clear the clouded vision so that we can see the truth, and even then we must learn what we can bit by bit, groping in the darkness which is inseparable from our fallen condition (*De Mor. Man.* i.1).

It was their realisation of the importance of freeing the mind from 'bodily images' which Augustine valued so much in the work of some of the Neoplatonists.

Augustine, like Boethius, was heir to a tradition in which the theologian and the philosopher were one in their aspiration upwards from the physical world towards the higher things of the mind and soul. Cicero says that it is a mark of great genius to be able to withdraw the mind from the senses (*Tusculanae Disputationes* I.xvi.38). Augustine thought the Platonists came closest to the Christian view among the pagans precisely because they saw *theologia* as a philosophical activity in this special sense. They understand that truth is to be perceived not with the bodily eyes, but by the mind alone (*De Ver. Rel.* III.iii.8). If they do not quite grasp the implication of this yet, Augustine is confident that he can quickly make it plain to the modern followers of Plato – as he could to Plato himself if he were still alive.

Other pagans mock those who say that something exists which cannot be seen with the eyes or envisaged in the terms of the senses, but only perceived with the mind and the understanding (*De Ver. Rel.* III.iii.10). They do not understand how the abstract differs from the concrete, the spiritual from the physical. If they did they would be won over at once to Christianity, because there can be no error in religion for the soul which worships God spiritually. Errors arise from mistaken attempts to worship a body or a bodily image (*De Ver. Rel.* x.xviii.51) as if it were abstract or divine. The *phantasma* is simply a false abstraction (*De Ver. Rel.* x.xviii.52).

Unfortunately, it is only too easy to let our thoughts run on these apparent abstractions, instead of on real ones, Augustine admits. It is difficult to seek the truth in the only proper way (*De Ver. Rel.* x.xviii.52), but if we succeed we shall find that we have understood the abstract in a higher manner than the body allows us to do, and approached the vision of God himself. Although he chastises Porphyry for failing to see that it was only logical to become a Christian when he had come so close to the Christian position in his thinking, he praises him for realising that a man can purify his soul without the aid of gods or demons, by 'chastity', that is, by separating himself from his body as far as he can (*De Civ. Dei* x.28).

One reason why Augustine thinks that we are likely to go astray if we use only our bodily senses in an attempt to arrive at an understanding of the nature of God, is clear enough (*De Mor. Man.*

xvi.39—48). We shall be stretching the senses beyond their capacity. There is an obvious limitation to seeing only with the eyes of the flesh (*De Gen. c. Man.* I.iii.5). Each sense can perceive only what is proper to it, which it admits into the memory by its own special sensory 'entrance', and which is stored separately (*Conf.* x.viii.12). We cannot, for example, perceive colour with our ears. Some things such as the forms of bodies, whether they are large or small, square or round, can be perceived with more than one sense – here, with the sight and the touch – but no sense can judge the perceptions of another.

We may postulate the existence of an inner sense (*interior sensus*), which is capable of perceiving both the *corporalia* sensed by the bodily sense and the bodily sense itself, and which can relate one kind of sense-perception to another. This even animals possess, for they can judge the accuracy of their perceptions well enough to move about the world successfully and find their food. In man there seems to be a higher faculty still, which is capable of perceiving, as animals cannot, what is eternal and changeless (*De Lib. Arb.* II.iii.8.25—v.14.56), but this faculty, the reason, does not depend for its information upon what it learns from the senses (*Conf.* x.ix.16). To telescope all these together and think that everything can be understood in terms of the perceptions of the bodily senses is, Augustine argues, nonsense. Yet that is what the Manichees are doing, because their minds are so muddled that they do not realise its absurdity. It is the height of madness (*summa dementia*) to claim that what we perceive with our senses pertains to God (*De Duab. An.* 2).

Common experience tells us that the body occupies a small space, and cannot be in two places at once, while the mind is capable of ranging over vast distances of heaven and earth (*Fund. Ep.* xvii.20). The mind has no material extension to correspond with its extensions of memory and imagination. The bodily senses cannot, therefore, act as a check on the mind's activities, or provide an infallible means of telling the difference between the real and that which is mere fantasy, and they certainly cannot be relied upon to yield analogies which will enable us to form an idea of the divine.

It is because they can think of nothing but the light they have seen with their eyes that Augustine despairs of being able to explain to the Manichees the 'inaccessible light' in which the Father dwells. From their knowledge of this visible light, with which beasts and even insects are as familiar as men, they form a vague idea (*phantasia*) and think that this is the light of the divine habitation (*Fund. Ep.* xviii.20). This is no fantasy in the Manichean judgment, for the Manichees believe that understanding truth means nothing more than thinking in 'bodily forms'; the images in which he places his trust are, then, the very images which are empty phantoms (*inania phantasmata*), by Augustine's reckoning. If the bodily senses cannot judge the difference for us, we must look to a higher authority. For Augustine, that means going beyond human reason to God himself and asking for enlightenment. In his own experience, once God has shown him how to look at things, everything falls into place. He is able to distinguish between those things he can perceive with his senses and such things as 'justice, chastity, faith, truth, love, goodness' and to see how great a separation there is between these and 'what I think are surely and obviously bodily things' (*C. Faust.* xx.7). 'Truth' and 'goodness' and so on are not in Augustine's eyes simply abstractions, ideas rather than concrete objects. They are attributes of God himself 'ideas' in something closer to the Platonic sense, in that they exist with a reality far beyond that of chairs and tables and the other objects the senses find so real. Boethius expresses a Neoplatonic commonplace at the opening of the second chapter of his *De Trinitate*, where he explains that the subject-matter of *naturalis*, natural science, is not abstract, because it is concerned with the forms of bodies together with their matter; the subject-matter of mathematics is not abstract either, because although it involves the study of the forms as though they could be separated from matter, the forms are really inseparable from matter in the created world. Only theology is truly abstract in its subject-matter, for only the substance of God (*dei substantia*) is perfectly free of matter. What is *abstractum* (in the sense which Boethius gives the term) is 'distinct from the corporeal' and is therefore both the contrary of 'concrete' and something which transcends the created world in its divinity (Boethius, *De Trinitate* II).

The *Enneads* contain a theory of evil which, like the Manichean view, Augustine rejected as a whole, but retained in many of its parts. He argues that the effect of evil upon our souls is to make them behave in a manner more appropriate to bodies, that is, to appear to be material not spiritual. They cannot behave as souls should, and strive for a purely intellectual perception. They are thrown back upon the body for their perceptions, and so they see everything in terms of the corporeal senses. The moral is the same as that which Porphyry and Plotinus draw. We must strive to purify our souls by separating them from the material (*Ennead* I.viii.4). We cannot do so literally; human beings are made up of body and soul, and until death our bodies are material not spiritual. The separation must take place in thought. If it does not, we shall still be able to think only in terms of the things we perceive with our bodily senses.

There was a persistent connection in Augustine's mind between matter and evil. While he was a Manichee he was able to equate the two, but even when he no longer held that matter is evil he found a persistent materiality in his thinking which he could only put down to the effect of evil upon his mind. Evil somehow clogged his mind and made it muddy.

(b) THE UPLIFTING OF THE MIND

In a letter of 412 to Volusian, one of the Roman exiles who had fled to Africa after the fall of Rome, a pagan with a Christian family (*Letter* 137.4), Augustine describes the way in which some contemporaries had been mocking the Incarnation. They think it absurd to suggest that God could have been encompassed in so small a human body. For then, they said, either he must have ceased to govern the world while he was in the world as a man, or else he must have concentrated his almighty power in the two hands of an infant. These are men who are not able to understand any substance except what is corporeal, says Augustine. The best they can do is to imagine 'refined' corporeal substances, such as air and light, but still material not spiritual substances. This kind of thinking is the result of men's failure to emancipate themselves from 'bodily images'.

Corporeal substances, however 'refined', do not behave like spiritual substances. When it is suggested that God somehow condensed himself into the infant Jesus and left the business of heaven unattended, it is implied that he behaved as a corporeal substance would. Only corporeal substances can be condensed, rarefied, contracted or expanded, and that is what these objectors were arguing must have happened to God when he became man. Such substances cannot be wholly everywhere at once, as a spiritual substance can, 'since they are necessarily composed of numberless parts, some here, some there'; for 'however large or however small the substance may be, it occupies an amount of space, and it fills that space without being wholly in any part of it' (*Letter* 137.4). Such a 'God' who became man would cease to be fully himself in a 'quantitative' sense.

If we are to emancipate ourselves from these crude ideas, which are based on analogies with the working of the physical world, our minds must somehow lift themselves out of the body for a time. This is by no means easy to do. Augustine tries to find common experiences that will show how this may be possible; he reminds us that we are used to perceiving things outside the flesh, when we see the sky or hear a sound from out of doors whilst inside a building. These things are in some sense present to us, although we remain some distance from them. It involves a greater leap of conceptual effort to understand how God may continue to be 'everywhere totally present' when he is incarnate in one body, but it is not beyond our powers to see that it may be possible (*Letter* 137.5). The mind must go out of the body, then, at least in thought, if it is to free itself from 'bodily images'.

i *The spirituality of the soul*

The mind is already in a sense 'out' of the body, because it is the soul not the body which reasons and thinks, but Augustine had to show that the soul is indeed a spiritual and not a bodily thing. This was a matter of controversy among the philosophers. The objectors would be being perfectly consistent in using 'bodily images' if they held that the soul is corporeal. Some of his contemporaries thought that the soul was a collection of particles, or made of a fifth element, or in some other way corporeal (*De Trin*. x.vii.9). He remarks in his letter of 415 to Jerome (*Letter* 166): 'Although it is difficult to convince those who are slow to understand that the soul is incorporeal, I am certain of it.'

The difficulty was partly one of definition. If we define a 'body' as the whole substance or essence of something, or use 'any better term which may be employed to express what something is in itself', then certainly the soul is a body (*Letter* 166), but that is a very different thing from saying that it is corporeal. On the other hand, if we restrict 'incorporeal' to things which are unchangeable and wholly present everywhere, then only God will fulfil the terms of the definition. Then we should have to say that the soul is corporeal. Yet that is not a definition of 'corporeal' which Augustine finds satisfactory. He

41

would prefer to define a body as that which occupies space and has a certain length and height and depth, which fills a larger space with a larger part of itself and a smaller space with a smaller part. If that is what a body is, then the soul is not a body, for it extends through the whole of the body to which it gives life, not by distributing itself spatially, but in the form of a life-giving impetus which is wholly present in every part of the body. Some of the Neoplatonists had given him precedent for the view, and Proclus has much the same notion in his *Elements of Theology* (*Proposition* 188). To take an example which became a commonplace, the soul is not reduced in size when a finger is cut off from the body, for, as Plotinus explains, 'life' cannot be broken into parts (*Ennead* vi.iv.3). He is confident that if his opponents can free themselves from the habit of thinking in corporeal terms, and if they can use technical terms correctly, they will find themselves in agreement with him here.

Augustine must convince his readers of the incorporeal nature of the soul, for on this point rests the whole weight of his argument about the dangers of allowing ourselves to use bodily images. If the soul were a body, such images would be perfectly proper to it. To those who will accept this, he points out that, if the nature of the soul is different from that of the body, the divine nature, who is the Creator of both body and soul, must be far different from both, more spiritual than the spiritual substance of the soul, able to be everywhere at once in a manner beyond that of the created spirit. How absurd it is, then, to suggest that God fills the world as water or air or even light fill it, so that a little part of himself is in a little part of the world (*Conf.* vii.v.7). (Here again, Augustine is pouring scorn on a naivety to which he himself had once been prone, in the days when he thought of the world as a great sponge, lying in the divine ocean) (*Letter* 137.5).

ii *The union of body and soul*

Before we can see how the soul may be able to separate itself from the body and pursue its 'upward' course towards the knowledge of the truth unencumbered by sense-impressions, we must clarify one further point: the nature of the union which exists between body and soul. A union there must be, if man is not, like an angel, a purely spiritual being. Augustine took this question as his starting-point in one of the Cassiciacum dialogues. 'Does it seem obvious to you that we are composed of body and soul?' he asks his friends in the discussion which is reported in the *De Beata Vita*. Only Navigius his brother was uncertain whether he thought so. 'Surely you at least know that you are alive?' Augustine asks him. 'Do you also know that you have a body?' Navigius concedes both points, but his difficulty is that he is not sure that these are all, that he is made up only of body and life (*De Beata Vita* II.7). The question which Navigius would like settled is whether something else is needed to complete a man and make him perfect.

The question arose partly at least because the philosophers differed on the constitution of the soul. Is this 'life' to be equated with the soul? Is the soul a separate thing from the mind, or the reason or the intelligence? Augustine's answer is clear. 'I, the soul, am one alone', he insists in the *Confessions* (*Conf*. X.vii.11); the mind is not a separate component from the soul (*C. Acad*. I.ii.5); life, reason and intelligence are faculties of the soul. Plotinus implies as much in the first *Ennead* (I.i.8) and in *Ennead* IV and V (IV.iii.23; V.i.10), he speaks of the reasoning-power of the soul. The soul itself is one and it is indeed life, says Augustine. Its existence, its knowing and its willing (*esse, nosse, velle*) (*Conf*. XIII.xi.12) are three things, but one life (*inseparabilis vita*). 'I am, knowing and willing, and I know that I am and that I will, and I will to be and to know.' There is no *diversitas substantiae* – these are all of one spiritual substance (*De Div. Quaest*. XXXViii).

In man this spiritual substance, the soul, is 'joined' to a material substance, the body. The way in which this may be possible is the subject of much perplexity to Plotinus. 'We must examine how the soul comes to inhabit the body – the manner and the process – a question certainly of no minor interest' (*Ennead* IV.iii.9). For Augustine and Plotinus alike there is no question of a combining of two substances into a third new substance, or 'man', for that would take away the identity of the first two substances. In the union of body and soul the body remains a body and the soul remains a soul.

Any closer union than that between body and soul (where the difference between the body in its material substance and the soul in its spiritual substance persists) would force us to conclude, by one of Augustine's borrowed arguments, that the body like the soul is immortal. Augustine's proof of the immortality of the soul, in *Soliloquies* II.xiii.24, rests upon the notion that if whatever is in a

43

subject is eternal, the subject itself must be eternal. This is Plotinus' argument in *Ennead* IV.vii, and Augustine makes use of it again in the treatise *On the Immortality of the Soul*. The knowledge or truth or reason which resides in the soul is itself eternal, and so the soul in which it resides must be immortal. It clearly cannot be the case that the soul resides in the body in the same way as the truth resides in the soul, or the body would be immortal too.

Nor can two substances of such entirely different kinds be united by any of the modes of conjunction which suggest themselves by analogy with the joining of material things in the world around us. If we try to envisage the two as merely juxtaposed, perhaps only the part of the body which was adjacent to the soul could be said to be 'animated'. Nor can body and soul be mixed together like wine and oil, for that is no more than a juxtaposition that has been given a good shake. The component parts have merely been broken up and mingled together as in an emulsion; they can still be separated. But body and soul cannot be separated or the man will no longer exist; even death separates body and soul only temporarily, for in eternity the resurrected body will be reunited with the soul. Whatever kind of union exists (Augustine wonders whether to call it a *harmonia*), it is such that body and soul adhere together *inseparabiliter* (*De Im. An.* II.2).

In Book IX of the *De Trinitate* Augustine explores the problem of union rather further, in an attempt to understand how the *mens*, *notitia* and *amor*, mind, knowledge and love, of the soul may be three and yet one. In a drink made from water, wine and honey, three distinct substances are mingled, and yet we speak of one liquor (*De Trin*. IX.iv.7). Here, and in Book X, where he considers memory, understanding and will in a further image of the Trinity in the mind of man, Augustine is looking beyond the mechanical junctions and unions which are possible in created things, in search of a mode of being 'many-yet-one' which is perfectly and uniquely exemplified in the Trinity.

The problem of the union of body and soul in man is of a simpler, but not unrelated kind, except that there remains the difficulty of the difference in kind between bodily and spiritual substance. The Persons of the Trinity, the faculties of the mind, are united in a way which is only possible because they are of the same substance. Even if we can get over the problem of the way in which body and soul are united, the difference in kind between spiritual and material substance raises a number of further difficulties. The soul has no length or breadth or depth. The soul has no 'place'. In no ordinary sense of the terms is it proper to ask whether the soul is *intrinsecus* or *extrinsecus*, 'inside' or 'outside' the body (*De Quant. An.* v.7). Here again, Augustine would have been able to turn to Plotinus for help. He shows that the soul cannot be 'in' the body in the way that something may be contained in a space (*Ennead* IV.iii.20).

In the *De Genesi ad Litteram* Augustine returns to an image of the *Confessions*, which had been used there to describe the way in which he envisaged God filling the universe, in the unregenerate days when he thought in 'bodily images': the soul does not fill the body in local space, as water fills a sponge or vessel (cf. *Ennead* v.v.9). If the soul cannot be *in corpore*, perhaps the body may be said to be 'in' the soul (*Ennead* III.ix.3; IV.iii.9; VI.iv.5), but certainly there can be no sense in which we can say that our souls are 'in' our bodies (*De Quant. An.* xxx.61). Yet, although we cannot properly speak of the soul as being 'located' in the body, yet the soul does entirely 'fill' the body in another way, to its fingertips, not part by part, but being wholly present in every part. It does so, not by 'local diffusion' (*non locali diffusione*) but by the *vitalis intentio*, a living and purposeful force (*Letter* 166). It is its liveness which it is so important to understand when we try to grasp the nature of the soul. In the *De Beata Vita* Augustine had been prepared to equate 'life' with 'soul'. Its 'life' is not a bodily thing, but independent of the body, conferring life upon the body (*De Trin.* I.vii.9). It is like Plotinus' description of the soul as lighting up the body (*Ennead* IV.iii.23).

The soul is thus the dominant partner, directing and controlling the body, inhabiting it whether it will or no, but nevertheless superior to the body, and capable of determining how far it will live in partnership with the body on its own terms. It is this dominance which gives it the power, if it chooses, to emancipate itself from the senses and rise above 'bodily images'. This is the aspect of the relationship or union of soul and body which Augustine wanted to emphasise.

It was essential that Augustine should make this point clear if he was to explain how it was possible for the soul to separate itself from the body intellectually, without breaking the indissoluble bond which ties it to the body. Only if the soul is in some way *alienata* from the body and its ways of seeing can it see higher things, because it requires its utmost spiritual insight to see anything at all of the spirit which is divine (*De Im. An.* x.17).

How far that may be possible depends, as many of the philosophers thought, upon the 'purity' of the individual soul. Some believed that the soul had fallen from a former state to which it must strive to return, even that its bodily dwelling was a temporary prison, a punishment. They envisaged the upward striving as a *reditus*. Plotinus taught that the understanding (*theoria*) must rise from the contemplation of the natural world, to the things proper to the soul, which nevertheless have about them some admixture of the bodily, and then at last to the realm of pure intellect (*Ennead* III.viii.8), which he calls Mind (*Nous*). Proclus was to put forward the view in the *Elements* (*Proposition* 184) that every soul is either divine (God), or enjoying perpetual understanding (intellection) and perpetually gazing upon God (the angels); or else subject, like man, to change from intelligence to unintelligence, sometimes beholding God and sometimes looking away. This third class of souls is eternal, but it acts within time upon temporal things (*Proposition* 191).

There are notions here which require careful scrutiny if they are to fit into the Christian system, and Augustine does not take them over uncritically. In the seventh Book of the *De Genesi ad Litteram* he considers various hypotheses. He explains why the text: *sufflavit in faciem eius* (Genesis 2.7) need not be interpreted to mean that the breath of life which God breathed into Adam was an infusion of the divine Spirit itself. The *flatus Dei*, the breath of God, is not itself the *anima hominis*, but the creator of the human soul (*De Gen. ad Lit.* VII.iii.4). He rejects metempsychosis (VII.viii.13), and the Manichean view that the human soul is a fragment of the divine (VII.xi.16); he reflects on the difficulty of characterising the stuff out of which the soul is made (VII.vii.10). Not all the questions which arise in connection with the soul seem to him to be answerable, and he feels obliged to defend the value of examining them at all. At the very least, he promises, they teach us how to search Scripture for answers to matters which may not yield easily to enquiry (VII.xxviii.43).

One principle, however, seems to him beyond dispute: the soul must leave the body and travel upwards in thought 'remove and take away the attention of the mind from the bodily senses' (*De Im. An.* x.17). That *vitalis intentio* which the soul directs upon the body and which animates it, must be directed away from the body, if the soul is to attain to the vision of God.

In *The City of God* Augustine emphasises that a man is a body and a soul, no more, and certainly no less. He is not body alone nor soul alone, but both together (*De Civ. Dei* XIX,3). The union is such as to make a single whole of the two parts. Augustine is in a paradoxical position where he must maintain the inseparability of body and soul while encouraging his readers to make every effort to separate soul from body in their spiritual and intellectual lives. The Christian must strive to ensure that his soul will bring the body up to its own level, so that his body may be resurrected as a spiritual body, utterly in harmony with the soul, but in the meantime it must deny their union with all its energies, or the body will act as an impediment to its upward striving.

iii 'Where I shall know as I am known'

The transcendent spiritual height to which the mind of man must seek to raise itself cannot be a mindless waste of sublimity, for that, to Augustine and his Neoplatonic contemporaries, would be a contradiction in terms. It must be a sentient being, a being with an intellectual power which far exceeds our own. When the heaven of heavens (Psalm 113) is described as the *domus dei*, the dwelling-place of God, we must understand that it is not like a house or palace made of some spiritual substance. God dwells in the heaven of heavens in the sense that the heaven of heavens has some spiritual participation in his eternity. It enjoys the sight of God; it is so fixed upon God by chaste love, so burning with joy, that it 'sees' God as clearly as it is possible for any creature to do (*Conf.* XII.xv.19). This being closely resembles the *Nous* of Plotinus' *Enneads* (v.vi.4). The *Nous* is a living intelligence, fixed upon the Good. It is not itself the Good, but it is conformed to the Good by knowing it (*Ennead* III.viii.8). The heaven of heavens enjoys the kind of freedom from 'bodily images' that the human soul must attain if it, too, is to know God. It is our pattern.

In this unimaginably high realm, which is itself a sentient being, the knowing and the thing known become one. 'Whether we speak of the "intellectual" or the "intelligible" we mean the same thing', Augustine explains in the *De Genesi ad Litteram* (XII.x.21). The *intellectualis* is the mind, which understands or knows; it is itself intelligible (*intelligibilis*), for mind can perceive mind – indeed mind can be perceived only by mind. If the heaven of heavens is a being which perceives God, it must be, like him, an intellectual and spiritual and rational being; and it must itself, by its very nature, be intelligible and accessible to reason. In the knowing of God it is known by God. Reason tells us, if we accept the underlying assumptions here, that it is only by developing those parts of man which most nearly resemble God that we shall be able to imitate the heaven of heavens, and 'know as we are known'. From far below, the upwardly striving human soul approaches that state in its own being, as it comes closer to God.

iv Alienatio

Proclus declares in the *Elements of Theology* (*Proposition* 186) that every soul is separable from its body. Augustine is in a difficult position here. He wants to separate the soul from the body not literally – for that would be to destroy the man who is compounded of both soul and body – but by a process of *alienatio*, a painful, step-by-step emancipation from the limitations of the bodily senses which the soul must undergo while it is still bound to the body. He describes three kinds of vision: the corporeal, the spiritual and the intellectual. They are parallel to the Neoplatonic rise of the understanding from the natural world, to the subject-matter proper to the soul in its involvement with the body, and then to the realm of the *Nous*. The first is simply sense-perception; the second (a little confusingly as to terminology) is certainly not bodily, but it is like a bodily perception; it is an image of a body which is not present, as distinct from an image of a body directly perceived by the senses. The third is a kind of seeing which Augustine would like to call 'mental' (*mentale*), but that would mean coining a new word and so he calls it *intellectuale* (*De Gen. ad Lit.* XII.vi.16).

The 'spiritual' vision involves signs which look like corporeal things, but which stand for higher, spiritual truths. As a *vis animae* the spiritual vision is inferior to that of the mind. Joseph is more of a prophet than Pharaoh, because although Pharaoh had the vision, Joseph was able to interpret it. Pharaoh's spirit was *informatus*, so that he was able to see an image of things (*rerum imaginatio*), but Joseph's mind was illuminated (*mens inluminata*) so that he could understand. Daniel is more of a prophet than either, because 'he saw in the spirit likenesses of corporeal things which were meaningful,

48

and he understood them by the liveliness of his mind' (*vivacitate mentis*), that liveliness which is peculiar to the soul, the life of the body (*De Gen. ad Lit.* XII.ix.20). The intellectual vision is, then, the highest of all (*De Gen. ad Lit.* XII.x.21); in it, the understanding and that which is understood become one; it is the vision of the mind alone (*mentis est proprium*).

This division into three modes of knowing, the 'physical' or 'natural', the 'mathematical' and the 'theological', as Boethius calls them in his *De Trinitate* (Book II), is a commonplace of Neoplatonist thought.[4] Boethius is concerned with a division of the objects of knowledge into concrete and mutable; that which, though it is in reality inseparable from the concrete and mutable, is treated as though it were abstract and immutable (as mathematicians treat the world when they make calculations about it); and that which is truly abstract, the divine; Augustine's interest is in the modes of knowledge appropriate to these three objects of knowledge.

Augustine first explored the problem of knowledge along these lines soon after his conversion, when he wrote the *Soliloquies*, the most solitary of the Cassiciacum dialogues. He explains that he did his exploring alone, 'myself asking the questions and myself answering, my Reason and I, as if we were two'.

Although his subject in the *Soliloquies* is the problem of knowledge, Augustine's opening prayer reflects his continuing pre-occupation with the problem of evil and its solution: 'God, by Whom all things come into existence, which would not exist by themselves . . . God, who has created the world out of nothing . . . God, who does no evil, and causes existence so that evil may not exist, . . . who reveals to a few . . . that evil is nothing' (*Sol.* I.i.2). He contrasts the light by which the Christian soul sees with the darkness which shrouds the sinner's mind. He describes God as 'the Father of our awakening and illumination' (*Sol.* I.i.2). God is himself the *intelligibilis lux*, in whom and by whom and through whom all things which shine intelligibly are able to shine (*Sol.* I.i.3). God's realm is beyond understanding by the senses, so God alone can help us to understand what he himself is, and, by contrast, what evil is not.

He asks what knowledge is, especially when it involves something beyond what may be attained by sense-perception. He sets himself the most difficult problem of all, but one which he must solve if he is to make sense of all the other kinds of knowledge. He asks his reason what it is to 'know'. God. How will he know that he has the knowledge he seeks when he has found it? How can a knowledge of God be tested? asks Reason. Augustine cannot answer, because he recognises that he has no standard of comparison; he can think of nothing else he knows in the particular way he desires to know God.

Augustine cannot see how he is even to begin his enquiry when he has no starting-point. Reason suggests that he should consider the way in which he knows his friends, and see whether he can learn anything from that – begin, that is, with a knowledge he possesses already, but this will not do. He insists that he does not know even Alypius fully.

Reason tries an example of a humbler kind of knowledge. What about the knowledge he has of the course of the moon? Is that real knowledge? Pressed, Augustine thinks that although his knowledge of the moon's course is satisfactory (*satis*) in terms of the senses, it is not complete. He can conceive of factors governing the moon's movements which are unknown to him since they are beyond sense. He 'knows' what he sees of the moon's course, but that is all. Full and perfect knowledge, not only of spiritual beings like God and Alypius, but even of the physical universe, is beyond the reach of the senses. In the pursuit of complete knowledge, even of the objects of sense-perception, sense-knowledge can be of only limited help; it is both partial and of another kind or degree from that which is required in the case of the knowledge of God or of a spiritual being such as the human soul. In fact, Augustine goes further. He wants, at this stage of his thinking, to eliminate it altogether (*Sol.* I.iii.8) in his pursuit of the higher knowledge.

Now he turns to the Platonists, who have explored this kind of knowledge further than any other pagans. They may be correct in some at least of the statements they make about the nature of God, but Augustine is not convinced that they really know God. He himself was, after all, able in his opening prayer to express in words the attributes of God he wants to know, but he does not yet 'know' them, or his search would be over. He was able to put together a list of divine attributes not because he understands them, by holding them in his understanding, but because he has collected them together from his reading and has them in his memory (*Sol.* I.iv.9). To know (*scire*) then, is something other (*aliud*) than the knowledge Augustine is seeking, in which he holds the object of his knowledge fully before him, and knows as he is known.

Augustine now looks for an example which he hopes will be sufficiently free from extraneous associations to make his point simply and clearly. He turns to geometry. His Reason asks him whether he 'knows' what a line is and what a sphere is. He answers that he does. He knows, for example, that every point on the circumference of a sphere is equidistant from the centre. His senses tell him so too, but they have done no more than corroborate what he already knows. Had he not known this by some inward sense, then his bodily senses would be like a ship bringing him to a point where he can see the shore, he says, but leaving him floundering in the waves at the end of his journey. They would not bring him to land.

These geometrical reflections take him a little further. Augustine knows that a line can be divided an infinite number of times (for it is made up of an infinite number of points), but lengthwise it cannot be divided at all (for it is only one point wide). He knows that a sphere has a single point at its centre. So he knows that the line and the sphere are different. Nevertheless, he believes that he knows about the sphere and the line with an equally sure knowledge (*aeque*), an inner certainty which makes them seem self-evident – for there is no evidence of the senses which can finally demonstrate such truths (*Sol.* I.iv.10). In the *Confessions* (VI.iv) Augustine says that he had at one time thought that the kind of certainty he sought in theological truths was of this intuitive and mathematical kind. He wanted to be as sure of them as he was that seven and three make ten. We have met the same example (an Aristotelian one in origin) in the *De Libero Arbitrio* where Augustine uses it to illustrate what will be true 'not only now, but always' (II.viii.21.83).

It is clear to Augustine that this intuitive, mathematical mode of knowledge is more direct and more certain than that got by sense-perception. Yet it is not in this way that we know God. He is beginning to think that his knowledge of the properties of the line and sphere belong to *una disciplina*, and knowledge of God to another order of knowledge altogether. If the two kinds of knowledge were really the same, so that we know God as we know geometry, he would expect to be as full of joy at perceiving mathematical truth as he is confident he will be when at last he knows God (*Sol.* I.v.11). He thinks of this joy as a response to the sudden 'appearance' of light where there was darkness before, knowledge where there was ignorance, a Good where there was an absence of good. Anselm, too, speaks in his Prologue to the *Proslogion* of the joy he felt when he hit upon the argument for the existence of God. It is as though the object of knowledge, God himself, were to switch on a light. We see mathematical truths by the light of our own understanding, but for theological truths we need God's illumination.

Reason proceeds to show him how the *intelligibilis Dei majestas* is superior to the *spectamina* of geometry in this way. He can, Reason says, 'see' God with his mind's eye, just as he sees the sun with his bodily eyes (*Sol.* I.vi.12). The two kinds of knowing are presented as two kinds of 'seeing', and the vision of the bodily sense is made to provide an analogy with the vision of the intellect. The certainties of such sciences as geometry are, says Reason, like the objects on earth upon which the sun's rays shine, but God illuminates them with an intellectual, not a physical light. Knowledge is therefore intellectual seeing. Reason itself is the faculty of intellectual vision, just as the bodily eyes are the instruments of physical vision. The truths of mathematics belong to the realm of *intelligibilia,* just as God does, but they differ in this: as in the corporeal realm the earth cannot be seen unless it is illuminated, while the light is visible of itself, so mathematical truths cannot be known unless intellectual light is thrown upon them, while God illuminates himself so that he can be known.

This highest intellectual vision, the vision of God, can function only if it is unimpeded by any trace of bodily corruption (*Sol.* I.vii.14). Augustine devotes the rest of Book I of the *Soliloquies* to showing that knowledge requires spiritual health, and that spiritual health and the resulting clarity of mental vision depends upon separation from all bodily ties. The answer to the question Augustine poses at the beginning of the *Soliloquies* is that the man who attains wisdom is the man who has learned to 'know' without the aid of his senses, which can only impede his soaring understanding of higher things. That remains the foundation of his epistemology; although as he entered more deeply into the exploration of the Christian faith it became a less insistent theme, it is always there beneath.

St Peter experienced the *alienatio mentis* when he saw the vision of a container full of animals let down by four ropes from heaven (Acts 10.10–20). He doubted whether he had really seen the vision when he returned to his senses because sense-experience would make such an event seem impossible. Only when he asked to have the meaning of the vision explained to him did he understand it in the intellectual sense (*De Gen. ad Lit.* x.xi.23). The moral is clear enough. The senses are not only incapable of understanding higher things, but if we trust them they will advise us wrongly. We must make our minds strangers to our bodies by an *alienatio mentis* if we are to see God.

3 Deceiving Appearances

(a) FINDING WORDS

So bright is the light which illuminates the understanding of the heaven of heavens, the *creatura intellectualis* which sees God face to face, that it would dazzle us. It is as if we were to look into a lamp or the beam of a torch; the light is inaccessible. Only to the *mens pura* is it a light to see by.

Therefore men need aids to understanding, something that they can grasp, to stand for the things they cannot understand directly. They need signs and symbols. Augustine saw signs everywhere in the world, natural signs, such as the smoke which tells us there is a fire somewhere (*De Doct. Chr.* II.i.2), and conventional signs, such as words and gestures, by which living beings exchange information about what they are thinking and feeling and perceiving (*De Doct. Chr.* II.ii.3). Such signs are necessary, for we cannot see directly into one another's minds, and we must give information to one another if we want to communicate with one another, but the sign is no more than an aid, to help us grasp consciously what we already know, if our minds were not too blurred with sin to see.

God uses signs not to convey new information to us, but to direct our attention to something he wants us to see or to realise. Augustine's claim that we can learn nothing from signs that we do not know already is perhaps the most startling of his epistemological ideas (*De Mag.* VIII.21). He argues that if God did not plant in our minds the knowledge which enables us to recognise the meaning of the sign, we should perceive only the sign and not its significance. The smoke would tell us nothing about the fire. The word would be an empty noise.

Augustine's theory of signs was worked out in full in the first books of the *De Doctrina Christiana*, written in the 390s. Already in his little book *De Magistro*, a 'Cassiciacum' dialogue in spirit, although it was written in Africa, Augustine was exploring its possibilities with his son, Adeodatus. The discussions of the *De Magistro* are dry and technical; yet they provide a foundation for the wider-ranging treatment of the *De Doctrina Christiana*: of all kinds of signs – the natural signs which are evidences that God has placed in the world to show us his goodness, beauty and power; the signs of our human language of words and gestures; the signs given by God in the words of Holy Scripture, which are given to us through the medium of the human beings who wrote them down (*De Doct. Chr.* II.ii.3).

In the *De Magistro* Augustine and Adeodatus ask a number of preliminary questions about the function of signs – whether signs can stand for other signs or whether they must stand for things, whether a sign can signify another sign, which in turn signifies the first sign (as the word 'sign' signifies a word, and 'word' signifies a sign). They examine a line of Virgil word by word (*Aeneid* II.659), to see what each word signifies, and they discover a special difficulty in the case of the word *nihil*, which, paradoxically, must signify something because all words signify something, while at the same time, it must signify 'nothing' because that is the meaning of the word *nihil*. He asks Adeodatus to sum up their discussion so that it will be clear what foundations they have laid (*De Mag.* VIII.21). A good deal of technical preliminary is disposed of in this way, to clear the ground for the main argument Augustine wants to put forward: that the sign is something which exists as a means to an end.

If that is so, the sign is of less value than the thing it signifies. It is also of less value than the knowledge of that thing which it recalls to the mind (*De Mag.* IX.26). The sign is a very humble intermediary, and knowledge of a sign is a lowlier thing than the knowledge of the thing it signifies. On this basis, Augustine now advances his principle that nothing can be learned from signs (*De Mag.* X.33). If a sign is used, no-one who does not already know the thing of which it is a sign will be any the wiser. I shall understand what a 'head' is, not by hearing the word alone, but by seeing a head and learning to associate the word with it. The meaning of the sign is learned, then, from our knowledge of the thing signified. We do not learn anything about things from signs. The best we can say for words and other signs is that they point to things, and suggest we seek them (*De Mag.* XI.36). They do not show us things in such a way that we know them, though they may prompt us to enquire.

Augustine regards the memory as the repository in which our knowledge lies. Ideas, notions, concepts, images, a vast equipage of inward signs crowds the memory, as Augustine shows in the tenth book of the *Confessions*. How do they get there? Each of the senses, he explains, takes in the things it perceives through its own channel: the eyes, light and all colours and shapes; the ears, all kinds of sounds; the nostrils, scents, and so on (*Conf*. X.xviii.15). These form images which are quite distinct in type and do not interfere with one another. For example, sounds do not intrude when we are visualising something. Yet sounds and other things perceived by the senses do not themselves enter our minds, but only images of the things. What we have in our minds are likenesses or symbols or representations of things (*similitudines rerum*).[5]

Here again Augustine would have been able to draw on Plotinus for guidance in framing his questions, if not necessarily for his answers. Plotinus discusses the soul's powers of taking in and storing knowledge in the fourth *Ennead*. He asks whether memory is vested in the faculty by which we perceive and learn (*Ennead* IV.iii.28), whether one principle of our nature is the seat of both awareness and recollection (*Ennead* IV.iii.29). Plotinus comes to a conclusion very much in accordance with Augustine's – that recollection is a matter of drawing images out of store, that the memory deals in images; and he, too, looks at the storing of sense-impressions.

Augustine sees no difficulty in explaining how these sense-images are used. If he wants to speak of Carthage, he looks inside himself to find what he is to say, and he discovers there a notion or image of Carthage. This is present in his memory because he has been to Carthage, and has received an idea of Carthage into his memory through his senses (*De Trin*. VIII.vi.9). The chain is complete. Augustine has been to Carthage and seen it; his senses have stored up an impression of Carthage in his memory; he can recall that impression at will and label it with the word 'Carthage', which he utters when he wishes to communicate his idea to someone else who also knows Carthage.

What are we to say of our knowledge of things we have not seen? If Augustine mentions Carthage to someone who has not yet been there, his listener must form an idea of it out of bodily features he already has in his memory. His image may or may not be accurate (*De Trin*.

VIII.iv.7). He can verify it by visiting the place and revising his image. In this way a word such as 'Carthage' comes to link the thing and our knowledge of the thing, with a sign or image in the mind.

This cannot be what happens, however, with abstract ideas, knowledge of the kind we seem to possess intuitively, as in Augustine's example of the properties of the sphere and the line. We do not know such ideas through our senses. We know them within our minds, in quite a different way. In such cases we hold, not an image of the thing, but the thing itself in our minds (*Conf*. x.ix.16; *De Gen. ad Lit*. XII.iii.6, x.21; *De Trin*. x.x.17).

If we ask how such things came into our minds, we shall find no door in the body through which they can have come. Augustine has looked, and found no points of entry (*Conf*. x.x.17). God must have given them to us directly, by implanting them in our minds. God is therefore the only teacher who can enlarge our vocabulary of ideas, the range of our knowledge, in areas where the senses are no help to us. Words themselves cannot teach us, because without God to tell us what they mean they convey nothing to us at all. Words are signs for things we already know.

Here again Plotinus has something to say which may have been helpful to Augustine. He asks whether all 'mental acts' are recorded by the 'imaging' faculty (*Ennead* IV.iii.30). There are some mental acts, he points out, which are not accompanied by an image. What role does the memory play here? Perhaps memory should be regarded in this case as reception into the image-making faculty of a verbal formula, which accompanies the concept, suggests Plotinus. The verbal formula in some way 'exhibits' the concept as if it mirrored it, while the concept itself remains hidden beneath. The memory retains the verbal formula or 'word'.

The image-making faculty would thus be responsible for forming the concept by an act of apprehension and holding it permanently in the form of a memory. This verbal formula is the model for the word we utter, a mere sign. The word does not vanish from our vocabulary as though we had used it up, when we speak it, any more than the image goes out of the mind when we voice it.

The word may be learned through the sense of hearing. The process by which it becomes attached to a concept is not strictly a learning process, however. The act of the memory is to store a verbal sign or formula for something it already knows.

We may think we learn something from what others tell us, but unless it is related in our minds to something we already know, we shall not come to knowledge that way. We 'know', in the strict and proper sense of the term, not what we have heard with our outward ears, but what we have learned by listening to the inward voice of the Truth which speaks to us directly. Someone speaking to our outward ears may encourage us to listen to God's word within, but only by listening to God himself can we come to knowledge. Every rational soul is capable of attaining knowledge in this way, but some listen harder than others, and so their knowledge is greater.

If these difficulties stand in our way in the case of learning to understand mere abstract ideas, how much greater are the difficulties of coming to know God himself? If we try to imagine God we are bound to form an inaccurate image, because our bodily senses cannot furnish us with reliable material. That is why bodily images are so misleading, and we cannot check the accuracy of the image by any means at our disposal, because our sinful minds cannot see God clearly. It is not perhaps very important that I should have an accurate picture of Rome or Milan; but it is of the first importance that my image of God should be a true one. How, then, are we to find the right 'word' for God (*De Trin.* VIII.iv.7–vi.9)?

(b) GOD'S WORD

In 415 Augustine wrote a letter to Evodius, a native of Thagaste who had been with Augustine at Milan and Cassiciacum and Ostia, and returned to Africa with him, becoming a bishop at about the same time as Augustine, at Uzalis near Uttica (*Letter* 168). He writes about the work with which he is busy. Books IV and V of *The City of God* are completed, and commentaries on Psalms 67, 71, 77. Augustine wanted to finish the commentaries on the Psalms, exercises in practical exegesis, with a largely pastoral purpose. *The City of God*, too, was an outward-looking book, in which Augustine was trying to make sense for his readers of the shocking and sudden changes which were taking place in the Roman world, to make them understand that Christianity offered a hope of something new in what appeared, after the fall of Rome, to be the last age of the world.[6] He did not want to be sidetracked yet into continuing with the books on the Trinity, which he had had on hand for a long time.

He found them demanding work. They were being written slowly and painfully and intermittently. The *De Trinitate* is a work of introspection. Augustine had a need of his own to meet in writing it. It is an exploration of the doctrine of the Trinity from within the human mind, in which Augustine tries to discover how closely he is made in the image of God in that most Godlike part of him, his intellectual being. He strives to find words in which to talk of God.

His starting-point is the paradox of the doctrine of the Trinity. It appears to be impossible for the human mind to grasp how what is 'one' may also be 'three'. A created intellect has limited capacities, but Augustine was sure that man ought to grasp this better than he does, that such understanding as men possess by nature is clouded by evil. He wanted to understand exactly what effect evil was having upon his mind, so that he could, as it were, see through it to the truth. We find him returning to his earlier reflections about the way in which it may be possible for man to form an idea of a God who is beyond bodily perceiving, without resorting to 'corporeal images'. Once again, he examines the faculties of mind which judge and assess and store the perceptions of corporeal things which are gained through the senses (*De Trin.* VIII.vi.9; x.v.7). He tries again to understand how it is that we are able to cross the boundary between ourselves and what surrounds us, by perceiving something outside us and, as it were, bringing it inside, in the form of an image or idea, for mental scrutiny, but above all Augustine is still concerned with the question he had been trying to answer as he wrote the *Confessions*: how can we be sure that we 'know' God as he really is, and not some phantom or fantasy of our own devising, some 'bodily imagining' fashioned from the perceptions of our senses?

In the course of the intervening decade, Augustine's method of enquiry had been modified. He had come to think that in a special sense – which does not undermine the epistemology of the *De Magistro* – we may come to know things because we have been told of them by reputable sources. In the philosopher's paradise of Cassiciacum he had employed a philosopher's methods; he worked by reasoning. In the *De Trinitate* reasoning has a partner, in 'authority'. It works in harness with the use of Scriptural proof-texts, interpreted to show that their teaching is in harmony with the arguments from reason which are being proposed.

The way in which we may come to 'know' something by authority already interested Augustine when he wrote the *Confessions*. There he notes that there are many things we cannot know unless someone tells us of them. We cannot come to know by observation that we had parents, and who they were, for instance (*Conf.* VI.v.7). Yet we are content to regard such pieces of knowledge as quite certain on the 'authority' of other people's assurances. How much more confidence, he argues, ought we to place in the knowledge we gain from Scripture than in what we learn on the authority of mere human beings? The same argument is put before Paulina in a letter written in 413 (*Letter* 147) in which Augustine tries to answer her question about the way in which it is possible for man to 'see' an invisible God. He divides the objects of human knowledge into things perceived directly and things 'known' by the testimony of others who have themselves perceived them, and report their perceptions to us. Again he gives the example of 'knowing who our ancestors were' (*Letters* 5–8), and again he emphasises that we ought to accept the testimony of Scripture more readily than that of the human witnesses whose accounts of ordinary things we find so convincing.

When did Augustine read the Bible thoroughly, to look systematically beyond Genesis and Paul's Letters and the Psalms he had come to love at Milan? Not, it seems, immediately after his conversion, or if he did begin then, it was not for some time that the influence of his reading began to make itself felt. The problems that crowded into his mind at Cassiciacum were approached philosophically, and there is little trace as yet of the knowledge of the Bible which became so detailed and so comprehensive in later years that he could scarcely write a paragraph without a quotation, because his head was so full of the Scriptures. He had long been acquainted with the book of Genesis – especially the part which touches on the creation of the world – because these were texts cited by the Manichees in their arguments against the Catholic position. The first Scriptural commentary he wrote was *On Genesis against the Manichees* in 388–90. The early chapters of Genesis presented him with familiar metaphysical and philosophical problems about the origin of evil.

Something new began to happen while he was a catechumen. He describes how he sang the Psalms (*Conf.* IX.iv.8) from the heart, and how it seemed to him that the Psalmist had expressed his own longings and uncertainties exactly. Like the Psalmist, he threw himself on God. He had been deeply moved by the Psalm-Chant when he went to hear Ambrose preach, and now his pleasure deepened. It is no accident that the style of the *Confessions* echoes that of the Psalms in its antitheses and climaxes and parallelisms. Its texture is entirely appropriate to Augustine's theme.

By 392 he had written commentaries on thirty-two Psalms. In 393–4 he began work on the *De Genesi ad Litteram*, which deals with a book already familiar to him, but in a new light – and with, significantly, a long *discursus* on the problems of epistemology, the theory of the way in which it is possible for man to know God, on which he had been concentrating his mind. The mid-390s also saw him writing on the Sermon on the Mount, a passage on which he had preached while he was a priest. Similarly, questions raised in discussion prompted him to begin on eighty-four 'propositions' connected with the Epistle to the Romans, at about this time, and to address himself to commentaries on Romans and Galatians, which he abandoned when he realised how long the task would take him if he went on with it in the same detail as he had begun. Augustine was not perhaps primarily an exegete. He was more at home with problems where he could bring his knowledge of Scripture to bear in finding solutions. In introducing Scriptural testimony into his discussions Augustine had redressed the imbalance he had begun to feel in the Cassiciacum dialogues and their companion works of the 380s and 390s. He had, by now, in every sense, little time for the pleasures of pure speculation. In a letter of 412 to Marcellinus (*Letter* 143) he writes that he is unwilling to 'expend much effort' on a question which has been put to him, arising out of something he had said in the *De Libero Arbitrio*. If this is a matter which cannot be settled by reason or by the Author whose statements cannot be disputed, then it is merely a matter of opinion, and Augustine cannot see that anything is to be gained by discussing it. He now wants to see reason and authority work together.

Augustine had not only become aware of the help to be had from the Bible; he had also become disenchanted with reason used as the sole method of arriving at 'proof', because it had proved misleading to so many. He sets out the categories of those who misuse reason at the beginning of the first Book of the *De Trinitate*. Some (including Augustine's old enemies the Manichees), try to apply to the spiritual world the ideas they have formed by sense-perception. They think in 'corporeal images', and they imagine that the spiritual can be conceived of and measured in that way. Others, he explains, try to think about God according to the models they have found in their own minds and hearts; recognising that God is spirit, nevertheless they can imagine him only in terms of what they know of the human soul. Others try to overleap such aids to understanding, and to rise above the whole created world in their minds, in order to try to understand God by direct perception. These men are arrogant and presumptuous, and, ironically enough, quite blind to the truth of which they think they have so clear a view. The first kind of thinker, limited by sense-perceptions, may try, for example, to say that God is red or white; the second may imagine God being like himself, sometimes forgetful. The third postulates some metaphysical non-sense, such as the idea that God brings himself into being. They are all grossly in error, and especially the last, whose ideas are wholly out of touch with the reality of things (*De Trin*. 1.i.1).

To question the power of reason was a serious matter for a Christian Platonist. It is, after all, in his reason that they believed that man most closely resembles God, and it would seem on the face of it that those who try to know God directly, without the aid of images, are approaching him in the right way. They go astray, Augustine is sure, because they try to know God entirely by their own efforts. It is not, he emphasises, the use of reason in itself that is mistaken, but the failure to allow the thing known to make itself known, the luminous truth to illuminate the mind.

In his letter of 413 to Paulina, *On Seeing God*, Augustine wrote about what he had come to see as a hierarchy of 'vision'. We see the sun with our bodily eyes, ourselves with an inward gaze (by which we perceive ourselves wishing or seeking, and so on), and God in another and higher way still. These different kinds of vision, bodily, introspective, spiritual, correspond with the three ways of thinking he has been outlining in the opening passages of the *De Trinitate*, with the difference that now God is being sought not speculatively but spiritually, by the light of the illumination he himself provides.

It is important that Augustine should find a proper place for these procedures, not only because his utmost inventiveness cannot suggest anything quite independent of them, but also because, as he acknowledges, Scripture itself makes use of the first and the second methods, those which have a contact with the created world; that is, Scripture uses 'bodily images' and analogies with the human mind and soul, to help enlarge man's limited capacity for understanding what is above and beyond him. In *Letter* 55, written to Januarius about 400, Augustine tries to explain the reason why Scripture employs 'figurative sayings'. He thinks that truths which are presented in figures excite our love (and stimulate our appetite) in a way that truths plainly set out and unadorned do not (although they satisfy our hunger). Some process of 'nourishing' and 'arousal' which they set in motion carries us upward and inward in response to the truth (cf. *De Doct. Chr.* II.vi.7). A soul sluggishly inert among earthly things can thus be carried along to the point where it understands 'bodily images', and then it can be brought to see some of the spiritual truths which are represented or symbolised by such images, until it is at last filled with love and burns with ardour. Thus the reason is enabled to function in the high region which is proper to it, but from which it is exiled by sin.

These divinely-granted aids to understanding must be distinguished clearly from the man-made aids which are more likely to be misleading than helpful. Man should direct his efforts, not to trying to make images of his own, but to purifying his mind, making himself receptive to God's illumination of his understanding (*De Trin.* I.i.3–ii.4). God's intention is that the *obscura* in Scripture should subdue our pride in our own mental powers by making us work hard to discover the hidden truth, as well as providing us with an indispensable aid to discovery. Edification and enlightenment go hand in hand (*De Doct. Chr.* II.vi.7). It is easy to see, given this view of the matter, why such a raising of the reason to its proper level should be progressive and why divine help is indispensable. No creature, even if he is *rationalis et intellectualis*, illuminates his own mind. The light must come from God, and full understanding of the spiritual sense is not to be achieved all at once. The distance reason has fallen is too great. There are several steps or *gradus* (Augustine lists seven) by which a man must strive to purify his mind (*De Doct. Chr.* II.vii.10) in order to proceed from the limited vision open to his bodily eyes to the higher vision of the mind. The divine illumination is of three kinds. It is perpetual, shedding light into the minds of the faithful, directly so that they may progress steadily in understanding.

On one occasion, it involved a specific act on the part of God. Christ 'spoke' himself as the Word, in the Incarnation, when he made himself perceptible to bodily eyes. He made himself a sign, a figure, a bodily image. He is everywhere present to the inward eye when it is pure (*De Doct. Chr.* I.xi.12), but for the sake of those whose vision of higher things is obscured by their sin, and who can see only with their bodily eyes, he appeared once in the body. (There is something akin to this in the *Manichean Psalm-Book* (ccxxii) where the Word of God is described as 'sowing in thee through what is invisible the remembrance of the hidden Judgment which thou hast forgotten since the day when thou didst drink the water of madness, O soul'.) He strung a bridge between bodily and spiritual perception from, as it were, the spiritual side, coming to meet man in his struggle to build one from the 'bodily' side in his own 'bodily imaginings'. Just as when we think of a word in our own hearts and then speak it, the thought is not converted into sound, but remains *apud se integra*, whole in itself, so the Word of God was not 'changed (*commutatum*)' but 'made flesh' by, as it were, a single 'utterance' (*De Doct. Chr.* I.xiii.12).

God 'uttered' the Word in a third way, too, in Holy Scripture, so that men might have something to read and hear, something they could take in through their bodily senses and which would, again, meet them on their own limited terms, in images and figures.

(c) TELLING LIES

Augustine's teaching about Scriptural interpretation is founded upon a great certainty. The Bible is telling the truth. It is God's Word uttered to us directly. Any apparent absurdities in what it says can be put down to our own inability to understand what the text means. Nevertheless, to all appearances Scripture is full of contradictions and anomalies, and Augustine faced a task which demanded all his ingenuity in explaining it.[7]

There are, as Augustine sees it, two reasons for the *absurditates* we think we perceive in Scripture. The first lies in the multiplication and diversification which was necessary if the Word was to speak to us in terms we would understand. The Word had to become many words, to descend even to the level of individual sounds for us. Scripture is full of words, and so the One Word of God is expanded or diffused and one Word sounds in many mouths (*En. Ps.* 103.iv.1). This was a descent indeed, for it is self-evident to Augustine's Neoplatonist way of thinking that what departs from unity departs from perfection.

Inherent in the varied language we humans speak is a lack of that perfect precision and clarity which lies in the single Word of God alone.

A second reason why Scripture appears not always consistent – and a far more important one – is our inability to read it aright, because our minds are clouded by sin. God has done all he can to help us here. In his concern to open up channels in the minds of men, God speaks in Scripture at several different levels, both literally and metaphorically. Scripture has distinctive usages (*En. Ps.* 105.18); Augustine speaks of: *locutio scripturarum; qua locutione divinae paginae* (*En. Ps.* 104.18); *locutiones enim tropicae propriis prophetico more miscentur* (*De Civ. Dei* XX.21). We must be alert to notice what kind of speech is being used (*De Civ. Dei* II.19) and to distinguish Scriptural usages from common usage (*communis locutio*) (*De Civ. Dei* IX.4) and daily usage (*quotidiana loquendi consuetudo*) (*En. Ps.* 108.23).

God has willed, too, that his Scriptures should be translated into many languages, so that all his people may understand them, and scholars must study the manuscripts carefully to make sure that they have not missed a nuance which cannot be rendered from the Greek into their own language (*En. Ps.* 105.31); in Psalm 104, for example, we have: *confitebor Domino nimis in ore meo*. In Latin, *nimis* normally means 'more than it should'; can the Psalmist mean that he will praise God more than he should? That is a quite unacceptable reading, but some Latin versions have *valde*, 'heartily', 'fully', and that is a much more acceptable version, which translates the Greek more exactly, for *nimis* in Greek is ἀγαν and the verse has σφόδρα (*En. Ps.* 104.32). Words in Scripture may even mean contrary things. Christ is described as a lion and the Devil is described as a lion; we are told to be wise as serpents; but Satan took the form of a serpent (*De Doct. Chr.* III.xxv.35–6).

God certainly does not intend us to be confused. He is trying to help our understanding, not confound it. Augustine proposes a collection of rules to help us here – as others had done before him, including the Donatist Tichonius. In interpreting the Bible's statements about the Trinity, for example, it is essential to distinguish between passages which speak of the respects in which God is one, and passages which refer to the Persons individually; if we do not confuse the two, we shall not find contradictions in Scripture (*De Trin.* I.xi.22). Scripture has different ways of speaking, and all failures to understand it arise from failures to read it in the proper 'mode'. Two apparently contradictory statements may both be true, if they are read in different ways (*De Trin.* I.xiii.29).

The moral is plain: we shall understand what the figures represent only when our minds are pure. Scripture is designed both to meet us at our own level and to improve our understanding so that we can see more deeply into it. God is not telling us lies in the Bible. Our sinful minds simply cannot see the truth, but the problem of *absurditas*, which exercised Augustine a good deal in his exegesis, takes on another appearance altogether when we remove it from the realm of the study of the Bible and consider it in the larger context of human talk and writing.

Augustine was in no doubt that here was an important aspect of the problem of evil, epistemologically speaking. A lie has all the properties he had learned to associate with evil, and which he had described in the *Confessions*. As good is opposed to evil, or light to darkness, so a lie is opposed to truth. There can be no compromise between them, no means of whitewashing a lie so that it can be told with a clear conscience. A lie may appear to be true, but it will have a hidden sense which is quite the opposite (*De Grat. Chr.* xxxiii.36); indeed, it must have some appearance of truth or it will not achieve its purpose, which is to deceive, for deceptiveness is of the essence of a lie.

Although Augustine was sure that the difference between a lie and the truth is clear-cut, he discovered that knotty problems arose when he tried to define a lie. Lying is a complex thing, eluding analysis like all its companions in the darkness we call evil. There are many *genera mendaciorum*. If a lie is a knot (*nodus*) (*De Mend.* ix.5), truth is a straight path, the *trames veritatis*, from which the liar turns aside (*deviare*) (*Contra Mendacium* vii.7).

It was in an attempt to untie these knots – and largely for the sheer intellectual satisfaction of doing so – that Augustine wrote his first treatise *On Lying* (*De Mendacio*) in 395. He criticises it in the last chapter of Book I of the *Retractationes* for its obscurity, and the complexity into which he has allowed himself to be led by intellectual curiosity. He had not published it. Indeed, he had almost decided to destroy it, but on re-reading it he thought it might be useful to the reader in more ways than one. It would certainly oblige him to exercise his mind, as he had intended when he wrote it, but it would also make the reader aware of aspects of the question which he had not touched on in his later book *Against Lying* (*Contra Mendacium*). He now thinks that a far better book, because it is directed entirely against lying, whereas in the first study he has marshalled every argument he could, both for and against the view that sometimes it is necessary to tell a lie. He is prepared to let the first book stand as a preliminary study, although he now values the importance of clarification less than he did. In the quarter of a century between the writing of these two pieces, Augustine had become less academically minded and more practical in his approach to problem-solving. His pursuit of the truth was a largely cerebral activity in his philosopher days; he had enjoyed tossing the question about, but now his chief concern was that his discoveries should be edifying to his readers.

The *Contra Mendacium* was composed in 420 to meet a specific difficulty (*Retr*. II.lx). At the time when he wrote the *De Mendacio* Augustine had not heard of the Priscillianists, a sect of heretics in Spain whose teaching had Manichean elements. Orosius had told him something of their customs when he came to Africa, and he was able to give a full account of their views in the catalogue of heresies he addressed to Quoduultdeus in 429.[8] The Priscillianist heretics thought it permissible to tell lies so as to protect themselves. Some Catholics had argued that they were, by the same token, entitled to pretend to be Priscillianists, if in that way they were able to get inside the Priscillianist cells, so as to be in a position to set about converting the heretics. Their lies would have a good intention.

This is a special case of the argument that lying is sometimes justified, but has much larger implications for the way the Christian is to respond to heresy. If a lie may be met with a lie with a clear conscience, to what other means may a Christian legitimately resort in order to attain a good end? What may he not be free to do in order to suppress heresy? Sometimes Christians were misled by such arguments into blurring the distinction between heresy and orthodoxy. One of Augustine's deacons had, he discovered, continued to attend Manichean meetings as a 'hearer' (*Letter* 236), apparently with no sense that he was living a lie. The boundary between heterodoxy and orthodoxy was too fine to allow anyone to blur it casually. A young man came to join the community at Hippo after hearing Manichean Scriptures (*Letter* 64.3), but he might have been led into heresy, not out of it.

The *De Mendacio* has an air of Cassiciacum about it. It deals with a philosophical question, a question of definition; what is a lie? A joke is not a lie, although it may be full of falsehood. The man who tells a joke makes it clear to his listener that he does not intend what he says to be taken seriously. His tone of voice, the sting in the tail of the joke, the revelation that he was jesting or teasing, when his listener has been taking him seriously, all make it impossible to confuse a joke with a lie, because the true state of affairs is made plain in the end (*De Mend*. ii.2). To tell a joke is certainly not to tell the truth, but it is not, properly speaking, to tell a lie, either; Augustine cannot think that perfectly good minds will want to engage in such activities, but they fall outside the scope of his immediate enquiry.

He approaches the definition of a lie by asking what is going on in the mind of the liar. 'The liar must be judged by the *sententia* of his mind, not by the truth or falsehood of what he says.' Not everyone who speaks a falsehood is lying; he may believe that what he says is true. The relationship between what is in his mind and what is on his tongue is an honest one. He is, as he understands it, saying that what is so, is so (*De Mend*. ii.3). He may not be entirely free from blame, if his error is the result of his own laziness for example (*De Mend*. ii.3), but the true liar is double-hearted: he has a *duplex cor*, a *duplex cogitatio*; there is one thing in his mind and another on his tongue (*De Mend*. iv.4).

In his treatise on the truth (*De Veritate*) St Anselm does not enquire into the psychology of lying, but restricts himself to the relationship between things as they are and the statements or acts made in relationship to them, either truthfully or mendaciously. To tell the truth is to say that what *is* so is so, not that what the speaker *thinks* is so, is so.[9] This primary relation between the state of affairs and the statement or action which tells others about it is distorted in the telling of a joke, or in a theatrical performance, but not in a way which will mislead anyone seriously. It is distorted in a seriously deceitful way in the telling of a lie. Lying involves the intention to deceive. There must, says Augustine, be a *voluntas fallendi* (*De Mend*. iv.4).

An intention to deceive no-one would be absurd. The liar must intend to deceive someone. Augustine therefore finds himself obliged to take into account the impact of the statement on the listener, who may also be subject to error or misunderstanding when he tries to judge what he has been told. Anselm's simple relationship between truth and reality (or 'things-as-they-are') involves no such complications, because he is dealing with truth. It is the presence of evil which makes for difficulties. Lying is full of *enodatio* because it is evil. Augustine puts two cases in order to illustrate the difficulty he finds himself in. Someone knows or thinks that what he has to say is false, but says it with no intention to deceive. Someone else knows or thinks that what he has to say is true, and yet says it so as to deceive. The first man, perhaps, knows that a certain road is beset by robbers. He knows that he will not be believed whatever he says, so he tells his sceptical friend that the road is not beset by robbers. He intends his friend to believe the opposite and not to travel on it. The second man knows that the road is beset by robbers. He knows his sceptical friend will not believe what he says, but he says that the road is beset by robbers, so that his friend will think it is not, and will travel on it. These arguments are full of negatives. Lying is an essentially negative activity, and that is why it is so full of perversity.

Which of these two is the liar? Perhaps they are both liars if lying is a saying with the intention of falsity behind it. The first man wills to speak falsely; the second wills to deceive. Or perhaps neither of them is a liar? The first man wills not to deceive; the second wills to speak the truth. That would be the case if lying were to be defined as a saying of someone willing to speak falsely. In each case the will is involved (and that, as we shall see, is of central importance for Augustine), but in the first definition, the intention is to deceive as to the thing; in the second, the intention is to deceive as to the statement made about the thing. In a perfect world these difficulties would not arise. The sceptical friend would believe what he was told, and his well-wisher could save him from the robbers by telling him the truth. The man who wants him to be attacked by the robbers would not be able to deceive him except by telling him a lie, that is, by making a statement which does not accord with things as they are. The negative element which is present in every lie (because it is evil, and evil is always negative), becomes a double negative when the listener to the lie is himself perverted by sin to the point where he cannot receive the truth into his mind.

The universe seems to be so disordered by evil that the well-wisher cannot save his friend from the robbers except by telling him a lie. Indeed, many people would say that lying is sometimes necessary (*De Mend*. iv.5). Augustine cannot accept that there may be *honesta mendacia* (*De Mend*. xii.20), which not only do no harm to anyone, but may even do good. He looks at the commandment 'Thou shalt not bear false witness', and points out that when a man speaks he bears witness to the state of his own mind. How can he then lie without denying himself? 'The mouth which lies kills the soul', he quotes (*De Mend*. v.6).

A not dissimilar problem arises over the passages of Scripture which are to be taken not literally but figuratively. Does Scripture lie in not telling the plain truth? We have seen that Scripture makes a concession to sinful man by speaking to him indirectly in allegory, by presenting higher truths to him in the form of bodily images. Is this, too, an *honestum mendacium* made necessary by the presence of evil in the universe? Not if we understand *mendacium* aright, says Augustine. 'Every saying is to be referred to that which it speaks of.' The figurative sayings of Scripture are in fact speaking of their hidden meanings, not of that which they appear to be saying, and so they do in fact signify truthfully what they ought to signify (*De Mend*. v.8). There is certainly no *auctoritas mentiendi*, no *carte blanche* to lie, given us in the figurative usages of Scripture.

The sayings of Jesus reported in Scripture fall into a class of their own here. There can be nothing but truth in the words of Truth himself. Augustine takes the opportunity to underline the point (*De Mend*. v.8), for it helps him to show that God cannot countenance lies in any form, or for even the best of motives. All lies are the property of Satan, who is the father of lies, because he 'did not stand fast in the truth' (John 8.44). Indeed, if we were to try to build up someone's faith by telling him lies, we should entirely subvert the discipline of faith (*De Mend*. viii.11). Augustine demands the utmost scrupulousness. A man is responsible not only for the deeds he does, but for the things he allows to be done by his consent (*De Mend*. ix.12). The act is certainly worse than the consent. To consent to something is not the same as to do it. Although murder is worse than theft, it is a greater sin to steal than to consent to murder (*De Mend*. ix.12–14). Nevertheless, to consent to a lie is wrong just as it is wrong to tell a lie, and the good end which may be in view is no excuse.

Nowhere is it so important to be clear that this point is understood as in the handling of heretics. A heresy is a lie or a system of lies about the faith. The heretic is a persistent liar. Sheer obstinacy of mind is characteristic of heresy, just as persistence in the truth is characteristic of a good man (*Contra Mendacium* iii.5). The heretic's lie may be unconscious. He deceives others by telling what he believes to be the truth. That is why he is so difficult to deal with: he sees nothing wrong in what he is doing. Even if he knows he is lying, he makes a virtue of it, saying that Scripture shows that prophets and apostles, even Christ himself, teach us to lie. The Priscillianists make a dogma of lying (*Contra Mendacium* i.2). Yet when the Priscillianist says that the soul is a *pars Dei*, of the same substance as God, a great deception takes place. The very nature of God is presented in a distorted light to the understanding of the believer (*captivetur, decipiatur, fallatur, conturbetur atque turnetur, damnetur atque cruciatur*) (*Contra Mendacium* v.8).

What are we to do about this? Are we to pretend to accept the teaching of these heretics, so that we may win their confidence and then lay bare their blasphemy (*Contra Mendacium* vi.8)? But that is to deny Christ, and we must not do that even for the highest motives. To learn the art of fallacy so as to beat the heretics at their own game can never be an honest act (*Contra Mendacium* vi.12). In the Apostles' time, there were those who preached the truth, not with a true mind (*non veraci animo*), but in envy and contentiousness. They were tolerated for the sake of the truth they were telling, but no-one could be praised for 'lying with a pure mind' even if that were possible (*Contra Mendacium* vi.16).

If, then, lying is never justified, even when there seems to be a good, even a necessary, reason for it, how much less acceptable is it in cases where all we hope to gain is pleasure? There is certainly a delight in lying (*De Mend*. xi.18). Some men seek that delight by lying so that others will think well of them. They do not mean to hurt others, but they deceive them with sweet words. This *suaviloquium* is offensive, because by its means a man represents himself not as he is, but as he would like others to think him. It breaks the first rule of truth-telling (*De Mend*. xi.18). Some take pleasure in the *fallacia* itself, in their sheer cleverness in misleading others (*De Mend*. xi.18). These pleasures are typical of the pleasures which evil brings. There is no difficulty in identifying them, once we look with the clear eyes of the mind purged of sin. Bodily modesty (*pudicitia corporis*), spiritual chastity (*castitas animae*) and truth of doctrine (*veritas doctrinae*) go together (*De Mend*. xix.40). Not to know a lie is an effect of the blindness of mind which sin brings upon us (*De Mend*. xxi.43).

Mistakes

In the *Enchiridion* (423) Augustine returned to the subject of lying, in a final attempt to set out the main principles of this 'handbook to the faith' of his old age. He remembers that he once wrote a long book (the *De Mendacio*) about the rights and wrongs of lying. Now he wants to make two main points: firstly, it is never right to tell a lie, and, secondly, lying is a sin which varies in magnitude with the intention of the speaker and the subject on which he tells his lie. The man who tells a lie believing it to be the truth is not so culpable as the man who tells the truth intending to deceive; the man who knows someone to be dead and tells others that he is still alive is in a better state than the man who is deceived into believing that Christ dies for ever (*Enchiridion* xviii).

These reflections lead him to consider error, boon companion of the lie and, like lying, possible only because of the presence of evil in men's minds. To accept what is false as if it were true is the essence of error (*Enchiridion* xvii). We can make such a mistake only out of ignorance. Ignorance is not bound to lead to error, but it will certainly do so if we pretend to knowledge we do not possess, that is, if we accept what is false as if it were true, placing faith in it without reason. That is what Pelagius has been saying, says Augustine in the *De Gratia Christi*, and he begs him not to add to the error and deception and wilfulness the Devil has inspired in him, by denying what he has learned, or defending his error (xxx.31). Were we free from the confusion of mind which evil brings about we should see too clearly to fall into error. There is, of course, deliberate and culpable error of this sort (cf. *De Ut. Cred.* 10–11) and Augustine is inclined to think that all error is blameworthy; it is, at any rate, certainly not a trivial thing.

The error in the soul which makes what is ugly seem fair, what is untrue seem plausible, is hideous. The *Manichean Psalm-Book* describes the way in which the Holy Spirit rescues man from the Error which permeates the world, an Error of universal scale (ccxxiii). Worldly men (ccxlviii), men who belong to Matter, are the children of Error (ccxx).

Nevertheless, God may use it for good. Augustine recollects an occasion when he took a wrong turning and by chance avoided the road on which a band of Donatists was waiting to attack him

(*Enchiridion* xvii), but error is always an evil in itself, even if it produces an advantage as Augustine's mistake did (*Enchiridion* xix). A small mistake which causes a petty annoyance can be turned to advantage by a good man; he will learn from his mistake and be spiritually edified; he will grow in patience; but an error of belief which will prevent a man's being a Christian is a serious matter. We should never regard error lightly. Large or small, it is a sign of the presence of evil.

So sure is Augustine of this that he is not prepared to say that even errors as to matters of fact in themselves neutral are not sins. It may be culpable to mistake a passing carriage for thunder or to take one identical twin for the other, although Augustine cannot see where the blame lies. He knows that the Academic philosophers taught that a wise man should never assent to anything in case he falls into error, for all things are uncertain (*Enchiridion* xx). On the whole he takes the view that error is not always a sin, but that it is always an evil (*Enchiridion* xxi).

We have moved from deliberate deception by lying to deception by mistake, where we must consider, not the guilt of the deceiver, but the guilt of the deceived, his own responsibility for the harm done to him by his error. Augustine is anxious that his readers should take responsibility for their own errors. In a later chapter of the *Enchiridion* (lx) he looks at Satan's attempts to deceive. If Satan appears in the guise of a man and deceives our bodily senses into believing that he is a man, that is comparatively harmless. 'When the Devil deceives with bodily appearances, no harm is done, because the eyes are mocked, if there is no error as to the truth of faith and understanding', he explains in the *De Genesi ad Litteram*. So long as Satan behaves as though he were good, and does things proper to a good angel, no damage is done if we believe him to be a good angel, but it is vitally important that we should be on our guard against Satan's attempts to lead us into his own perverted ways of thinking by presenting evil to us in the guise of good. Satan is a deceiver, a purveyor of error. Knowing that, we must, unfortunately, regard all our fellow men with suspicion, and trust nothing we are told until we have examined it carefully.

Nowhere is this more necessary than in guarding against intellectual deceit. If our senses are deceived, it is not important, but if our minds are deceived, far more is at stake.

Fallacies

The Devil may have all the best tunes, but there is no need for the Christian to envy him his arguments. Indeed, he cannot argue except in fallacies, because his reasoning is perverted. His arguments may appear impregnable; but that is the way with sophistries; they would not be able to deceive if their fallaciousness were obvious. Heretics are men whose powers of reasoning suffer under the same disabilities. Augustine wrote to his fellow bishops Eutropius and Paulus in 415 to explain where the fallacy lay in a series of definitions or *ratiocinationes* which Celestius had drawn up in defence of the Pelagian position. (We shall hear more of Celestius and Pelagius.) Jerome condemned the arguments as 'not syllogisms but solecisms' (*Letter to Ctesiphon*, 413 or 4). The definitions all rest on a single principle (it is perhaps a feature of Celestius' sin-darkened state of mind that he does not realise that all his arguments can be reduced to one). Celestius appeals to the idea of divine justice in order to show that it must be possible for a man to become perfect by his own efforts.

What, he asks first, is sin? Is it something that can be avoided, or something that cannot be avoided? If it cannot be avoided, surely it is not culpable, for a man cannot be blamed for what he cannot help. Therefore sin can be avoided, and so a man is responsible for avoiding it (*De Per. Just. Hom.* II.i). Augustine attacks his premiss. Certainly sin is something which can be avoided, and a perfect human nature could perhaps avoid it unaided, but our nature is *vitiata*, and it can only be healed of its flaw by the grace of God through Christ. Otherwise it can neither see what is required, because it is blind, nor carry it out, because it is weak (*De Per. Just. Hom.* II.i).

The same refutation can be used against Celestius' second argument. Is sin a matter of will or of necessity? If it is a matter of necessity, it cannot be avoided, and we have already seen how that would remove the blame from the sinner, and make his sin no sin at all. If sin is a matter of will, it can be avoided by an act of will. Yes, says Augustine, sin is certainly a matter of will, but the human will is blinded by sin and weakened by sin, and only with the aid of grace can a man resist temptation (*De Per. Just. Hom.* II.ii), If we put Celestius' third question and ask whether sin is *naturale* or *accidens*, the argument will follow the same pattern. If it is natural, a man can hardly be blamed for sinning, and if it is an accident it can be removed; what can be removed can be avoided, and so on. Augustine replies that sin is not in human nature, but is an attribute of nature, that is of flawed nature, and flawed nature needs the help of grace (II.iii). Celestius' point is that if God is just it must be possible for man to avoid sin; it would be unjust in God to condemn man for something he cannot help. Augustine has no quarrel with that, but he wants to emphasise the role of divine mercy in making the impossible possible: with divine aid man can do what otherwise he could not do. Certainly God is just (*certe iustus deus*), but it is a fact that he imputes every sin to the man who committed it, and that would be unjust if there were any sin which could not be avoided (*De Per. Just. Hom.* VI.v) says Celestius in a summing up of the points he has been making. Does God wish man to be without sin? Certainly. Who would be so insane as to say that what God wants cannot be so? (*De Per. Just. Hom.* III.vii). God made man good in nature, and over and above that, he ordered him to do good. It cannot be that God has ordered man to do something he cannot do (*De Per. Just. Hom.* IV.x). Again and again Augustine returns to his own single argument from grace, an argument which alone, he feels, can straighten out Celestius' crooked thinking.

The Manichees, too, are muddled thinkers. The eyes of their minds are so clouded that they do not understand the inconsistency of their position. In the *De Moribus Manichaeorum* Augustine took pleasure in showing them how their arguments about evil could all be turned back upon them (*De Mor. Man.* viii.11), how inconsistent their statements about evil were (*De Mor. Man.* ix.14), 'What a confusion of ideas! What an amazing fatuity!' there was in everything they said (*De Mor. Man.* ii.2).

This is not an altogether innocent muddle-headedness. The Manichees are deliberate deceivers. In the *De Moribus Ecclesiae Catholicae* Augustine tries to show in their true light the two tricks the Manichees use for catching the unwary. They make a false show of chastity and abstinence; that is, they set an example which is deceptive, and they misinterpret Scripture, making out a plausible case by their arguments and exegesis. Augustine's anti-Manichean writings are much concerned with the second of these. In the *De Moribus Manichaeorum*, for example, he takes examples of the claims of the Manichees and shows how self-contradictory they are; in the *De Utilitate Credendi* he distinguishes three ways in which the

Manicheans go astray in their interpretations. The *Reply to Faustus* includes a series of exchanges, in which Augustine presses Faustus on his readiness to accept the Gospel, the Old Testament and other parts of Scripture.

Augustine asks himself where he can best begin if he wants to show the Manicheans their errors, and although he maintains that in the natural order of things, authority must come before reasoning (for if a reason requires an authority to support it, it is clearly weak in itself) this will not do for the Manicheans. They prefer to begin with argument, and so Augustine does the same (*De Mor. Ecc. Cath.* II.3). He argues that to be happy a man must both love and possess his chief good, that a man's chief good is that than which there is nothing better, God himself. A man's own chief good is his soul, and the soul grows more good by following God. We learn about God from Scripture, both the Old Testament and the New. Augustine wants to arrive at a point where he can attack the Manichees directly on their views about the Bible, and demonstrate the harmony of the Old Testament with the New, so that they will be forced to concede the authority of the Old Testament which they want to deny.

Augustine wants to use logic for its traditional purpose of distinguishing truth from falsehood, but he insists that first its sphere of reference must be made clear. The rule that the logicians have laid down, which states that two contrary attributes cannot be predicated at the same time of the same thing does not apply in the case of good and evil. No body is simultaneously black and white, but something may be simultaneously good and evil; indeed, since evil cannot exist except by borrowing the existence of the good in which it inheres, there can be no evil unless there is simultaneously good and evil. If there is no good for evil to diminish, it is not there at all (*Enchiridion* xiv.1). With such provisos in mind, Augustine sets out Faustus' argument in the form of a syllogism so that he can show exactly where it breaks down, technically speaking (*C. Faust.* xxv.1).

> If evil does not exist, God is infinite. Otherwise he must be finite.
> Evil certainly exists,
> Therefore God is not infinite.

He himself uses a syllogism to demonstrate that Faustus is deliberately trying to mislead:

> Faustus uses an argument which is either deceitful or stupid.

Faustus is not stupid.

Therefore he tends to mislead the careless reader

(*C. Faust*. xvi.26). In the case of Faustus' argument that:

If these things are not written of Christ

And if you cannot show any others,

It follows that there are none at all,

Augustine acknowledges that the form of the argument is valid, but he points out that the two premises remain to be proved true. To prove the second false is easy, and then the whole argument collapses (*C. Faust*. xvi.26). In this way he hopes to avoid the muddled thinking the Manichees are given to, and to avoid it in such a way that his readers will be able to see how admirably clear Christian reasoning is, when the mind is lit by the divine Light. The very disorderliness of Manichean thinking about evil proves that evil is nothing. Just as their 'bodily' thinking about spiritual things is associated with their notion of evil as a material substance, so the muddled thinking to which they are given is associated with the disordering of reality which evil brings about. Augustine has shown to his own satisfaction a correlation between the misguidedness of the Manichean theory of evil and the shortcomings of their philosophising. They cannot handle abstract ideas because their 'metaphysics' is really 'physics', restricted to the concrete objects of the created world.

That would not matter perhaps if the Manichees were content to restrict themselves to the discussion of matter in its own terms, but they pretend that matter is what it is not. If they meant by *Hyle* only the unformed matter which is capable of taking bodily forms there could be no objection to their teaching, but they want to contribute to *Hyle* the power which belongs to God alone, that of making the forms by which bodies exist, and so they make *Hyle* a god (*C. Faust*. xx.14–xxi.4). Augustine notes in the *Confessions* that there came a moment when he felt he had made a breakthrough. He now hopes to help the Manichees through the same 'gate', so that they will understand the implications of this talk of matter and substance and existence as clearly as he does. When they pass through it they will see before them a clear-cut, methodologically exact procedure for analysing the problem of evil, in which there is no risk of falling into fallacy (*De Mor. Man*. vii.10).

(d) THE ABSURDITY OF THE TRUTH

As, day by day over a period of many years (*En. Ps.* 101.ii.1) Augustine preached on the Psalms, he unfolded before his listeners a method of practical criticism which they could use themselves when they read the Bible. The 'foundations' of the method are systematically set out elsewhere (especially in the *De Doctrina Christiana*) but they emerge clearly in the course of the exegesis, as Augustine pauses to explain a procedure in detail, and he repeats his principles as he puts them into practice. He emphasises that it is important that the reader does not abandon the foundations as he builds his 'edifice' of interpretation (*In John* 98, no. 7; *Letter* 93.7). He must build a solid structure, which will not show weaknesses, for those weaknesses will be absurdities.

Perhaps the most important principle to emerge from Augustine's lectures on the Psalms is his emphasis on the need to ensure that there is no *absurditas* in the interpretation of Scripture.

We must be conscious of the danger of falling into absurdity in connection with both words and things, he warns. In the case of a passage (*En. Ps.* 104.8), where the Latin texts vary, we are dealing with an apparent absurdity in usage. In Psalm 104, verse 12, we are told that there were 'few men in number, few and strangers in the land of Canaan'. Latin usage requires that *paucissimi et incolae* should be in the nominative to accord with: *cum essent numero brevi*. The accusative case cannot follow *esse*, but some manuscripts have: *paucissimos et incolas*, in which they seem to follow Greek usage. Augustine points out that this cannot be transferred to Latin without some absurdity (*nisi cum absurditate*), and he is insistent that that is not to be endured. In any case, it would be grammatically unacceptable for Greek usage to be imposed upon Latin, but it is especially so in the case of Scripture, where everything must be done properly and in order.

It may also seem that the Bible makes absurd statements about things, and here again we must look for an interpretation which removes the apparent absurdity. In Psalm 103 we meet the statement that God 'walks upon the wings of the wind' (verse 3). The winds may, not absurdly, be said to be souls; the interpretation is acceptable for several reasons, but chiefly because the wind is invisible, like a soul, although it is in fact a bodily thing, capable of moving bodily things about. It therefore bears a sufficient resemblance to a soul for it to represent a soul *in allegoria* without absurdity (*non absurde*) (*En. Ps.* 103.i.12).

There are, then, two ways in which our interpretation of Scripture may run into absurdity: when we make nonsense of the words and when we make nonsense of the meaning, that is, of the words' relation to the things they stand for either literally or metaphorically. In the latter case, it is clearly more likely that a metaphorical sense will prove to be nonsensical than a literal one; there is more room for error where the interpreter has a world of figurative meanings to choose from than where he is trying to point to the straightforward meaning of a word. Nevertheless, there are terms, as Augustine points out, which have more than one plain meaning, and where it is important to distinguish the appropriate meaning in the Scriptural context. In cases where one meaning is unworthy, this is especially important. A term may have a usage which is *ludicrus* and *non honestus*, whose proper place is in the theatre (*in scena*) and not in the Church (*in ecclesia*) (*En. Ps.* 103.i.13).

Augustine's objection to *absurditas* in the interpretation of Scripture is that it is incompatible with the clarity and rightness of the truth. It is deceptive, dishonest, a mockery. The Word of God is deliberately mocked and derided by sinners in their empty-headedness (111.8). Are Christians to mock it too, by suggesting absurd interpretations? *Absurditas* is an evil thing because it displays all the characteristics of emptiness and perversity which signal the presence of evil for Augustine. An absurd interpretation is both a twisted interpretation and no interpretation at all because it tells us nothing about the text in question.

What, then, are we to say of allegory, which, by definition, is a substitution of something else for the plain meaning of the words: 'We speak of allegory when something seems to say one thing in words, and to mean another thing in understanding'. Surely that is a perversion? When Christ is called a lamb or a lion, surely he is not said to be a beast; when he is called a rock, surely he is not said to be hardness; when he is called a mountain, surely he is not said to be a swelling of the land? The words do not mean what they say, and if we took them at their face value they would seem absurd, but this *allegoria* has no more to do with the theatre than the word *parabola* in its Biblical meaning of 'parable' has to do with its other meaning: the speech an actor makes in the amphitheatre.

In Scripture, allegory is a device for expressing a holy mystery in figurative form (*En. Ps.* 103.i.13). Augustine has put himself in a position where he has to tread a narrow path between false representations which are 'empty signs' and 'deceptive symbols', and the true signs which Holy Scripture contains in its allegories. Similarly, the signs and symbols of the liturgy used in Christian worship are to be carefully distinguished from the deceitful signs of the 'theatre'. In his remarks on Psalm 53 (verse 10) Augustine distinguishes between the sacrifices of pagans and the sacrifices of the Christian heart. The pagan offers a sheep or a ram or an ox. Shall we offer God such a return for his mercy, or something from within ourselves, that which comes to the tongue and is conceived in the heart, and is then uttered by the voice as it is retained in the mind.

(A comparison with a passage in the *Manichean Psalm-Book* is irresistible here: 'Thou [the word] leapest from the heart to the tongue, from the tongue to these hearers' ('Psalm to the Victorious Soul', p. 118)). There is nothing of the theatre in this. It is not a matter of theatrical performance, of pretending to be what we are not. The mark of such worship is its utter sincerity. 'Willingly shall I sacrifice to you', says the Psalm. True worship proceeds from right will; it can come from nowhere else. This 'coming-out' of the word from the heart guarantees the sincerity of what such a worshipper says. There can be no 'absurdity' in that, but only when the word enters his heart in an equally direct way can he be sure of avoiding 'absurdity' in his interpretation of Scripture. If his heart is clogged with the weight of the bodily images which lie upon it (Augustine speaks of *grossa corda*, *En. Ps.* 113.i.4) the acuteness of his perceptions of higher things will be dulled (*De Doct. Chr.* I.ix.9). The 'heart' is the seat of understanding in Scripture, but more, it is that deep core of the mind in which faith and reason come together.

If a man is to avoid absurdity in his interpretation of Scripture he must see what he reads not only with the eyes of the body, which view the words on the page, but also with the eyes of faith which help him to understand it (*En. Ps.* 103.iv.6). What is the relationship between these 'eyes of faith' and the 'eyes of the mind' with which we perceive those things which are beyond the reach of our bodily senses? Hebrews tells us, in a passage much-quoted in connection with the definition of faith (11.1), that 'faith is the evidence of things not seen'. It is in some sense a 'seeing' of the invisible, but a putative 'seeing' only. It provides us with a working hypothesis, a confidence that things are so which we cannot know for certain in this life. There will be no need for faith or hope in heaven. The 'eyes of faith' are therefore of only temporary use. They are a substitute for the 'eyes of the mind' or perhaps it would be more exact to describe them as spectacles which help the eyes of the mind to see better while their vision is still clouded. They therefore help us to avoid absurdity by holding our judgment steady.

The avoidance of *absurditas* is more difficult in the case of allegorical or spiritual meanings. They are full of pitfalls for those whose eye of faith is not working properly, because the bodily eyes so readily interpret them in a carnal way. The only way in which it is possible to guard against absurdity is to match the spiritual to the bodily eye – just as we ought to join together in one the worship within the soul which is a *vox perpetua* and the outward worship perceptible to the bodily sense in which the voice utters a prayer (the sound of the voice with which we praise God) (*En. Ps.* 102.2). The eye of faith is the God-given means of joining the two in a common effort. A similar harmony exists between the spiritual and the literal sense in Scripture, its inward and its outward sense (*En. Ps.* 104.35). We must learn to use the outward and literal sense to lead us into the inward sense, the 'body' of the Psalm to show us its 'soul' lying within, 'in, as it were, outward words' to see the *interior intellectus*. The spiritual sense will be found to fit the literal, but this natural harmony within Scripture will be apparent to the reader only if his soul is full of faith and his body in due subjection to it. To such a student any *absurditas* will be apparent at once, and he can be trusted not to interpret foolishly.

The truth, then, is characterised by its solidity and fullness, its integrity and the united front of interpretation it presents. Absurdity is empty and perverse. '*Vanitas* and *veritas* differ *a contrario*. They are opposites.' (*En. Ps.* 118.xii.1.) The mouth of those who speak vanity (Psalm 108.8) is contrasted with the mouth which speaks truth. What is absurd in interpretation is *vana et falsa*. Its essentially evil character is plain enough, for Augustine has typically evil qualities.

Augustine has practical suggestions to make to help the reader exercise the eyes of faith effectively. In the *De Doctrina Christiana* he emphasises the importance of distinguishing the literal from the metaphorical. The search for harmony must not lead us to forced comparison, or there will be *absurditas*. The natural harmony of Scripture should be clear to the eye of faith without elaborate contrivances to make it seem so.

Indeed we should be reluctant to depart from the literal sense without good reason. Only if the literal sense does not refer to purity of life or soundness of doctrine is a figurative sense to be preferred (*De Doct. Chr.* III.x.14). In the opening passage of his commentary on the literal sense of Genesis, Augustine lists the four levels of interpretation which were becoming established, the anagogical sense ('what eternal things are intimated there'), the tropological ('what we are admonished to do'), the allegorical ('what things to come are foretold', that is, what types of New Testament figures and events are to be found there), and the literal ('what facts are narrated'). The higher senses raise difficulties of their own, but Augustine is concerned to show that even the literal sense is by no means as straightforward as we might expect. He deals with the great metaphysical questions raised by such statements as 'In the beginning God made heaven and earth', by the Genesis account of the creation and the fall of Satan. In his *Questions* on Genesis he takes this a little further, and considers the often petty questions which are asked about details of the rest of the Genesis narrative. These questions, as he shows, arise when sinful men, whose minds are full of 'bodily images' ask about the apparent anomalies in the narrative when it is taken literally. Could Noah's Ark, made to the Genesis measurements, have been large enough to contain all the animals and their food (Q. 4)? (Yes, if, as Origen says (*Hom. in Gen.* ii.2), a *cubitum geometricum* is the equivalent of six ordinary cubits.) How could the lions and eagles, which are carnivorous, have been fed, unless Noah took more than two of each animal, so as to provide them with meat (Q. 7)? Abraham and his seed were promised as much land as he could see to the four corners of the earth (Genesis 13.14–15). How far is it possible for the bodily sight to reach (Q. 28)? How can Abraham have been frightened if he was a good man, and therefore not subject to perturbation of spirit (Q. 30, Genesis 15.12)? Abraham behaved inconsistently when he offered the 'three men' food. If he understood that they were angels or gods, he should have realised that food is necessary for mortal flesh but not for the immortal angels (Genesis 18.4–5, Q. 34). Perhaps Sarah thought they were men, seeing with a bodily eye, and Abraham, recognising them as angels, saw with a spiritual eye (Q. 37)? A similar difficulty arises in the case of Lot's invitation to the angels to eat (Genesis 19.1, Q. 41).

Some simple rules can help us here, where our spiritual vision fails us. We must look to the implications of the meaning we choose. If a passage seems to suggest that God is severe, the literal meaning will hold if he is thus shown to disapprove of evil will, that is, of lust (*De Doct. Chr.* III.xi.17), for in such matters he is indeed severe. Some sayings or actions attributed to God and the saints may seem to be wicked, but we must consider the circumstances and the intention. When the Lord allowed his feet to be anointed by the woman with precious ointment, his purpose was not the same as that of luxurious and profligate men who have their feet anointed at banquets. The Lord cannot be accused of a wrong act in allowing his feet to be anointed (*De Doct. Chr.* III.xii.18). We must look for a literal sense, in accordance with the time, the place and the person, which is good and acceptable. In interpreting figurative expressions, we must look for the most edifying (*De Doct. Chr.* III.xv.23). Commands and prohibitions are to be taken literally if they forbid a sin but figuratively if they do not (*De Doct. Chr.* III.xvi.24). We must bear in mind that some things were done by men of the Old Testament which would now be condemned (*De Doct. Chr.* III.xxii.32). We must not assume that we are free to imitate them. The rules are plain enough, and based on common sense, but they are not easy to apply without the aid of the eyes of faith.

It is not intended that wicked men shall see as clearly as the good what Scripture is designed to teach them, and not all the mysteries in Scripture can be explained. In the *De Trinitate* Augustine takes the example of God's appearance to Adam in the Garden of Eden. He wants to make clear some of the difficulties that arise when we try to determine whether a given passage refers to God as One, or to a single Person of the Trinity (*De Trin.* II.x.17). According to the rule he has laid down for such passages, we must decide whether God is being spoken of in respect of that in which the Persons are one, or in respect of that in which they are individual. God must, it seems, have appeared in the form of a man, because we are told that he walked in the garden, and that he talked with Adam. That would suggest that it was the Son who appeared to Adam, especially since we should expect 'speaking' to be done by the Word, but this was before the Incarnation. God had not yet become man. Besides, God is invisible, because he is spirit. Even the human soul is invisible (*De Trin*. II.vii.14–ix.15). Unless someone can so 'penetrate this secret with his mind's eye' that he can see clearly either that the Father is able to appear in visible form like the Son, or that the Son only, and not the Father, can so appear, the problem remains insoluble (*De Trin*. II.x.18). We do not know whether Adam saw God looking like a man, and speaking to him in a human voice.

This leads Augustine on to other 'appearances' (*De Trin*. II.xii.20–xiv.24). When Moses saw the burning bush, did he see God who had assumed a creature, so as to give himself a visible appearance, or an angel? When the children of Israel saw the pillar of cloud by day and of fire by night, they certainly did not see God in his own substance, but in a created corporeal substance which he had 'used' for the purpose. On Mount Sinai (*De Trin*. II.xv.25), the people saw the cloud and within the cloud Moses, granted a spiritual vision, saw the Son of God. In all these cases visible and sensible things appear, not the divine substance, and God uses them in some way to 'signify' his invisible Being, and to make himself intelligible.

Augustine's ostensible purpose as he examines these samples, is to try to determine whether the Trinity or one of the Persons individually makes these 'appearances', but the underlying question with which he is concerned is whether God assumes creaturely substance in order to 'appear'. If so, God is making a 'bodily image' of himself, and coming half-way to meet his creatures by taking on a form they can understand directly.

There is, however, Augustine is sure, no possibility that God can show himself in his own substance, 'whereby he himself is what he is', his very essence, in any bodily image or likeness, whether to someone who is asleep or to someone who has a waking vision (*De Trin*. II.xviii.33). We cannot know God as he really is by bodily images, even when he himself is their author.

Indeed, he is not necessarily directly present in all such appearances. In Book III Augustine asks whether when God appears in a creaturely form, he creates the creature which is to be his vehicle, or causes one of the angels to take on the appropriate form. He is not concerned with the way in which the angels may do this, whether they assume corporeal properties from the elements and fit them to themselves, like a garment, which they can make into any bodily form they choose, or whether they transform their own spiritual bodies directly (*De Trin*. III.i.5). These are practical details. However it happens, God is the high and ultimate cause of all such change. The angels appear in bodily form only when it is his will that they should do so (*De Trin*. III.ii.7). It is, therefore, immaterial whether God makes new creatures for his own appearances or employs the angels. In either case, the 'bodily image' is sent by God, manifesting himself visibly by means of invisible things (*De Trin*. III.iv.9). Augustine is inclined to think that the appearances recorded in the Bible are all to be explained as angelic appearances. That would remove the difficulty about the appearance of God to Adam in the Garden, walking and talking like a man, and if it is objected that Scripture says, for example, 'The Lord said to Moses', not: 'the angel said to Moses', we have only to remember that God is the author of the saying, the original speaker, and that Scripture is therefore perfectly proper in its usage (*De Trin*. III.xi.22–3).

Now we are coming to the point. What is the difference between these manifestations 'to bodily and mortal senses' and the manifestation of the Son at the Incarnation (*De Trin*. III.xi.27; IV.xxi.31)? What does the Incarnate Christ do for man by becoming man in person, which is not achieved by God's manifesting himself in the bodily appearances of the Old Testament? *Cur Deus Homo*? Why was it necessary for God to become man himself? We have seen how we may learn something of God from divinely-caused 'bodily images', but we have also seen that we cannot learn what God is 'in himself' in this way. God comes down to our level of understanding in such appearances. We need aid of a different kind if we are to replace the figments of our imaginations with truths (*De Trin*. IV.i.1, Preface). The Incarnate Word gives just this aid. He is the 'light of rational minds', not a corporeal light visible to the bodily eyes. He it is who illuminates our minds and makes it possible for us to understand what is otherwise beyond our capacity as created beings.

After the fall of Adam, human nature was no longer naturally receptive to the divine light, as God made it. All human minds lay in darkness until God should purge them and make them again what they were by nature ('as we were created, and not as we were by sin'). Then man would be able to see clearly to contemplate God as he had been designed to (*De Trin.* IV.xviii.24). When St John describes how the Light shone in darkness and the darkness comprehended it not, he refers to the foolish minds of men, which could not comprehend the Light that shines upon them (*De Trin.* IV.ii.4). Christ, the Light, was the proper Person to remove the darkness and allow the Light to shine in.

It seemed to Augustine only proper that a fault in a created and temporal thing should be put right by an act within the temporal sphere. God restored fallen humanity by entering time in the Person of the Son, bringing Light to us in our fallen condition, and then leading us from the first beginning of faith to a knowledge of divine truth (*De Trin.* IV.xviii.24). The process is put succinctly in *Letter* 140 (iii.7), written in 412. 'Thus he became a man whom men could see, so that, healed by faith, they might afterwards see what then they could not see.' It was essential for such a task that the workman and the substance he was sent to clean should be of the same kind (*De Trin.* IV.xx.27). It was certainly not possible, as the Pelagians claimed, for the substance to cleanse itself. 'There are some', Augustine notes, 'who think themselves capable of being cleansed by their own righteousness', so that they can 'penetrate with the eye of the mind beyond . . . the creature, and touch, though it be in ever so small a part, the light of the unchangeable truth' (*De Trin.* IV.xv.20). God had to make human nature clean because man could not do it himself, and he had to do it by himself becoming man so that he could reach the source of the trouble.

God became man, then, so that man could know God better than he had been able to do since the fall of Adam. Christ made a bridge of Light between himself and human understanding, and the Christian can now cross that bridge and go outside his mind in search of God. As early as 389, in *Letter* 11, to Nebridius, Augustine was advancing the theory that the Incarnation ensured that 'a certain method of living and example of precept has been conveyed to us under the majesty and clarity of His teachings', but now he is saying something much more profound. We learn not only how we should live, but how we should *think*, from Christ.

'Natural man', the non-believer, cannot understand what a difference the Incarnation makes, precisely because he is still in the position in which Augustine found himself for so many years before his conversion, unable to think except in terms of space and solidity and physical size, his mind full of 'images of bodies' (*De Trin*. VII.vi.11). Such a man will not be able to grasp the doctrine of the Trinity. He will not be able to understand how Father, Son and Holy Spirit may be three Persons in one God, while his mind is in its clouded state, but he can take the help Christ offers him, and hold by faith what he cannot yet understand, until his mind has been sufficiently cleared for him to see the truth (*De Trin*. VII.vi.11–12). Human nature cannot join itself to God but God has joined himself to human nature, to make this possible (*De Trin*. XII.xvii.22).

A considerable part of the difficulty lies in the inadequacy of human language, its inherent absurdity as the speech of fallen man. Just as God is beyond our comprehension as fallen beings he is beyond our description in our language (*De Trin*. v.i.1) and for the same reason. This was brought home hard to Augustine himself as he tried to explain the doctrine of the Trinity. He looks at the problem of terminology which arises. God is a substance (though it might be 'better' to call his substance *essentia*). The Greeks use the word *ousia*, but current usage threatens confusion. The Latins mean the same thing by 'essence' and 'substance', as we have seen. They lack an adequate vocabulary. The best word they can think of for the 'three' of the Trinity is 'persons'. The Greeks use *ousia* and *hypostasis* as the Latins use *substantia* and *persona* (*De Trin*. v.ix.10; VII.iv.9).

God's substance is unique in that it admits of no accidents. Accidents (by definition) can be altered without destroying the nature of the substance in which they inhere. A man remains himself if his black hair turns grey, or if he stops walking and sits down. God's attributes never change, because they are all substantial and not accidental. God is always good and just and merciful (*De Trin*. v.ii.3), but this special usage of *substantia* for God can lead to confusion. The Arians say that the term 'unbegotten' like any other term predicated of God applies to his substance. Therefore, either both the Father and the Son are begotten, or else the Father (who is unbegotten) and the Son (who is begotten) are different in substance. In either case, if this were true, the doctrine of the Trinity would have to be modified (*De Trin*. v.iii.4). Augustine believes that there is in fact one category that may be predicated of God apart from substance, and that is 'relation'. This allows us to speak of the Persons singly as having different properties.

The only way in which these linguistic difficulties can be got over at all is by frequent usage, by repeating and handling the words and ideas we use in stating the doctrine of the Trinity until they are thoroughly familiar (*De Trin.* VIII, Preface), and we do not inadvertently slip into error. Nowhere is this more difficult than in speaking of the Trinity. Even Plotinus ran into difficulties here when he tried to describe how the One can be 'from' himself or 'towards' himself or 'through' himself, how he can 'will' himself or 'cause' himself, for all such statements would involve two distinct entities in normal usage, but the One is one alone, and so when we say such things of him we speak 'incorrectly' (οὐκ ὀρθῶς) (*Ennead* VI.viii–ix). Augustine wants the reader to be conscious all the time of the thing that lies behind the Word. When we speak of the evil will, we should remember that the will itself is good, for God made it. Evil is one thing; the will is another. 'Evil will' should be understood as a harnessing of two things together in an unequal yoking (*De Trin.* VIII.iii.4) of something and nothing. We must make ourselves masters of an 'inspired authority' in order to understand these things. The truth itself is bound to seem absurd to us while our minds are dark with sin, and that is why it is doubly important that we should interpret Scripture without absurdity.

What testing-ground can remain to us, where we can assess the absurdity or rightness of our interpretations, if we cannot be sure that we perceive things rightly? Augustine is confident that God has provided one. It is not a test by sense-perception, for we have seen that 'carnal perception' cannot understand how three Persons can be no more than one. Although it can perceive things as they truly are in a limited way (if the things in question are objects in the created world, and therefore susceptible of sense-perception), it cannot perceive the Truth itself which made them, and which is beyond their reach (*De Trin.* VII.i.2). Augustine looks at some of the traditional analogies which suggest themselves to carnal perception, between the relationships created things bear to one another, and the relationship the Persons of the Trinity bear to one another. No *imago* or *similitudo* will help us here. It is useless to think of any touch or embrace in physical space, such as three bodies might make; or of three things joined together in any of the ways in which solid objects may be joined. Any such image makes the three together more than each singly – for three of any bodily thing must be more than one of the same thing. Therefore it seems that every idea formed from

observation of the physical world must be rejected (*De Trin*. VIII.ii.3).
Nor can we get at the idea of God by thinking of any single thing that
we know (such as the light of the sun) and magnifying it in
imagination, so as to make it greater. God is not simply higher or
greater than created things; he is of another order altogether. The
divine Light is not the same light as that which the bodily eyes see,
but our minds are so constituted that as soon as we ask the question
'What is truth?' a host of such 'bodily images and clouds of
phantasms' clutter our minds (*De Trin*. VII.ii.3). Nevertheless, in the
human mind Augustine discovers by introspection that he has the
ingredients of an analogy that is not bound to fail him as soon as he
tries to apply it to the Trinity. In its love and knowledge, the human
mind resembles the Trinity. Indeed, it is itself an image of the Trinity.
The mind is like the Father, in his relation to the Son and the Holy
Spirit. Knowledge is that by which the mind knows itself and love is
that by which the mind loves both itself and its own knowledge (*De
Trin*. IX). These three are one in substance and inseparable. There can
be no knowledge without the mind and no knowledge without love
(for Augustine believes that we do not know what we hate) (*De Trin*.
IX.x.15). If we take away the lover, there is no love; if we take away
love, there is no lover. The loving mind and the love of the mind exist
in a mutual relationship, and yet they are one (*De Trin*. IX.ii.2).

By introspection we have learned something about the nature of
the Trinity which could not have been learned from observation of
the world which lies outside ourselves. The 'word' or image we form
of God in this way is formed, not from sense-perceptions, but from
what we have seen 'in the eternal truth' (that is, by loving God by
faith) (*De Trin*. IX.vii.12). We 'see' it, then, by 'the sight of the mind',
not by bodily sight. We 'conceive' the word or image within us, and
by speaking it we 'beget' it in some way from inside ourselves; when
we utter it, it does not depart from us by being 'born', but remains
within us to be uttered again an infinite number of times (*De Trin*.
IX.vii.12). In corporeal matters things are very different. An animal
conceives its young and gives birth, and is thereafter separated from
its offspring. Even in the love or knowledge of carnal things, the
conceiving of the word is one thing (a result of sense-perception) and
its utterance another, but in spiritual matters the conception and the
birth are one. A man who knows and loves righteousness is himself
righteous; he conceives the idea of what he himself already is, and

'utters' the idea or word 'righteousness' by being righteous himself (*De Trin*. IX.ix.14). Thus the intellect and the intelligible are one.

Love and knowledge are not identical; two 'Persons' of the mental 'Trinity' are involved here. Knowledge is the offspring of the mind, just as the Son is begotten by the Father. Love is not 'begotten', just as the Holy Spirit is not begotten (*De Trin*. IX.xii.17). Love proceeds from the mind, and loves both the knowledge of the mind, and the mind itself. In Book X Augustine tries to explain the implications of this point more thoroughly, in order to show clearly how the human mind is constructed. Then, he hopes, we may be able to direct our 'mental vision' more effectively (*De Trin*. IX.xii.17).

Now the love of a mind which is directed towards knowledge is the love of that which it already knows (*De Trin*. X.i.3). A man may desire to know what he does not know with a passionate urgency, but he cannot be said to love something until he knows it (*De Trin*. X.ii.4). How, then, does the mind fall into absurdity? In order to answer that question we must first ask what it loves during the period when it is seeking ardently to know itself, but does not yet know itself (*De Trin*. X.iii.5), the period when it is still in the darkness of sin.

Perhaps it loves what is like itself, that is, what it knows of other minds? But it is hard to believe that it can know other minds well enough to love what is like itself if it does not already know itself, for what can be more present to the mind than itself? The mind cannot see itself, just as the eyes cannot see themselves (except in a mirror, and there are no mirrors that will reflect a mind). There is a mystery here, but one thing is clear: the mind knows itself as a seeking thing, and it knows that it does not yet know itself; it knows that it must seek to know itself (*De Trin*. X.iii.5). So it goes about the search in the only way it knows. It has loved certain things it learned of through the senses, so it tries to carry them inside itself, where it can both know and love them, but corporeal things cannot be literally carried into the mind. They cannot themselves be images or words (*De Trin*. X.v.7). Therefore the mind lends them something of its own substance in an effort to modify them so that they can be contained within the mind.

In so doing the mind errs; it gains a false opinion of itself, thinking itself to be a corporeal thing like the things it knows through the senses and loves (*De Trin*. X.vi.8). That is how it comes about that some men's minds have thought themselves to be a kind of 'body', or a part of the body (for some have thought the mind to be blood or brain or heart – the latter misunderstanding the metaphorical sense of 'thou shalt love the Lord thy God with all thy heart'. Others have thought the mind to be made up of tiny bodies, corpuscles or atoms; others have thought it air or fire, or some kind of glue joining together soul and body), but the mind which has broken free of these errors and shaken off its bad habits by faith, can come to have an idea of God simply by being what it is. As it learns to love God it comes to know him. The 'word' or image thus formed is a true, if incomplete, image of God.

Augustine's enquiry is not now a single one; he wants to understand, not only how man may know God, but how man may know the Trinity in its 'oneness' and its 'threeness', and Christ in his humanity and divinity. A search which was at first almost identical with the Platonists' search for the Highest Good has become a wholly Christian matter, confronting the vastly greater conceptual difficulties involved in grasping the doctrines of Trinity and Incarnation. The reality of God evades human understanding because it is of a higher order than our own reality. That is not difficult to understand, at least in principle, but the impossibility of understanding fully by human reason how one Being may be three, and how the three can act in such a way that one does what another does not do, while remaining one (*De Trin*.I.v.8), all but confounded Augustine, and he knew that he would not easily make himself clear to his readers.

The *De Trinitate*, then, is an exploration of the alternatives to 'bodily images' provided by Scripture and by divine illumination of human reason, an attempt to understand how God intends himself to be known by man, and, above all, it is a vehicle for the working out of Augustine's greatest discovery: the idea that God intends the incarnate Christ to provide a living substitute for the 'bodily images' into which our minds so readily run, by being himself an image of God in the body.

If this truth appears absurd when first we meet it, that is because the evil in our sinful minds distorts our perception of the truth. What is straight appears crooked to us; what is clear and luminous appears obscure. If we recognise our own condition we shall not be surprised to find the truth apparently absurd.

IV · EVIL IN THE UNIVERSE

1 A Channel Blocked by Fallen Leaves

At Cassiciacum, under the gentle stimulus of one another's company, the small community explored the great problems of the universe. When he edited the discussions that became the *De Ordine*, Augustine put in a preface, in which he reflects upon the importance of considering questions on a universal scale. It is far from easy, he says, for men to grasp the order of reality proper to each thing and then to see the order of the universe as a whole by which all individual things are held together and governed. Yet there is a strong desire in the most gifted men to look at the problems they try to solve in this way against the background of the whole.

In the case of the problem with which he is concerned in the *De Ordine* the adoption of a universal scale of reference is particularly important – indeed, indispensable. It is obvious to every observer that the world is full of evils: perversity and unpleasantness and disruptions of the natural order. How are these to be explained, if we believe that a divine Providence is watching over creation? Are we to infer that Providence is not concerned with details but only with the overall plan? Or are we to think that God himself is the Author of evils? That would be worse, for to impute negligence to a kindly God is more acceptable than to impute deliberate cruelty to him (*De Ord.* I.i.1).

A Greek contemporary of Augustine, Nemesius, Bishop of Emesa in Phoenicia, wrote a treatise *On the Nature of Man* (*De Natura Hominis*), a little before Pelagius, Nestorius and Eutyches had begun to trouble orthodox churchmen on the subject. In it, he briefly reviews the views of the philosophers who had gone before him on the subject of providence. Plato held that there were three providences, which together governed all things, down to the particular and detailed. The first is the providence of the supreme God himself, which is concerned with the maintenance of the universal order, genera and species, with the very structure of creation: this is true providence.

The second is the providence of the lesser gods, which looks after the creatures, that is, everything that is generated or corrupted: this is more accurately described as fate. The third, and lowest, level of providence is that by which the *daemones*, the lesser spirits, supervise man's exits and his entrances, the *minutiae* of life: this might be thought of as fortune (PG 40.793B–6B). The Stoics have no place at all for providence in their system. All is fate. Democritus, Heraclitus and Epicurus say that God foresees neither universals nor particulars (PG 40.796B). Aristotle allows providence over universals but thinks particulars are under the control of nature alone. Euripides and Menander are of the same mind (PG 40.796B).

Like Nemesius, Augustine was anxious to put the Christian case for an all-embracing Providence. He is sure that we must attribute to divine power and divine government whatever order there is in small events and in the details of the construction of creatures, too. If we do not, we are obliged to regard the marvellous details of animal bodies, their adjustment to the needs of each creature, as a matter of chance. Augustine has a striking image of what happens when a man looks at the world in search of a pattern. It is as though he were scrutinising a mosaic pavement from a few inches away. The details of the *tesserae* are clear enough, but he cannot see the picture (*De Ord.* I.i.1).

Before he became a Christian, Augustine had dabbled for a time in astrology (*Conf.* IV.iii.4). He had respected the astrologers because they did not make sacrifices or invoke spirits but seemed to proceed by scientific methods, making calculations on the basis of the movements of the heavenly bodies by which, as they taught, the future might be predicted. The mathematical certainty of the horoscopes cast in this way rested upon the belief that the universe is ruled, not by providence, but by fate. Fate is necessity. It is not under the direction of a God who keeps an eye upon his world, adjusting events and their outcome so that they conform to his divine plan; it is a blind force. Augustine defines fate in Book v.1 of *The City of God* as that which happens independently of the will of God and man, by the necessity of a certain order. Augustine, now that he was a Christian, found fate to be irreconcilable with a belief in providence.

The same is true for fortune. In the same passage (*De Civ. Dei* v.1), he defines as fortuitous what has no cause at all, or what does not proceed from an intelligible order. If divine providence is indeed in charge of even the smallest events, nothing can be left to chance.

To set aside fate and fortune as Augustine does, with the determination to have no recourse to them at all, is to bring sharply into focus some difficulties that arise in connection with the Bible's account of the death of Christ. Jesus said, 'Father, the hour is come' (John 17.1). Did he mean an hour ordained by fate, an hour that it was necessary should come, whether God willed or no? Some had argued, from this and other passages (*In John* 37.8) that Christ was subject to fate. Augustine explains why this cannot be so in his discussions of John's Gospel. God made everything by his Word. Those who believe in fate say that it lies in 'the order and changes of the stars'. How, asks Augustine, can fate rule him who made the heavens and the stars (*In John* 37.8)? The hour Christ awaited was not the 'fated', but the 'fitting and voluntary' hour. How could he have been under the necessity of fate when he himself said in another place, 'I have power to lay down my life and I have power to take it again' (John 10.18)? When he said, 'Father, the hour is come; glorify your Son', he showed that all time, every occasion when he did anything or suffered anything to be done, was arranged by him who was not subject to time. It would, then, be foolish to suppose that this 'hour' came by any necessity of fate. It came by divine appointment. The Passion of Christ was not tied to its time by any necessary law of the heavenly bodies. 'We may well shrink from the thought that the stars should compel their own Maker to die', says Augustine (*In John* 104.2). His conclusion is that as Christians we should think not of fate or fortune but of providence as Governor of the universe.

THE FRAMING OF THE QUESTION

One night at Cassiciacum Augustine was lying awake thinking – a habit with him at that time, he says. He heard water running in the bath-house, and he noticed that it made not a uniform but a varying sound (*De Ord.* I.iii.6–7). He was puzzled as to the reason for this. A sound made him realise that Licentius was also awake. Augustine told him his thoughts and Licentius suggested a rational, scientific explanation. If the channel was blocked by fallen leaves the pressure of the water might cause them to move, and the water would make different sounds as it was alternately impeded and allowed to flow freely.

This helped Augustine to recognise the question which lay at the back of his mind, and which he had not been able to identify during his sleepless night. The next morning, he asked those of the 'school' who were present (Alypius and Navigius had gone into town that day), what explanation they could offer. What gives rise to an event outside the ordinary course of events? Can anything happen by chance, or must we look for order even in such apparently random things? We might postulate that there were causes for the placing of the trees, and for their branches growing in certain directions, and for the wind blowing the falling leaves in certain ways (*De Ord*. I.iv.11).

In order to understand this problem clearly – and that is his aim in all these early dialogues – Augustine lays down the fundamental axiom that nothing happens without a cause (*De Ord*. I.v.14) and that nothing can therefore lie outside the order of things. The important word here is 'happens'. He is discussing, not a static order, but an order of events. Movement and change are involved. 'Nothing comes about or is brought into existence which is not brought into existence by some cause' (*De Ord*. I.v.14). Here Augustine is taking Plotinus' starting-point, and working 'on the assumption that all happens by cause' (*Ennead* III.i.1). Plotinus' discussion of the theories of causation he knew is to be found in the third *Ennead*, where he is concerned with exactly the complex of problems about chance, fate, fortune and providence upon which Augustine and his friends had stumbled, and in which even chance has a cause. Boethius defines a 'chance' as an 'unexpected event (*inopinatum eventum*)' which results from a coincidence of causes (*ex confluentibus causis*) (*Consolation of Philosophy* v.1), and that is the light in which Augustine sees it, too.

The first 'chance', or mischance, the Fall, may be described as a *lapsus* from the unity of God (*ab unitate dei*). By the *perversitas*, the turning-away of the soul (*De Ver. Rel.* xxi.41; xxii.43; xxxiii.62), man's soul is set in chaotic motion, made subject to perturbation; we may reasonably conclude that disorderly movement is an attribute of evil. (Orderly motion, such as that of the planets, is not in question here. That is divinely ordained, and in its regularity it imitates the divine stillness.) The mutability of things is a sign of the effect evil has upon their intrinsically good natures. Even if we can postulate a cause, and be confident that God ultimately has all in hand, it seems that there is an anomaly here, a special kind of event. The first manifestations of evil, then, were chance events – the fall of Satan and the fall of man (*De Ver. Rel.* xxi.41). Evil is a happening that ought not to be, a *defectivus motus*. Much of Augustine's vocabulary for describing the ways in which evil manifests itself has to do with turning or falling away or movement from the good: *perversus, perversitas, aversio, defectio, lapsus, deformitas, deviare, infirmare*.

Now if we are to consider not merely the state of things in a static universe but the order of events and the disorderliness of certain events, we may reasonably ask when evil came into the picture, as Licentius does in Book II of the *De Ordine* (II.vii.22). He suggests that if order governs everything, there can be no room in the universe for what is outside order. If we accept that chance events originate in evil, we cannot speak of an 'order of events' at all, unless we postulate that evil is contained within the universal order.

There is, however, a further complication. An evil event is not a mindless happening. Inanimate objects cannot spontaneously do evil. Beasts can behave only according to their natures, and their natures are good because God made them. The only creature capable of acting against the good and bringing about an evil happening is a creature with a mind of its own. Augustine located the source of evil (as we shall see) in the rational will, which is free to choose between good and evil. In *The City of God* Augustine emphasises that the nature of all the angels was the same when they were created. The contrary propensities of good and bad angels do not arise from any differences in their natures, but from a difference in the direction in which they use their wills. The bad angel differs from the good not by nature but by fault (*De Civ. Dei* XII.1). In *De Natura et Gratia* he shows that the nature of man, too, was created faultless (*sine ullo vitio*), having all good things from God: life, senses, mind. The fault that darkened and weakened those natural goods did not come from the Creator but from the good free will he gave them (*De Nat. et Grat.* I.iii.3). It is in this sense that every evil event may be said to have a mind behind it.

This does not bring us to a solution by any means. On the contrary, it appears to put us in an impossible position. If evil is orderly, perhaps that is evidence that God himself gives rise to evil; it would certainly seem that he embraces it (*De Ord.* I.vii.17). If we reject that possibility (as we must, if we hold that God is good and the source of nothing but good), it seems that there must be something that is contrary to order. But that possibility has already been eliminated. We seem to have reached an impasse.

Licentius thinks he sees a way out of it. Perhaps order came into existence solely because of evil. When evil appeared, it was taken by God into a divine order (*dei ordine inclusum est*), and thus made governable. There would seem no need for order at all unless and until disorder threatened (*De Ord*. II.vii.23). Augustine cannot let that pass as it stands. The divine attributes are eternal, he reminds Licentius; order and justice were always present in God. Perhaps, though, they did not need to be exercised or brought into play until evil was present? In any case, it is clear that once we begin to allow for the possibility of change and movement in the universe, the problem of evil takes on a new dimension. We are no longer concerned with the crude Manichean notion of a ' territory ' of evil, but with an active force, with the way evil brings about events. It should be emphasised that it is not to be concluded from the fact that evil is contained within the divine order that God loves evil, says Augustine. God loves order, and it is not ' in order ' (that is, it does not belong to order) that God should love evil. He loves order precisely because by order he does not love evil, and evil is ' in order ' in being not-loved by God (*De Ord*. I.vii.18). God exercises his justice by giving to each thing in the divinely appointed order exactly the place it ought to have. God thus accommodates evil by making of it something intrinsically good (*De Ord*. I.vii.18), for there can be no doubt that order is good if God loves it. God can make an event good, even when it is contrary to the ordinary course of things and would otherwise seem disorderly. We commonly say that such an event is contrary to nature, and so it would be, if it were evil in origin, but since God is the author of all natures, when he causes an event out of the common run, he does nothing contrary to nature. When Jesus healed the man blind from birth he did something against nature, but we call such an event a miracle.

The order God imposes might be described as bringing a kind of stillness back into movement. By arranging the disordered multiplicity of things so that they stand in a proper relationship to one another, God ' fixes ' them. He gives them the beauty that at its highest belongs only to those things that are at one and without motion. It is not beyond his power to do something of the kind with evil. In poetry, apparent disorders may create great beauty (*De Ord*. II.iv.13); poets love to introduce solecisms and barbarisms as stylistic devices. In a not dissimilar way, God makes beauty out of disorder by using it as what we may call a 'stylistic device' of the universe. In the universe as it was originally created a purer order obtains, governed by laws like those of the mathematical arts, which have the 'necessity of numbers (*numerorum necessitas*)' (*De Ord*. II.iv.14). There is the fixed order of the universe, the order God put into his creation (foreseeing that it would need to be made an active not a potential order when evil arose), and a disorder brought to order, which is evil restrained by divine providence.

This is a task he is still carrying out in the human soul of each wicked man. There remains a *perversitas* here which must be straightened (*De Ver. Rel.* xxxiv.63) or the due order will remain out of order, what is 'below' will be 'above' and what is 'above' will be 'below'. This is as ugly a state of things in the soul as it would be in the body if the limbs were attached in the wrong places (*De Ord*. II.iv.12). The disorder in such a soul is certainly not static. The wicked man is in a state of disorderly motion. He is constantly being moved to do evil deeds. He causes evil things to happen. The subject of the *De Libero Arbitrio* is what it means to 'do evil' (*Quid sit male facere*) (*De Lib. Arb.* I.iii.6.14). 'To do evil', Augustine thinks, 'is nothing but to go astray from discipline (*male facere nihil est nisi a disciplina deviare*)' (*De Lib. Arb.* I.ii.3.6), that is, to go away from the proper path.

The more clearly Augustine understood the implications of Adam's sin, the simpler and more clear-cut the matter seemed. Adam lost the power to do good because a permanent twist arose in his will. He lost, in effect, his freedom of choice, because he could choose only one thing. This had a universal effect, a long way beyond man himself and his activities, penetrating deep into the natural order, and it required a major act on God's part to put it right. The scale of the problem is easy enough to understand if we remember the runaway nature of evil as Augustine saw it. Once it was let in it could not be stopped. And given his conception of providence, as a Christian he could not but see God's act of putting right in equally large terms.

We have yet to establish how the evil in the perverted will is able to affect matter and cause events in the created world. For Augustine, 'natural evils' are a question of very subordinate interest. He would not attribute them to God but to man. For him, there is no such thing as a 'natural evil' (for that would be either a God-made evil or a Manichee, alien power coequal with the good – by far the more acceptable option to fifth-century thinkers). All evil arises in the will. Plato has an explanation that must be regarded as Augustine's too, if we are to accept the view that all the evil in the universe, even the evil of an event such as an earthquake, which is apparently quite unconnected with anything the will of man or angel can bring about, is ultimately traceable to an act of will. In the *Timaeus* Plato says that bodies are first moved by souls, whether good or evil. The motion of any body so moved necessarily communicates itself to another body, and this transmitted motion is neither intelligent nor purposive but random – as if Achilles pushed Hector and in falling Hector dislodged some of the leaves of a tree he chanced to strike. This disorderly motion is an inevitable consequence of soul acting upon body, but it is incidental.

It is entirely in keeping with the random nature of evil that it should be so. We should expect an element of chance to twist the chain of cause and effect that leads from the evil action of a rational will to its ultimate consequences. It may be difficult to discover all the links in the chain, but then we should expect some of them to be hard to find, because evil shrouds things in darkness. It may indeed be easier to see how God incorporates evil events such as earthquakes into the natural order than to understand how a human or angelic sin may have caused it, but that again is what we should expect, for the divine ordering of things is clear, and the evil disordering of things is hidden. If Augustine has correctly identified the properties and behaviour of evil, his case looks impregnable.

2 The Angelic Darkness

In the monastery at Bec in northern France in the late eleventh century, St Anselm's pupils used to ask him why, if evil is nothing, it matters whether or not we sin, for it would seem that to sin is to do nothing. 'If sin is nothing', they said, 'why does God punish man for sin, for no-one ought to be punished for nothing?'[1]

In asking how 'nothing' could be so serious and damaging they had put a finger on a question that was beginning to arise pressingly for Augustine when he set about the task of composing *The City of God*. Faced with what was surely a very great evil, the fall of a Christian Empire, Augustine had to account for the catastrophe in such a way as to show that it was none of God's work, and yet at the same time within his providential purpose. Most urgently of all he had to explain how evil can be so terrible and powerful an influence in the world, if evil is nothing.

Evil changed men so radically that they became mortal. It ruined the angels who fell. It is to be feared because it distorts God's good creatures, letting loose in the world damaged beings who are actively malevolent, exercising their wills for evil with a terrible energy, making the negative appear positive by the force of their desire. We must, therefore, fear, not an abstraction, but the terrible 'angelic darkness', darkness personified, the brightest creatures bereft of light and intent on destruction. In the wills of rational beings who have turned from the good there is power and substance, that which makes the 'nothing' of evil a 'something'.

As a Christian philosopher, Augustine had asked with the philosophers whether the divine power extends to the limits of the universe, whether even a benevolent God can be supposed to concern himself with every detail of his creatures' lives, what are the underlying principles of providence's supervision of events, and he had found himself assured of God's omnipotence and all-embracing care. Now, confronted by the progressive erosion of the Christian Roman Empire by pagan invaders, he had to move from metaphysics to history, and to a more than human history. The vast scale of the disaster would suggest that a more than human malevolence lies behind. There is angelic wickedness here. We must look to the beginning of the world to find its origins, and to the heaven as well as earth to see its effects.

When did evil enter the world? At the very beginning of creation, Augustine thinks. In Genesis we read that 'God divided light from darkness.' This passage, Augustine believes, refers not only to the institution of the succession of days and nights, but also to the separation of the good angels from the evil angels when Satan sinned. He thinks that there is nothing absurd (*non absurda sententia*) in the view that when the light was first made, the angels were created too, for they are like personified light, radiant with the illumination of the truth (*inlustratione veritatis intelligibiliter fulgens*). The angels who fell turned from that light (*aversi a luce*), and so they became, of their own free choice, the darkness from which the light was divided (*De Civ. Dei* XI.19). We are told that when God made the light 'he saw that it was good'. We are not told that he approved the darkness in the same way (*De Civ. Dei* XI.20). He certainly 'ordained' the angelic darkness, making it part of his plan (*De Civ. Dei* XI.20), but the *tenebrae angelicae* was not approved (*non adprobandae*); only the light pleased the Creator.

The evil in the universe thus made its presence felt so early that we must be careful not to fall into the error of thinking that it was actually created by God, along with the world. Scripture says 'the Devil sinned from the beginning' (I John 3.8). How are we to understand this? Augustine insists that if the Bible says that Lucifer fell (Isaiah 14.12) that implies that he was once unfallen. If it tells us that he did not abide in the truth, it implies that he must once have been in the truth (John 8.44). He was, therefore, not a sinner from the moment of his creation. It is not possible that he was created evil in nature, as Augustine is anxious to emphasise, because if God had made him sinful his sin would be natural, in accordance with the will of God, and therefore it would be no sin at all (*De Civ. Dei* XI.15). Besides, the goodness of all created natures is axiomatic with Augustine. The flaw (*vitium*) in Satan cannot have been built into his nature or substance, because it is contrary to nature (*De Civ. Dei* XI.17), and it is clear that a non-flawed nature (or substance) must have existed before it could be flawed. A flaw can exist only as a damage or fault in a good nature. It cannot exist as a nature in its own right, because evil, in Augustine's metaphysics, cannot be a substance (*De Civ. Dei* XI.17). We must conclude that Satan sinned, not from the beginning of his very existence, but from the beginning of his sin. Evil, then, had a beginning, and is therefore a historical phenomenon, affecting, not the changeless and eternal, but mutable created natures, and the events in which they are involved (*De Civ. Dei* XI.15). It does its work, not by exerting a force in its own right, as if it were a god, but through the efforts of wicked beings, which have become evil by turning away from the good, of their own volition.

That said, it was not the origin of evil that was in the forefront of Augustine's mind in *The City of God* but its operation. Most pressingly, he had to clarify for himself and his readers, many of them educated and highly articulate pagans who had come to North Africa when Rome fell, the Christian position on the 'demons' which were so confusingly described by pagan authors of different persuasions, and which were held in respect if not honour by many of his contemporaries. Such pagans held that it was a sign of the anger of these spirits at the desertion of their former worshippers that present events had overtaken the world.

Augustine is perhaps at his remotest from the concerns of present-day thinking on the problem of evil in these pages of *The City of God* because he is trying to meet a difficulty of his own time. He has a vivid sense of the reality of the powers he describes.

Augustine fully accepts the existence of such spirits. He explains in the *Ennarrationes in Psalmos* (103.15, *Sermo* 1), that the word 'angel' properly describes the angel's task, not his nature. It is an *officii nomen*. Angels are spirits sent by God to work in the world. The fallen angels, Augustine believes, also work in the world, but not as God's messengers. Their work is a hideous parody of the mission of the good angels.

Much of Book IX is given up to discussion of various current hypotheses on the subject of the power over *The City of God* these spirits had. There was general agreement that demons were dis-embodied beings, dwelling in the air above us, but there was no consensus of opinion as to what they could do. There is, Porphyry notes, great confusion over demons. In his treatise *On Abstinence from Animal Food* (II.37), Porphyry distinguishes two classes of demons that Plato, he says, 'indiscriminately' calls demons. Some have names and are worshipped as gods. Others are nameless and held in respectful fear by the common people as dangerous spirits. Augustine saw two tasks before him; first, he needed to determine what the demons were and whether, indeed, they really existed; secondly, he needed to show whether they really had any power over men's lives, as their worshippers feared.

Some of these beings are commonly called *daemones* and others *dei*, he explains. The word 'demon' often has a pejorative meaning; even the worshippers of demons commonly worship out of fear rather than love. If we say that a man 'has a demon', we mean that he is accursed (*De Civ. Dei* IX.19). We can speak of a 'good demon' only by qualifying the noun. 'God', on the other hand, has a good meaning. It is used in Scripture, where both good angels and good men are called 'gods' (Psalm 95) (*De Civ. Dei* IX.23).

We must be careful not to become confused. The statues the pagans call 'gods' are not gods in this sense, even if Hermes Trismegistus is right (*De Civ. Dei* VIII.23) and spiritual beings come to dwell in the man-made 'bodies' of the images. The vessels we use in celebrating

101

the sacraments are honoured but not worshipped (*En. Ps.* 113.ii.5).
How much less should we worship the idols of the pagans. They have
mouths and do not speak; they have eyes and do not see; they have
ears and do not hear. Even a beast is better than these *fictilia
simulacra* that have no more than a *similitudo membrorum*, a likeness
in the form of their limbs, which makes them resemble a living man.
Thus Augustine ridicules the worship of images in much the same
terms as Athanasius does, but his purpose is to show that it is the very
tendency to think in 'corporeal images' that dogs the minds of
unbelievers which makes it dangerously easy for them to be fooled by
these statues. The bodily likeness to a man deceives the mind that is
given up to bodily perceptions (*En. Ps.* 113.ii.3).

We must beware, too, of the confusion into which Apuleius falls
(*De Civ. Dei* IX.11) when he argues that the souls of men become
'good' or 'bad' demons after death. Men are a separate order of
beings, and they cannot turn into demons. These are not the demons
the Christian has to fear. If we follow this line of thought we shall be
sucked into a great 'whirlpool' of misunderstandings (*quantam
voraginem aperiant*), as the Manichees are, when they try to prove that
the souls of men are fallen angels, sent to earth to redeem themselves
by living virtuously.

Devils or demons, strictly speaking, are fallen angels, the first
sinners, the very originators of evil, that, and that alone, is the
reason why Christians must take the threat they pose seriously.
Augustine warns us that we must believe them to be evil spirits,
anxious to harm us (*nocendi cupidissimos*), wholly separated from
righteousness (*a iustitia penitus alienos*), deceitful and envious. They
have been cast down from the higher heaven and they dwell in the air
above our world, which makes a suitable prison for them (*De Civ. Dei*
VIII.22).

There are some who distinguish three kinds of rational soul, that of
the gods, which is celestial, that of the demons, which is aerial, and
that of men, which is terrestrial. With the gods (or good angels) the
demons share immortality of body; with men they share a capacity
for perturbation of mind (*De Civ. Dei* VII.14). In this 'hierarchical'
arrangement it seems as though the demons or devils are in some
sense 'better' than men, because they have immortal bodies, and
because they dwell in a higher place. Augustine will have none of
this. Certain animals can run faster than men, and some beasts are

stronger than men. Do we therefore consider them better than ourselves? And birds inhabit the air, like the demons. Are birds to be reckoned higher beings than men merely because they live in a higher place? Men can prove themselves better than demons by leading virtuous lives; they should certainly not feel it necessary to worship the demons as if they were beings worthy of respect. Their wickedness robs them of any claim to honour that they might have had as 'gods' before they fell (*De Civ. Dei* VIII.15).

Augustine is trying to meet the pagans on their own ground here, to make it plain to them in their own terms why there can be no justification for treating demons with anything but contempt (coupled with a wary alertness to their evil intentions towards mankind).

Apuleius himself acknowledges that demons are subject to distress and perturbation (cf. Porphyry, *On Abstinence from Animal Food* II.37). They are affronted at dishonour done to them, placated by gifts, pleased by being honoured, delighted by various rituals and angered if any point of ritual is omitted (*De Civ. Dei* VIII.16). Why should we honour such petty-minded beings, these 'animals of the air', which are rational only so that they may be capable of misery, able to feel only so that they may be miserable, immortal only so that there may be no end to their misery? None of their finer attributes is a cause for worship when their better points are so manifestly vitiated by the evil that is in them. This lack of tranquillity is, for Augustine, the significant difference between 'good and evil demons', angels and devils (*De Civ. Dei* IX.3). The minds of Satan and his followers are disturbed; *animi moribus*. πάθη; *affectus*; *perturbationes*; *affectiones*; *passiones* are to be found in them (*De Civ.Dei* IX.4). They lack the divine peace that they had as an attribute of their angelic nature when they were created. In terms readily comprehensible to his contemporaries, and fully acceptable to more than one contemporary school of philosophers, Augustine has shown why demons are unworthy of worship.

Need we do more than refrain from worshipping them? Can they safely be ignored? No, says Augustine. The disturbance of their minds affects us directly. Their thinking is distorted and they try to win us to their cause by distorting ours. They are actively at work to deceive us, and so we must be on our guard (*quibus maxima est fallendi cupiditas*) (*De Civ. Dei* IV.32). This is not merely a matter of

103

keeping our thinking clear on specific points where the demons would lead us into error. Much more is at stake. No-one in his right mind would follow the Devil, as Augustine has demonstrated, but if the demons can deceive a man to the point where he thinks their lies are the truth, his will, as well as his intellect, will be perverted. He will become like them, and they will possess him because he has freely bent his will towards them (*De Civ. Dei* IV.32). This is an important passage for what it shows us of the assumption underlying Augustine's teaching about the working of evil in the world. Evil cannot change directly the good natures God has made. The alteration of those natures is possible (Augustine has a great deal to say about *naturam mutare* in the later anti-Pelagian writings). It takes place in this way: evil arises in the will of rational creatures and makes itself felt by clouding their reason and making it impossible for them to think clearly or to see the truth. They then act upon the world in such a way as to twist everything they touch out of its proper and good nature into something diminished or perverted – as far, that is, as God allows. It is in the mind, then, and specifically in the will (which, together with the memory and the understanding, makes up the mind) that we must look for signs of evil. We need not fear what the demons can do to the outside world; but we must be constantly on our guard to prevent them making us evil within by presenting what is unreasonable to our minds in the guise of something eminently reasonable and desirable, and persuading us to will what they want us to will.

How is it possible for these beings to deceive us? What have they in common with men that allows them to communicate with us? Perturbation of mind, certainly, and the animal nature and rational mind that the Platonists claim makes them like men. Their aerial bodies separate them from us, and their immortality (*De Civ. Dei* IX.12), but they have quite enough in common with men to enable them to see how to set about deceiving them, and they are in fact, as some thinkers had pointed out, 'closer' to man than the good angels; they are in a position to mediate between heaven and earth. It was because they believed that they could do so that many of Augustine's contemporaries worshipped demons, tried to propitiate them and employed their aid in magic and other superstitious practices, in augury and prognostication.

Augustine's comment on the wisdom of doing so is predictably brisk. We know that we cannot trust what the demons tell us; we have already seen that they are deceivers, twisted by sin in their intentions towards us, but if we propitiate them, some would argue, we may find them trustworthy. They will not deceive their own. Augustine has doubts about that, but in any case, he suggests, it is by no means certain that the demons have accurate information to impart to us even if they can be trusted to look after their followers. He makes a table to clarify the different ways in which the good and evil angels 'know', so as to show that the demons may themselves be in error without realising it. The good angels and the evil angels alike have a knowledge of material things, but the good angels rate their knowledge at its proper value and despise it, while the evil angels are proud of their knowledge. They therefore place a distorted value upon it. The good angels can see the eternal causes of things because they see the truth in the wisdom of God. Demons see some things that are hidden from us, so they can foresee something of the future, but their knowledge of cause and effect, present and future events, is incomplete. What they have to tell us can, then, be at best only part of the truth. Angels are never wrong, but demons are often deceived. They can conjecture probable changes in the future, but their knowledge clearly cannot be fully trustworthy. The reason for this is easy enough to understand. If the effect of evil is to cloud the mind, then the fallen angels must be confused in their thinking like fallen man (*De Civ. Dei* IX.22).

One of the effects of their confused thinking is to cause them to prefer false representations on the part of their worshippers to true worship from the heart. They love deceiving appearances; they are flattered especially by theatrical performances given in their honour. Augustine is sure that those 'gods' who love scenic displays (*ludos scaenicos*) prove by their preference that they are evil. This 'play' is mockery of the truth. To be *ludibundus* is not to be innocently playful but to be full of cruel laughter (*De Civ. Dei* VIII.13). Numa experimented with hydromancy so that he might see the images of the gods in the water, but these were *ludificationes*, appearances by which the demons made sport of him (*De Civ. Dei* VII.35). In the theatrical performances in which they delight, the gods love to have iniquitous acts portrayed as their own deeds, so that their worshippers will feel they may safely imitate them in wickedness; in this way, they lend, as it were, godlike authority to wicked deeds (*De Civ. Dei*

II.25). All these are 'false signs', instructions gone wrong, which will lead men, not to knowledge of the truth, but into lies. These *prodigia mendacii* are to be a sign of the coming of Antichrist. Mortal senses are to be deceived by such *phantasmata* so that it will seem to men that they do what they do not do; and they will believe what they see to be *vera prodigia*, such as can be performed only by God, for they do not know the power of the Devil (*virtutem diaboli nescientes*) (*De Civ. Dei* XX.19).

We are on familiar ground here. These are the very *phantasmata* and *corporales imagines* from which Augustine strove so long to emancipate himself, and which he associated with the thinking of the Manichees.

His conclusion is that if we want the help of an intermediary we should make use of the benevolence of the good angels: *quasi medietatem*. We can resemble them by possessing a good will, and thus there is a link between us which they can use to help us (*De Civ. Dei* XIII.25) but, best of all, we have a Mediator who is united to us here below by the mortality of his body, but at the same time able to give us divine help in purging our mental vision of sin, so that we can see clearly, and pass beyond the limitations of bodily images to a higher mode of thought. This is the state of mind the Incarnation was designed to bring about in Christ's followers (*De Civ. Dei* IX.17). We may, at any rate, be quite confident that the demons have nothing to offer us as intermediaries.

Just as the demons only 'appear' to be able to reveal things beyond our understanding, so it is only 'apparently' that they can affect events. They can do nothing to alter the course of events unless God permits, and therefore any alteration that really takes place comes from God and not from them (*De Civ. Dei* II.23; VII.35). They only *seem* to have power. In the *Adnotationes in Job* Augustine describes how Satan was allowed to test Job. 'It is to be noted that he had power over men and over the elements, but it was given by God (*sed tamen data a deo*)' (*In Job* I.i). The demons have power only because it is delegated to them, and they have it only for the purpose of trying and ultimately glorifying the saints (*De Civ. Dei* X.21). In the *De Doctrina Christiana* Augustine explains that the demons have been given charge over the lower world for that purpose (*De Doct. Chr.* II.xxiii.35).

It is God's intention that we should not set too much store by worldly prosperity, and that is why he sometimes gives prosperity to wicked men and withholds it from the good. Then men will not be tempted to be good only for the sake of the advantages it will bring in this world (*De Civ. Dei* II.23; XX.3). The worshipper of the demons thus sometimes seems to be rewarded by his gods, but this, too, is a reward more apparent than real, for it is not really in the power of the demons to grant; such as it is, it comes from God. Misinterpreting the evidence, and concluding that their superstitious tricks have worked, men become ensnared in error (*multipliciis laqueis*).

God turns the demons' attempts to influence events to account in another way, too. He intends the devils to be objects of mockery, and to present an example to men which is not at all the kind of example they had in mind; they are to be a terrible warning (*De Civ. Dei* XI.17). Their followers, too, men who yearn after evil things are handed over to be mocked and deceived as a reward for their evil will (*De Doct. Chr.* II.xxiii.35). The angels who sinned did not disturb the order of divine providence (*De Civ. Dei* XIV.27). God is able to use even this cosmic event for good, and in smaller matters he turns the evil intent of the wicked angels back upon itself, using them indeed as go-betweens between God and men, but not for the purpose they think.

It would be a foolish religion, he points out, which says that men are not fit to mingle with gods but which sees no objection to postulating that demons may fittingly 'mix' with both gods and men, that is, that demons may act as the only intermediaries between two orders of beings that can have no direct contact with one another (*De Civ. Dei* VIII.18). He can see no reason why gods should be more willing to have intercourse with demons than with men; and he has already shown that good men have in common with gods the good will that is all that is needed to unite them.

Magic is a case in point of a practice that depends for its credibility upon the hypothesis that demons can act upon objects in the material world. Magic cannot work without the assistance of malign spirits (*De Civ. Dei* VIII.19). It involves a pact between men and devils (*pestifera societas*), in which the devils bring about things that do not occur in nature. Here again, the effect devils have is a mere appearance. The signs they do are empty (*nugatoria*), fancied, not real (*imaginaria signa*), and they are therefore misleading. Even to interpret them requires foul play. The augurs take note only of the flights of birds they choose to consider significant. Such signs deny the true function of signs. They lead to worship of the creature instead of the Creator (*De Doct. Chr.* II.xxiii.36).

Augustine takes an especially careful look at the stories of transformations brought about by the work of demons. There are, he concedes, many tales of such changes. Circe changed the companions of Ulysses into beasts and the Arcadians were turned into wolves. Augustine finds himself in a difficult position here. If he says that such stories are not to be believed, he knows that some will say they have heard them on the best authority, and indeed had experiences of their own which confirm the possibility that such things may happen. Augustine himself has heard tales about a part of Italy where the landladies of the inns supplied themselves with beasts of burden by giving a poisoned piece of cheese to travellers. They were immediately changed into beasts, did the work that was required of them, and then reverted to human form; but he cannot believe that if such changes do happen, they involve the real substances of men. The demons to whose agency the changes are attributed do not have the power to create substances. The only possibility Augustine can envisage – and here we are again on the familiar ground of 'bodily images' – is that a *phantasticum*, a phantasy of a man's mind, could perhaps take on the form of a body by some kind of projection, and be somehow presented to the perceptions of others. It may even seem to the man himself that he is changed (*De Civ. Dei* XVIII.17–18).

The difficulty in which Augustine finds himself is that it seems to him – and he knows it will seem to his readers – that there is good authority for the view that magicians can sometimes really perform the marvels credited to them, just as there is evidence that soothsayers and seers are sometimes correct in their predictions. It is no good his simply dismissing these evidences of the powers of demons, if he wants to convince his pagan readers of the soundness of the Christian view. Instead he proposes a compromise. We are dealing, not with real change, but with deceiving appearances, and those, as we know, are well within the capacity of demons.

Demons mislead men's minds, then, by a diabolical *ludus*, playing with their perceptions and mocking reality. The effect of the demons is not to change the substance of things but to work upon the *oculus mentis*, the eye of the mind. However large-scale their operations appear, it is here, in the deception of individual minds, that they begin. Nowhere is this more obvious than in the case of heresies.

Heresies spread alarmingly and yet each individual heretic has been seduced by the same trickery. The Devil, seeing that the temples of his demons were being deserted, and the whole human race was turning to Christ, moved the hearts of heretics who, under the name and guise of Christians, resisted Christian truth. Satan's plan was to present something that was not Christianity as though it were the true faith and thus deceive would-be Christians who followed the heretics into thinking that they were followers of Christ (*De Civ. Dei* XVIII.51), but God used the Devil's stratagem to the benefit of the Church, for the true Christians perceived the danger and strengthened the Church against it; and for the sake of its beneficial effects upon the Church, heresy is allowed to persist.

In his remarks on the Apocalypse, Augustine speaks about the period of 'release', during which Satan will be free to do what he will in the world (*De Civ. Dei* XX.8). It is, on the face of it, difficult to understand why he should have been released at all. God's intention was certainly not that he should seduce the elect; but he is allowed to get up a war with those who are strong enough to resist him, and in that way God will demonstrate his malign power to the world, and manifest his own glory by contrast. 'If he had never been released, his malign power would never have been evident, the most faithful patience of the Holy City would never have been tested, and it would not have been clear how great was his evil.' The Devil is to be made a public exhibition so that everyone may see how thoroughly unattractive evil really is. Again, it is upon men's minds that such demonstrations work. The deceptiveness of the deceiving appearance is made plain to the minds of the faithful by a divinely-appointed piece of theatre.

This device of using the Devil's attempt to deceive, so as to consolidate the truth, is a divine irony, God's own *ludus*, a bending back of the perverse twist the Devil has given things in his *ludus*. By such illuminating contrasts the faithful may see the Devil's stratagems for what they are. As Tichonius says in his seventh Rule, as Christ is the head of the body of Christ, which is the Church, so the Devil is the head of the body of those bound for Hell (*De Doct. Chr.* III.xxxi.44–xxxvii.37). This is what is to be done throughout the universe at the end of the world: there is to be a change, not a total disappearance of the world. That *mutatio* is to involve a turning back of what is bent to the straight (*De Civ. Dei* XX.14). It is a *figura* that is to pass away, not the substance or *natura* of the world. Until then, we have to contend with *mala* and *ficta*, what is evil and what is fictitious (*De Civ. Dei* xx.19).

There is a final irony in the fate that awaits the wicked. The purpose of the judgment on the Last Day is to consign the Devil's followers to the fate that overtook Satan himself when he fell (*De Civ. Dei* xx.7, xx.14). Even the bodies of the wicked must be resurrected, for a dead body without its soul is a mere *cadaver, caro exanimis*, empty flesh, and unless the souls of the wicked are restored to their bodies they will not be able to feel the torments that await them (*De Civ. Dei* xx.21; xxi.2). Here lies the irony. The demons have deliberately confused the minds of men by filling them with corporeal images, bodily fantasies, so as to prevent them from thinking spiritually and coming to a knowledge of the truth about God. Those they have seduced are now to have their perceptions limited for all eternity by bodily sensations of pain. The wicked are to feel their torments in the body, and, in Augustine's scheme of things, there can be no greater torment than to suffer for ever an obscured and clouded vision of God. That is darkness indeed, the *tenebrae angelicae* in which Satan and his followers already dwell, adapted to the human condition.

There is, he is confident, no need to be afraid of demons or superstitions. The demons are all in God's hand. The evil in the world is 'contained' already, although it is still abroad among us. After the end of the world it will be removed to a place set apart for it, where the saints will be able to watch the wicked suffer, not by a *corporalis motus*, a movement of the body, but by a journey of the intellect (*per scientiam*). The darkness will become outer darkness, not in the crude sense that the Manichees envisaged, where the realm of evil and darkness is seen as a region abutting onto the realm of the good, but in the sense that the knowledge of God which the elect will share with the good angels will be purged of the evil that is mingled with it at present. The evil will be cast out. Above all, the purging is to be a cleansing of the faculties of knowledge. Its result will be a power in the elect to know the truth. Satan is, above all, the Father of Lies, and that means he is the source of ignorance and error.

In the meantime it is not necessary, Augustine thinks, to cast out the learning of the pagans with their religious banalities. No aid to understanding is to be despised, even if it comes from a profane source (*De Doct. Chr.* II.xviii.28; II.xl.60; II.xlii.63). We should not refuse to learn letters because the pagans say that they were discovered by the god Mercury. 'The Christian can recognise the Truth of his Lord, where-ever he finds it.'

V · THE ANTIDOTE TO EVIL

1 On the Freedom of the Will

When he came to take stock of his writings in 427 Augustine found himself embarrassed by the controversy surrounding a book he had begun in Rome, after his mother's death, while he was waiting for a ship for Africa. He reconsiders it in the longest of the entries in the *Retractationes*. 'While we were still staying at Rome', he says, 'we wanted to trace the cause of evil' (*Retr.* I.ix.1). He was prompted by a desire to refute those who denied that evil is a result of a free choice of the will, and who said that even if it is, then God is to blame because he created the will. 'We discussed so many problems', he says, that some questions arose which could not be solved at the time, and indeed it was to be seven years before he finished the third book, in Africa, in 395.

The *De Libero Arbitrio* takes the form of a dialogue with one of the Cassiciacum circle, Evodius, who was to return to Africa with Augustine. Now that he was free of them, Augustine discovered in himself a considerable strength of feeling against the Manichees. Even thirty years later, when he was writing the *Retractationes*, the sheer vigour of his denunciations is striking. 'Now that I was baptised, while I was in Rome, I could not endure in silence the tossing-about of falsehoods by the Manichees' (*Retr.* I.vi). The treatise *De Utilitate Credendi*, 'On the Profit of Believing' of 391–2, was written 'to my friend, who, deceived by the Manichees, was still, I knew, held fast in that error' (*Retr.* I.xiii). He was to write an exposition of Genesis to demonstrate the absurdity of the Manichean account of the beginning of the world. In 391–2 he composed a work on 'the two souls' against the Manichees, and although the principal works against the Manichees, against Manicheus' *Fundamental Epistle*, the *Contra Faustum*, the *Contra Felicem*, and so on, were written over a period of years, it seems clear that Augustine felt the urgency of the task which lay upon him (for who was better-equipped than he to refute the Manichees? Who understood them better?), even before he came back to Africa.

The problem which now lay before him was that of the *cause* of evil. 'Our plan of debate aimed at understanding by means of thorough rational enquiry . . . what we believed about the matter on divine authority.' The Manichees objected, perfectly logically, that, since evil is undeniably a fact, it follows that God cannot be both omnipotent and perfectly good. He is either perfectly good and unable to prevent evil, or else he is all-powerful and able to prevent evil, but unwilling to do so, and that would show that he is not perfectly good.

This presented itself to Augustine, fresh from Cassiciacum, largely as a philosophical problem. 'Divine authority' did not yet mean 'Scriptural authority' to him, but the authority of reasoned argument conducted prayerfully and in whatever light God might be willing to shed on the matter. Seven years later, in 395, a good deal more theology comes into Book III as he completes the work, Evodius withdraws, and the air of a philosophical dialogue is gone. But even then he had not seen the problem he was trying to resolve in the way he was later to see it. Looking back, he distinguishes his attempt in the *De Libero Arbitrio* 'to enquire into the *cause* of evil' from the enquiry into 'how we may return to the good we had before or reach a greater good' (*Retr.* I.ix.2) into which he was later led by his campaign against the Pelagians. His emphasis then lay increasingly upon the indispensable work of grace in helping men recover from the effects of sin. In the *De Libero Arbitrio*, he explains, 'I did not mention God's grace, because this was not the subject with which I was concerned' (*Retr.* I.9.4). As it proved, he had put the Manichees behind him only to move to a position which the Pelagians could claim to be close to their own, because in order to clear God of blame, he insisted that the free will of men and angels is the cause of sin and sin the origin of evil. If the will is the cause of sin, said the Pelagians, then by an act of will a man can return to the good. He has no need of divine assistance. Grace need not come into the picture.

Here lay the source of Augustine's embarrassment in later years. The Pelagians were able to point to the *De Libero Arbitrio* as a step on Augustine's part in their direction. He was to make it clear to them, most vehemently, that they had misinterpreted him, as we shall see, but in one thing they were right. It was a turning-point of a book in which he moved finally and decisively away from the Manichees and into a position which neither a Manichee nor a philosopher could hold: a position distinctively his own and at the same time distinctively Christian.

The discussion begins with a metaphysical question of the Cassiciacum sort: 'Is God the cause of evil?' asks Evodius. Augustine's response at once brings the discussion into a human context by defining the two senses of the word 'evil' in which it directly affects a man. There is the evil a man does and the evil he suffers. We may postulate that God is the source of the second when he justly inflicts just punishments. Such unpleasantnesses are good for us. They restore things to order. There is no reason to suppose that God cannot be their author, but what are we to say of the source of the first? Augustine claims that there is no single source, for every man individually is the author of his own evil deeds. Evil cannot take place without an author or source. God cannot be its author. If we reject the Manichean alternative, that evil is an independent power, we are left with only one possibility: that the wicked man is the source of his own wickedness.

Evodius first puts forward the possibility that men learn to do evil from someone or something else; they are not initiators of evil but imitators of a bad example. Augustine counters this by pointing out that all learning is good. It imparts knowledge, indeed it is the only path to knowledge, and so we cannot, properly speaking, 'learn' evil. To do evil is to stray away from the discipline of learning (*De Lib. Arb.* I.i.2.5). To teach evil would be to teach something that is not capable of being understood or known, for knowledge is always good; we cannot, by definition, 'know' evil. If a man had been 'taught' evil, he would not, even then, know or understand it. He could not be said to have learned it. The purpose of the teaching would have been thwarted. We can, it seems, dismiss the idea that men do evil because they have learned to do so (*De Lib. Arb.* I.i.3.7–8).

If we are left with the view that we do evil of ourselves, it is difficult to see why souls which God has created, and which are therefore good, should act wickedly, and if they do, it seems that their wickedness is to be attributed in some measure, even if only obliquely (*parvo intervallo*) to the God who made them (*De Lib. Arb.* I.ii.4.11). Without divine aid, Augustine admits, he would never have found the solution to this problem, which puzzled him greatly from his youth.

The first essential is to stand fast by the principle that God is good (*De Lib. Arb.* I.ii.5.12). Any explanation that implies a diminution of goodness in God must be unsatisfactory. That is where the Manichees were wrong in postulating that God's infinity was limited on one 'side' by evil.

We are discussing, not the nature of evil, but what it is to *do* evil (*male facere*), what it is for a man to *act* wickedly (*De Lib. Ab.* I.iii.6.14). Augustine and Evodius begin by taking the example of an act of adultery. To say that adultery is wrong because the law is against it, or because no man would like the sin of adultery to be committed against him by his own wife, is not satisfactory. These are external considerations. The evil itself lies within the act; the evil thing in adultery is lust (*De Lib. Arb.* I.iii.8.20). Evodius and Augustine agree when they have considered other examples that the common factor in all evil acts is lust in some form, *libido, cupiditas* – desire, in other words, or that misapplication of the will which makes a man want what he should not want. The evil lies in the will, then, and is transferred to other things by an act of the will.

Can a man's will be compelled to evil? No, says Augustine, for nothing is more excellent in man than a wise, rational and virtuous mind. Only something superior to such a mind can compel it to serve lust, but something superior to it would itself be even more wise, rational and virtuous, and would certainly not compel it to act wrongly. Anything inferior, which might want to do so, will be too weak to compel what is superior to itself. Nothing, then, can make the mind lustful except its own free choice (*De Lib. Arb.* I.x.21). We have still not arrived at an explanation of the reasons why the will ever leans towards evil, but Augustine has shown to his own satisfaction that it is in the will alone that we must look for an explanation. Clearly, a definition of sin is needed, which will enable us to understand where in a man it may come from, and that is what Augustine sets out to find in the remaining chapters of Book I. His account is not entirely satisfactory because the argument proceeds by elimination, and by way of a number of wanderings. We are not led purposefully to the conclusion that sin arises in the will but, as it were, by default, by discovering that sin is not merely doing that which one would prefer not to have done to oneself; nor is it simply desire; nor is it merely breach of human law, which is an unreliable measure.

The best Augustine can do in Book I is to define wrongdoing as neglect of eternal things (which we cannot lose if we give them our love), or pursuit of temporal things (which it is easy to lose). It is, in other words, misdirection of energy, perverted desire, misplaced zeal; where energy, desire, zeal are good in themselves, but given up to an end God does not intend.

Why do we do wrong, then? Through free choice of the will. Why does God give us free choice of the will, if we can abuse it? That is the question with which Book I ends. Augustine tries to answer it by looking at that which is undoubtedly good: the will itself and its freedom.

Two tasks remained to Augustine in the second and third books. First he must show why God gives man free choice in willing, so that it is possible for him to sin, when, on the face of it, it would seem better for him to have ensured that that was impossible. Secondly, he must show where the impulse to do evil comes from in the will of man, for both the will and the freedom must be, in themselves, good.

We may be sure that all the organs and powers a man possesses are good in themselves, even though they can be used wrongly, because God gave man his bodily organs. Augustine divides the goods a man may possess into three: bodily goods are the lowest of our goods; the virtues are the highest, for they cannot be misused. It is among the middle-ranking powers of our souls, of which the will is one, that we must look for the goods a man may either use or abuse. The will can turn to the good or away from it. Will is a good, even if only an intermediate good (*medium bonum*) when it attaches itself to the unchanging Good, and it attains for a man those virtues which constitute his first and greatest goods (*prima et magna bona*). If the will turns to its own private good, or to anything exterior or inferior, it sins, but it remains itself a good; even the things sought are good, in themselves, for all that exists is good. The evil lies in the *aversio*, the turning away (*De Lib. Arb.* II.xix.53.199), not in the nature of the will or its objects, since they are the creation of a good God.

It is not difficult to see why God should have given man that 'middle' good of a free will, which can be used either way, for therein lies man's freedom and his potential righteousness. A stone or a tree cannot act rightly or wrongly. A man can. He can do so only because he has the power to make a free choice of the good. That is surely a sufficient reason for him to be given free will. If he had made no contribution of his own to his actions, both punishment and reward would be unjust (*De Lib. Arb.* II.i.2.3). It would be absurd to punish a tree because its leaves fall in autumn. If we look at it in this light we shall see that free will is a good thing, and in that way we shall be sure that it is God-given (*De Lib. Ab.* II.xviii.49.186).

Evodius is still not satisfied. We have still, he presses in Book III, not accounted for the movement towards evil in the free will, which Augustine has shown to be a good thing and rightly given us by God so that we can act rightly and deserve reward. If God so made the will that it has a natural built-in tendency to turn towards evil, Evodius protests (*De Lib. Arb.* III.i.1.2), then God alone is to be blamed for our sins, for he has imposed a necessity on us, and we can do no other. Augustine is obliged to draw his attention back to their earlier discussions. They have already settled the point. Nothing can compel a free will to evil, so every motion of the will must be voluntary, that is, it must proceed from the will itself. There is no *positive cause* of the will's turning to evil because such a turning is negative, a defection. Nevertheless the turning away is under our own control, and we are responsible when it occurs.

Headed off at this juncture, Evodius now reveals the larger problem which troubles him, and which underlay his question: how can it be that we do not sin by necessity, when God knows beforehand that we shall sin, and what God foreknows must come to pass (*De Lib. Arb.* III.ii.4.14)? Augustine's solution to this classic difficulty, which Anselm was to call 'that most famous question', is to distinguish between things that happen according to God's foreknowledge, where there is no intervention of man's will at all, and things that happen because man's will has been exercised. In the latter case, God has foreknowledge of our willing and also of our power to will, but the power, or freedom, is not taken away by his foreknowledge (*De Lib. Arb.* III.iii.8.35). Nor does God compel a man to sin by knowing in advance that he will do so (*De Lib. Arb.* III.iv.9.36).

Augustine was to shift his ground on the question of compulsion in his last years, as he became more and more firmly convinced that divine grace chose those it would rescue from the consequences of Adam's sin, and made their wills capable of choosing the good whether they consented or not. God thus has not only foreknowledge but an active role in bringing about that which he foreknows, and because he is omniscient he is irresistible. His final position is already implicit in his thinking here, at the time when he had become a Bishop at Hippo and moved beyond philosophy into a psychology of evil. But the catalyst in advancing his thinking was to be his writing against the Pelagians.

2 Compelling Questions

By the end of the first decade of the fifth century, Augustine had been Bishop of Hippo for fifteen years. He was well into his fifties, and since his conversion he had been working out his position on all sorts of practical and doctrinal aspects of the Christian faith, under unremitting pressure. He, himself, felt the forcing of the pace, and he was certainly not satisfied that he had dealt adequately with all the questions that had been put to him. Nevertheless, the circumstances in which he had worked had encouraged him to knit together everything he wrote into a coherent system. We have seen how familiar arguments and principles occurred to him constantly in fresh connections; he never hesitated to repeat himself if he thought a point he had made before could usefully be made again in a new context. We have seen something of the result in the progress of his thinking about the way 'bodily images' impede our thinking about higher things. A similar process was to bring about the long, slow development of his view of the work of grace in bringing the will of fallen man from evil to good.

The God who makes the dark angels his instruments, who cannot be outwitted by the most diabolical cunning, who takes the perversion out of his creation and makes it good again, is a powerful and active God, not the passive 'Good' of the Manichees. The God who is so vigilant in the universe that not one demon can entertain a scheme of destruction in a corner of his mind without God's knowing of it and making it part of his providential plan, is a God with an eye for detail. This is a God who takes a personal interest, who will take trouble over the individual in whose damaged human will is a source of evil. 'It is one thing to ask where evil comes from; it is another to ask how we may return to the former good, or come to a greater good' (*Retr.* I.ix.2). Augustine had been moving steadily away from the metaphysical aspects of the problem of evil, and the academic questions they raised, towards a preoccupation with practical and pastoral aspects which became by far the most important for him in the last decades of his life. The change of direction in his thinking came about naturally, as he exhausted the possibilities of philosophical development which he could see in the notion that evil is nothing. But he needed some fresh stimulus to set him actively to work in a new direction, and the pastoral needs of his flock were not, on their own, quite sufficient. They were stimulating, however; Augustine found his thinking being gradually advanced by his efforts to answer the questions he was asked, but the circumstances in which he was forced to work made it impossible for him to build to a plan. He rarely sat down to write a book on a subject he had chosen simply because it interested him (except in the period immediately after his conversion). When he was Bishop of Hippo people from all over the world resorted to him with their difficulties; questions were put to him by friends and acquaintances and complete strangers, sometimes at random, sometimes because he himself had left a point open to question in one of his books or letters. Everything he said or wrote brought him more work. He describes in the *Prologue* to the *Questions* on *Genesis* how during Bible-study classes questions would be asked 'as they came to mind', sometimes small points which could be quickly settled, sometimes large ones which required lengthy answers. The *Questions* on the *Gospels* were again put together in about 400, just as they arose.

It was not until he heard about Pelagius that a major new development took place. His thinking began to move forward again at a great rate when he felt 'compelled' (*Retr*. II.xxv) to address himself to the errors of his followers.

Pelagius, a provincial like Augustine, had gone to Rome from Britain, but unlike Augustine, he had stayed in Italy. There, baptised but still a layman, he had remained for thirty years, building up a following among noble Christian families with his letters of exhortation to the living of a Christian life of energetic striving for perfection. Pelagius' aim seems to have been to foster the growth of a Church whose members would all be perfectly good. His was a muscular Christianity, and he would countenance no excuses for flabbiness. The idea that man's nature was so flawed by original sin that he could not help himself, and would, inevitably fall into sin if he tried to resist temptation by his own efforts, seemed to Pelagius just such an excuse. Man, he held, was made good by a good God, and there can be no inherent fault in his nature. His faults are therefore his own responsibility, and he can cure them by effort. 'How could that which lacks substance [evil, which is nothing] weaken or change human nature?' (PL 48.601).

Augustine defines his position cautiously at first, that to hold a created nature to be evil would be to fall into the Manichean error. Every nature is good; that is axiomatic, for every nature (or substance or essence) is the creation of a good God, but human nature behaves in a way which is not good. If we cannot entertain the possibility that God made it flawed, we must conclude that something has damaged it (*De Nat. et Grat.* III.iii). This is the point the Pelagians will not concede. Augustine thought that they had failed to make a necessary distinction between the constitution of human nature, which is undoubtedly good, and the restitution it requires in its damaged state if it is to be made sound again. In the *De Natura et Gratia* he began to try to work out the respective roles of 'nature' and 'grace', what God gave man at his creation, and what he gives him in redeeming him from his sin (*Retr.* II.xliii). He is sure that grace acts upon the damage which sin has done to human nature (*De Nat. et Grat.* XI.xii). Thus grace co-operates with the good in man's nature to make man wholly good again.

This distinction will not seem important or helpful to the Pelagians as long as they argue that human nature has not been corrupted by sin (*De Nat. et Grat.* XIX.xxi). Pelagius rests his case on the 'nothingness' of evil. His contention is that something which lacks substance, and sin is surely not a substance, could not have damaged the substance of human nature. Augustine tries to answer this with an analogy. To abstain from food is not a substance, but a withdrawal from a substance. Yet if we do not eat, the substance of our body is damaged, we grow thin and weak. God is the sustenance of a rational creature, and to withdraw from him results in damage to the substance of man. Here he is thinking again along lines laid down in the years when he was working out the flaws in the Manichean position. These are very much his reasons for believing that evil, although it is not a substance, can affect substances, making them less in some way, so that they tend to non-existence. If we accept that evil diminishes substances, we can see that sin can certainly damage the substance of human nature. Augustine could take no other view without upsetting the structure of his hard-built theory of evil. He could make no compromise which would enable him to meet Pelagius half-way on this.

The description that follows of the effects of sin upon human nature shows clearly enough that Augustine's mind has run back to his own experience in the years before and immediately after his conversion. Sin brings with it its own penalty, for sin and the punishment of sin are the same in their effect (*De Nat. et Grat.* XXII.xxiv). Sin makes us blind, and so we stumble in the darkness of our clouded minds and commit more sins because we can no longer see what we are doing. Thus the punishment of sin leads inevitably to more sins. This is the meaning of Romans 1.21, 'their foolish heart was darkened'. Pelagius is impossibly far removed from this position when he claims that there is no need to pray for divine aid to help us avoid sin. (The only reason for prayer, he holds, is to ask for forgiveness for sins when they have been committed, for what has been done cannot be undone by the power of nature and the will of man.) (*De Nat. et Grat.* XVIII.xx.)

Augustine's *Confessions* was being widely read in Italy, as well as in Africa. When a copy came into Pelagius' hands he found Augustine's approach to God deeply distasteful. Augustine threw himself on divine aid as if he could be expected to do nothing about the state of his soul without it. To Pelagius' mind too much quarter was being allowed to human weakness, if it was implied that man could not achieve perfection simply by striving wholeheartedly for it (*De Don. Persev.* xx.53). Pelagius' attitude thus contradicted everything Augustine had been trying to express when he wrote the *Confessions*, about the way in which God works in man to convert him to the dependence on divine help without which he cannot even think clearly, let alone live rightly. Perhaps, too, the notion of a Church made up of *perfecti* came too near the Manichean conception to be tolerable to Augustine.

Pelagius' hypothesis was that if a man can make himself evil by a wrong exercise of his will, he can make himself good by a right exercise of his will. Augustine found two serious faults in this view: it implies that a man can himself be the source of good, and that is a creative act Augustine holds to lie with God alone; and it takes no account of the effect Adam's sin had upon all his descendants.

121

Adam's sin so flawed the very nature of man, that the free will God gave him is no longer in balance; man can no longer turn his will Godwards, and allow God to enable him to do good; he can only turn his will away from God, towards nothing, and thus he can only do evil. Only when God intervenes directly and compels the will of man can man do good. This was an extreme position to which Augustine came only gradually, but it was the logical working-out of the stand he took against Pelagius and his followers from the first.

THE OPENING OF THE CONTROVERSY

What Pelagius was saying did not at first cause general alarm. It did not touch on traditional areas of unorthodoxy, where a man had only to raise a question to make himself suspect at once: those problems concerned with the doctrines of Trinity and Incarnation which had exercised the best minds of the Church for two centuries at least (*De Grat. et Lib. Arb.* iv.6). It was Augustine himself who gradually made a system of Pelagius' thought, by working out its theological implications, and he himself did not see until some years had passed that there was in fact a distinct 'heresy' which could be called 'Pelagianism'. At first, indeed, he did not address himself to Pelagius at all, but to some difficulties raised by the tribune Marcellinus in a letter from Carthage in 411, but as he was drawn further into the conflict, twenty years of work opened up before him. He found himself trying to resolve the 'most famous question' of the relationship between human free will and the foreknowledge, predestination and grace of God. His sense of the importance and urgency of the task was kept alive not only because the difficulties multiplied on inspection, but also because the Pelagians refused to acknowledge themselves refuted. In 420, writing *Against Two Letters of the Pelagians*, he says that he feels it necessary to try to prevent the Pelagians confirming themselves and their friends in error. In 427–8 he was still anxious. Writing *On the Predestination of the Saints* he speaks of 'those things which now by the warning of the Pelagian errors must of necessity be discussed with greater copiousness and care'.

Whatever rumours had reached him, he had, as he notes in the *Retractationes*, hitherto done nothing more systematic to combat Pelagius' teaching than preach against it when occasion demanded, but in 411 Celestius, one of the most forceful of Pelagius' followers, came to Carthage to join the community of Romans in exile there, and applied to be made a priest. He was condemned by the local Church leaders because he had been putting forward the opinion that infant baptism served no purpose (for there was no reason to doubt the salvation of children who died before they had had time to commit sin). This was a perfectly logical extension of Pelagius' teaching. If there is no inherent flaw in the new-born child, there can be nothing to be purged by baptism. Celestius' arguments were causing some controversy in Carthage when Marcellinus wrote to Augustine asking for a clarification of the issues involved; Augustine was sufficiently concerned to set aside the work he was engaged on in connection with the Donatists and write a long letter of systematic rebuttal. Marcellinus, an Imperial commissioner, recently arrived in Carthage and a keen lay theologian, represented a class whose needs Augustine was anxious to meet. They were influential and articulate, and it was possible for them to lead others astray if they fell into error.

In the forefront of Augustine's mind as he wrote *On the Deserving of Sinners and their Forgiveness* (*De Peccatorum Meritis et Remissione*) was, as its title implies, a strong sense that the sinner deserves nothing but condemnation. The sinner must somehow be set right with God. Pelagius does not understand the damage that sin has done. Pelagius' simple rule, that he must try hard to be good, will not meet the difficulty which Augustine outlines at the very beginning. The effect of sin goes beyond anything the individual can repair by his own efforts. Men die because of sin. If Adam had not sinned, he would not have died, but his body would have been changed into a spiritual body. He would not even have grown old. Before the fall he was capable of dying, certainly, but there would have been no reason why he should ever have done so if he had not sinned, just as there is no reason why a body should suffer illness unless disease strikes it, although it is capable of suffering illness (*De Pec. Mer.* I.ii.2–v.5). There is, then, an effect of sin which cannot be put right by plain effort. A man cannot restore himself to the condition of unfallen Adam. Something therefore has to be done on his behalf.

Yet before we can generalise from Adam to the rest of mankind, we must show that the sin of Adam had consequences for all Adam's progeny. There is no difficulty here if we lodge the original sin in the body and say that Adam was physically altered; it is easy then to see how sin must pass from Adam to all men by natural descent, but Augustine had demonstrated that sin begins in the soul. The will is the only source of evil, and the will is a faculty of the mind not of the body. Original sin must therefore affect the will so that it wills evil; from nowhere else can sin proceed.

Augustine recognised a classic difficulty here. It is easy to see how original sin may be transmitted to the soul if all souls are derived from the soul of Adam, as all human bodies are derived from his body. It is far from easy to explain the matter if we argue that all souls are freshly created. For some reason this was a question on which Augustine preferred to keep an open mind (*Retr.* II.lvi), even though it was a topic of considerable contemporary interest. In a *Letter* of 412 (143.8) to Marcellinus he lists various opinions that are popularly held. Perhaps all souls were generated from that of Adam. Perhaps the soul comes into existence individually in each person. Perhaps each soul is separately created and introduced into the body at some stage of its development before birth. Perhaps souls make their own choice of body and spontaneously plunge themselves into bodies. In *Letter* 165 (*c.* 410) to Marcellinus and Anapsychia Augustine again lists various current theories about the origin of the soul. Pythagoras and the Platonists and Origen think that it comes down from heaven. The Stoics, the Manicheans and the Priscillianists imagine that the soul is an emanation of the divine substance. Some Christians are foolishly led to believe that God has a store-house of souls, waiting until it is time for them to be united with their proper bodies. Scripture suggests that souls are daily created by God and sent into bodies (John 5.17) as they are made. Tertullian, Apollinarius and many Western scholars claim that it is derived from a root stock, that is, from the soul of Adam.

Augustine preferred to take the view that this is an unnecessary question, merely adding to the 'clouds' which envelop the 'lurking-place' of the Pelagians (*Against Two Letters* III.x.26). In the same letter to Marcellinus (143.11) he says that it is better to leave the question alone unless a definitive solution becomes clear. 'If anyone wishes to support and defend any of those theories about the soul,' he says, ' he should either offer such passages from the Scriptures, vouched for by the authority of the Church, as cannot be subjected to different interpretations: for example, that God made man, or else he should prove his case by an argument so solid that it is impregnable, and only a madman would try to contradict it.'

Augustine himself came back to the question in 419, in the writing of a treatise *On the Soul and its Origin* in which he hoped to put right the errors of Vincentius Victor. Vincentius was a native of Mauritania, once a member of a splinter-group that had separated itself from the Donatists, but now a converted Catholic. Vincentius had been writing on the subject himself, because he disagreed with two of Augustine's opinions. He took exception to Augustine's unwillingness to commit himself on the origin of the soul, and he thought that Augustine was wrong in maintaining that the soul was incorporeal.

The second, for reasons we have already looked at, seemed to Augustine a matter of the first importance. He would prefer to think that Vincentius has simply misunderstood what he is saying, that he has not yet learned to conceive of something which is not a body, although it may seem like a body. Augustine himself had had exactly the same difficulty in his Manichean years (*On the Soul* v.5).

The first question ceases to be neutral only when one of the current theories of the origin of the soul is made to bear interpretations which lead to heresy, and that is what has happened here (*On the Soul* vi.6). Vincentius seems to be trying to maintain that each freshly-created soul in some way 'deserves' to be polluted by the body (which is transmitted directly from Adam) and that original sin, lodged by inheritance in the body, moves, as it were sideways, from the body into the soul. This is a view that would take sin out of the will, and for that reason alone Augustine felt it necessary to make it clear that it was a mistaken view.

The Pelagian sympathisers among Augustine's contemporaries preferred to avoid all these difficulties by taking the view that the sinner merely imitates Adam (or indeed, Satan, the first sinner of all) (*De Pec. Mer.* I.xiv.18). He could choose not to do so if he wished. The Pelagian challenge was not to the notion that sin lies in the will, but to the idea that sin is a universal imperfection, a flaw in every human soul. If he was to rebut their arguments, it was necessary for Augustine to emphasise the difference between regarding Adam as an example whom sinners imitate (and so 'learn' to sin), and holding that he is the originator of sin in the human constitution; then the sin is transmitted inwardly, directly into the individual, and not outwardly, by example. Augustine has no quarrel with the idea that Adam set an example to sinners, provided it is understood that he also transmitted sin to his descendants directly. He draws a parallel. Just as men imitate Adam in sinfulness, so they must learn to imitate Christ in goodness. Just as sin works inwardly in man, so the grace of God works inwardly to counteract it (*De Pec. Mer*. I.ix.9–x.9). There is a symmetry in the arrangement that seems to him an indication of the rightness of the view of sin he is putting forward.

Confusion can be avoided if we distinguish carefully between original sin and actual sin. The Pelagians do not wish to deny the existence of the sins which the individual commits. Augustine's quarrel with them is over the existence of original sin. For if the Pelagians are right, and imitation alone makes men sinners (when they commit actual sins after Adam's example), then surely imitation of Christ alone can make men righteous (*De Pec. Mer*. I.xv.19)? In that case, a man can achieve perfection by his own efforts. On the other hand, if sin enters the individual by natural descent, or natural generation, then only re-generation can put it right, and that can come only through God's direct action, that is, through grace, and a man cannot become perfect merely by trying hard.

What conclusions does Augustine draw from all this? First, it leads him to consider the work of grace – a line of thought he was to pursue a very long way, because the more he thought about it the clearer it seemed to him that grace was the key to a vast complex of problems about the working of human free will, God's foreknowledge, and predestination. This divine intervention covers not only the original sin but also all the actual sins a man has committed. He wants the Pelagians to acknowledge the need for grace independently of the question of original sin, to concede that, even in the case of his personal sins, a man cannot avoid or make up for sin on his own. This was a point on which Augustine was to expand considerably, later in his anti-Pelagian writings. The role of human effort in attaining perfection was very much a subordinate one in his mind from the first, and it dwindled as he scrutinised it.

Secondly, if we insist on the presence of original sin even in new-born children, we must assume that God takes it seriously. Since personal sin cannot be attributed to infants, the condemnation that awaits them if they die in original sin will be very mild, but condemnation there must be, Augustine is sure. Only grace can save them. That is why infant baptism is necessary, so that grace may be made available to the child (*De Pec. Mer*. I.xi.14; I.xvi.21–xvii.22), for baptism confers grace as nothing else can do.

An immediate problem was the series of difficulties raised by contemporaries over this point, some of which Augustine feels require an answer, if his case is to stand up to the assault of sympathisers with the Pelagian position. Some moderates would accept the necessity for infant baptism, but only on the grounds that infants are thereby spiritually reborn. They see no need for the purging of original sin (*De Pec. Mer*. I.xviii.23). Others object that baptism is efficacious only for believers and penitents. How, they ask, can an infant be said to be a believer and a penitent (*De Pec. Mer*. I.xix.25)? Is it necessary, others enquire, for an infant to eat and drink the body and blood of Christ in order to be saved – for that is required of the full member of the Church (*De Pec. Mer*. I.xx.27)? If God is merciful, and yet insists upon baptism before he will give the grace which is needed for salvation, why does he allow some infants to die unbaptised (*De Pec. Mer*. I.xxi.30)? That, Augustine confesses, remains a great mystery, but for the other objections he has a ready answer, and he is very anxious indeed to rebut the last of these objections (*De Pec. Mer*. I.xxii.31) that souls are put into bodies suited to their merits, on the basis of the way they have lived their previous lives, and that that is why infants are born full of sin. This is a Manichean argument, and he is determined to allow it no quarter at all.

At the beginning of the third book of the *De Peccatorum Meritis et Remissione* Augustine pauses to survey what he has achieved so far. He thinks that, even if he has not covered in detail all the points the Pelagians have raised, he has built a firm base on which the defenders of the faith may confidently take their stand. The foundation is an acceptance of the doctrine of original sin, with a concomitant recognition of the need for a more than human aid to counteract the effects of original sin. To complete his platform, Augustine had to explain the nature of the aid provided by divine grace, and the connection between grace and baptism. He needed to make it clear what baptism could achieve and what grace could do, so as to determine the proper place for human effort in the process of striving for perfection. That done, he could tackle the further question: is it possible for man to achieve perfection in this life? It was important to place the teaching of the Pelagians in this larger context, so as to show how unconvincing was their view that perfection could be achieved by human effort alone.

3 Grace

There is no doubt that Augustine's own position was modified during the years when he was writing against the Pelagians. He acknowledges as much in the *Retractationes*, in reconsidering his first treatise on the freedom of the will, the *De Libero Arbitrio*. When he wrote it, he had wanted to understand how evil arises in the will. The Pelagian controversy had made him think about the process of putting right the damage. He asks why the man who sins by an effort of will cannot turn from sin by an effort of will and be good, unless God helps him. Is fallen man a creature without freedom? Writing *Against Two Letters of the Pelagians* in 420 Augustine argues that freedom of choice did not perish entirely with Adam's sin, only the freedom to be fully righteous which Adam had (*Against Two Letters* I.ii.5). The wicked certainly retain their free will, for no-one is forced into sin, but because they have given themselves up to sin by their own free will they are hurried along in their sin to commit further sins (*Against Two Letters* I.iii.7). Satan does not cause the sinner to act; each sinner is the source of his own wickedness (*Against Two Letters* I.iii.7). In no way for which the sinner is not himself directly responsible can sin be said to be coercive; it is simply that a man remains free only in evil. He cannot be made free in good until God makes him so, because Adam lost that freedom for all his progeny (*Against Two Letters* I.iii.7).

This is the human freedom of will that grace must help, a damaged and restricted freedom, perhaps, but still a freedom, and it is in its power to will good that the human will needs help. It has no difficulty in willing evil unaided.

As he came to be more and more firmly of the opinion that some direct action by God is necessary, Augustine moved towards an extreme position. His developing conception of the huge generosity of the Creator in helping man's damaged will to function properly, gradually blotted out any notion that man might contribute to his own salvation by trying hard; if a man could deserve God's grace that would make grace a lesser thing; only if it is utterly undeserved is it truly a free gift. And if man has no say in the matter it is also a gift he cannot refuse. It is a gift which compels him to be saved.

This view of things rests ultimately upon Augustine's theory of knowledge. Just as the perversion of the will is reflected in a perversion of the understanding and the memory which prevents them from functioning properly, and divine illumination is needed to show man the presence of the Trinity in his own mind, so there is a parallel between the exercise of the free will of man in co-operation with divine grace, and the exercise of the other faculties of the mind in co-operation with divine grace.

Augustine explores this thought in the tenth Book of the *Confessions*. It would seem, on the face of it, that the divine beauty reflected in the created world ought to be visible to all beings whose sense-perceptions are intact. Yet it clearly does not say the same thing to all men. Animals do not possess reason and so they cannot understand or 'judge' what they see, so as to realise its meaning. Men are rational beings, but not all of them have their judgment in proper working order. Only those who can set what they see beside an inner measure of the truth can judge correctly, and only such men can perceive the beauty of God in the beauty of the world. Their minds are flooded with divine light and they have eyes to see what it shows them, but that divine illumination is a free gift of God.

Reasoning is the process of judgment in the mind. It is, as Augustine defines it in the *De Ordine*, a 'mental operation' which is capable of distinguishing the things that are learned and connecting them together in appropriate ways. Only rare individuals are able to use reason as a guide to the knowledge of God or the soul at all effectively without divine aid (*De Ord*. II.xi.30). Even then, the senses must first be employed (*De Ord*. II.xiv.39). We habitually say that something is 'reasonably' sweet or 'reasonably' well made (*Against Two Letters* II.xi.32). By taking orderly steps from there we can progress to the use of reason to judge higher things, but only with the aid of illuminating grace. This requires hard work on our part. (Augustine admires ratiocination because it is effortful.) Reasoning is a 'movement of the mind' (*De Ord*. II.xi.30). Reason aspires effortfully upwards, trying to retrace the downward progression of the soul which took place in Adam's fall, for that *regressus* ought to be made by the highest faculty of the mind. In this right directing of effort it is like the will, when it is exercised for good, and as grace co-operates with the will, so it co-operates with the reason, to illuminate the understanding and make the memory work efficiently.

Like the reason, the will cannot even make this effort for the good;

it cannot work effectively and consistently choose the good, without the help of grace. Perseverance in good is a gift (Augustine wrote a book on *The Gift of Perseverance*). Augustine came to the conclusion that the doing of even one good act is a gift of grace, as he learned to attribute more and more to grace and less and less to human effort. If all good things come from God, how can a man do something good by himself?

The Pelagians claim that grace shines freely on all: the True light lights everyone who comes into the world (John 1.9). They say that children are enlightened as soon as they are born. Augustine cannot agree. He has seen infants struggling and crying when he has baptised them too often to believe that they are enlightened already. They clearly do not understand what is happening to them, or they would not resist baptism (*De Pec. Mer.* I.xxv.36). He interprets St John's words as meaning that although the light is shed on everyone, not everyone sees it, only those whom God chooses. Just as some are blind in their bodily eyes, so those who are not given spiritual sight are blind to the light of grace (*De Pec. Mer.* I.xxv.37). Unbaptised infants are in inward darkness. Their rational intellects do not function properly and they are ignorant of God; that is why they struggle against baptism. A strong proof of the devastating effect of Adam's sin is that human infants are more ignorant than the young of animals, which can find their way to their mother's breast and walk about unaided as soon as they are born. Adam was not formed in ignorance. From the beginning he could understand what he was told and he was able to name the animals, but his offspring's minds are clouded (*De Pec. Mer.* I.xxxvi.67). Here again we find a theme of the *Confessions*, an experience of Augustine's own being brought to bear on a doctrinal problem. Scripture is consistently expounded in the light of that experience.

Grace, then, works by aiding our mental sight, so that we may see to do good. Without it we should be confused, and we could certainly not arrive at a state of perfection by travelling in the dark (*De Pec. Mer.* II.v.5). Grace counteracts specifically a specific effect of original sin. Augustine emphasises that baptism was divinely instituted. God had a purpose for it, and that was to provide an instrument for making Christians members of the body of Christ (*De Pec. Mer.* I.xxiv.35). In baptism we are incorporated into Christ as his members. Members of the body of Christ must of necessity be illuminated by grace, so we may conclude that baptism confers grace (*De Pec. Mer.* I.xxviii.55), but that is too general a conclusion.

It is important to be clear what baptism achieves and what it does not achieve, if we are to show up the inconsistency of the Pelagian position, says Augustine. Baptism purges all the wrong a man has done in the past and it takes away the penalty which would otherwise be due for the original sin which distorts his very nature. It does not, however, take away the urge to sin at a stroke. It merely sets in motion the process by which a man changes towards his everlasting renewal and his ultimate perfection. The urge to sin remains, to do battle with the grace which now illuminates the Christian, but he has the aid of grace and so he can make progress.

The physical body is not directly affected; it goes on dying, but it now becomes merely a matter of time before it will be changed into a spiritual body. The soul begins to be renewed at once, and it is renewed day by day thereafter (*De Pec. Mer.* I.xxxix.70; II.vii.9). Baptism does not turn an evil will into a good will; that would be to take away a man's freedom of will, for good will comes only from God and the possessor of the will would lose all freedom of choice if he could choose only the good which he himself cannot initiate. He must remain free to choose the evil so that there will be some freedom in his giving himself up to the good. Throughout his life the choices will go on, and only with the aid of grace can he choose the good consistently, and so, by the exercise of his free will hand in hand with grace, become perfect by co-operation with the good. Without baptism, he could not make a beginning, but baptism does not make him perfect. It merely cleans the slate for him.

What do the Pelagians have to say to this? Some of them do bring infants to baptism, on a pretext that Augustine can only regard as absurd. They cite John 3.3, 5, 'Except a man be born again, of water and the Spirit, he shall not enter into the kingdom of God.' Unbaptised infants, they say, will have salvation and eternal life. There is no reason why they should not, if there is no such things as original sin, for they cannot have committed any personal sins, but Scripture says that they will not enter into the kingdom of God without baptism, and so their parents must have them baptised so that they may be with Christ in the Kingdom (*De Pec. Mer.* I.xxx.58).

Augustine points out that the actual form of baptism makes nonsense of this practice. The sponsor renounces the Devil on behalf of the infant, but the Pelagians do not acknowledge that the Devil is in the child at all. The sponsor says on the child's behalf that he is converted to God, but the Pelagians do not allow that the child has ever been turned away from God. The sponsor says that he believes in the forgiveness of sins, again speaking for the child, but the Pelagians deny that the infant has any sins to forgive (*De Pec. Mer.* I.xxxiv.63). The Pelagian position is untenable because it is inconsistent. If they think baptism is necessary, then they are, whether they realise it or not, implicitly accepting the existence of original sin. Augustine is impatient with the Pelagian notion of the general usefulness and edification of baptism.

They certainly have no case to make when they claim mockingly that if baptism purges original sin a baptised man ought to beget children who are without original sin, and not themselves in need of baptism (*De Pec. Mer.* II.ix.11; II.xxv.39). They would not think like this, Augustine explains, if they understood what baptism does. It makes it possible for a man to be counted righteous by the operation of the Spirit, but it is not by the Spirit that he begets his children. They are begotten by an act of the old concupiscence (legitimate in marriage, but still a legacy of Adam's sin). We have already seen that the body is not changed by baptism. There is a parallel case in circumcision. The children of the circumcised are not born without foreskins (*De Pec. Mer.* III.viii.16). Baptism brings about a spiritual change, and grace acts within, not externally.

If the path to perfection begins in earnest at baptism, we may legitimately ask whether the Pelagians are correct in their view that perfection is attainable, but wrong merely in thinking that a man can achieve it unaided. Pelagius claimed that perfection must be attainable, for God commands us to be perfect, and God does not ask us to do the impossible. For the Pelagians the matter was simple enough. We commit no sin unless we will to sin. We must not will to sin, and then we shall be perfect. Augustine agrees that God intends perfection to be possible for man. He would certainly not command us to do something we could not do, but he insists that we cannot do it unaided, for the reasons he has already outlined. The will of man requires the assistance of grace if it is to refrain from sin. Good will comes from God, as all good things come from God. Man himself can be the author of nothing at all, but only the evil which is a negation of good.

4 Contradictions?

Augustine's thinking about the problems the Pelagians were raising involved him in an increasing number of apparent contradictions. He was confident that these were illusory, but he knew that they gave difficulty to many people. He wrote the treatise *On Grace and Free Will* in 426 or 427 because he was aware that some people were maintaining that despite what he had said, grace and freedom of the will were incompatible, that the operation of grace must limit freedom of the will (*Retr.* II.lxvi). It seemed to such objectors that eternal life cannot be both a reward for faithful service and a free gift of grace (*On Grace* viii.19). Augustine's solution of this, and other similar paradoxes, was to look for a formula which encapsulated both sides of the contradiction. In this case, the problem disappears if we understand that even our good works are prompted by the grace of God, so that, although they remain ours because we have done them by a free act of will, yet they are free gifts of grace, too, because God has made them possible for us (*On Grace* viii.20).

The first hint of the existence of problems of this kind had already appeared in Book II of the *De Peccatorum Meritis*. It arises again in *On Nature and Grace* (VIII.viii) where Augustine returns to the question whether it is possible for there to be a man without sin. He sets out two principles: if something exists, it follows that before it existed, it was possible for it to exist, but the converse does not follow: if it is possible for something to exist, it is not necessarily true that it does exist. Now Pelagius had been asking in what lay the 'possibility' that a man might be without sin. It was, he thought, not a mere 'possibility' or 'power' of a man's will, but a very necessity of his nature (*De Nat. et Grat.* XLV.liii). We can, for example, speak or not speak as we choose; the act of speaking is subject to the will, but the power of speaking is not. We are always able to speak, because the power to speak resides in our nature; it is, in this special sense, a *necessitas naturae*. The same is true of the capacity to hear, smell or see (*De Nat. et Grat.* XLVII.lv).

Augustine is not happy with these analogies. He cannot see that our desire to be happy (which is surely inalienable from our nature) has nothing to do with the will (*De Nat. et Grat.* XLVI.liv). He perceives a number of difficulties arising in the case of God if we try to separate the action of the will from the power-to-act, in this way. (Does it detract from God's power that he cannot will to sin, die or destroy himself?) (*De Nat. et Grat.* XLIX.lvii). Pelagius is found to be inconsistent, implicitly allowing that a man cannot avoid sin without the help of God's grace when he asserts that the power-to-avoid-sin lies in man's nature and not in his will. For in the present state of things a man may will to be able to avoid sin, but be unable to do so without grace precisely because of the flaw in his nature (*De Nat. et Grat.* LI.lix). Augustine marshals a series of Scriptural texts to show that the flesh wars against the spirit even in baptised persons; how, then, can the capacity to avoid sin be an inseparable part of our nature, as *necessitas naturae* implies that it is? (*De Nat. et Grat.* LIII.lxi). Augustine dispatches Pelagius' arguments by roundly asserting that what is needed is a true confession of the weakness of human nature, not a false defence of its capacities (*De Nat. et Grat.* LIII.lxii).

Nevertheless, this talk of necessity was to have long-term results in Augustine's painstaking working out of an explanation which would reconcile divine foreknowledge, predestination and grace, which have an absolute necessity, with the freedom of choice of the human will.

Augustine's ideas on predestination were not formed all at once. Indeed, they changed as he thought more deeply about the problem. He confesses to some early misconceptions (*De Praed. Sanct.* iii.7). Late in the 420s he wrote a treatise on the *Predestination of the Saints* in the hope of bringing finally to heel some semi-Pelagians who had understood that grace works together with the will of man and that no-one can begin a good work, or complete it, entirely by himself, but who had not yet grasped the total dependence of human will upon divine grace if it is to do any good at all (*De Praed. Sanct.* ii.6).

Augustine sets out for their inspection the obvious truth that many people hear Christian truth expounded to them, and while some believe, others do not. There must be a reason why their responses differ. Augustine suggests that the reason is that God has prepared some but not others (*De Praed. Sanct.* vi.11). Those who receive the truth are the elect, and those who do not have not been chosen to be Christians.

On the face of it this appears unjust in God. Why should some men be favoured over others? Augustine has two points to make here.

First, he emphasises again that it is an act of mercy in God to save anyone at all. No-one deserves to be saved. We should be marvelling that the truth is received by some, not quibbling because it is not received by all.

More to the point, perhaps, is his second line of argument. We must distinguish between what God 'foresees' and what he 'causes to happen' in the future. Those to whom the faith was never preached at all were those God knew would not believe. He did not unjustly deprive them of an opportunity for salvation. Those he knew to be potential believers he prepared for the Kingdom of Heaven and the company of the angels (*De Praed. Sanct.* ix.17).

At first, Augustine says, he deliberately confined himself to the problem of divine foreknowledge. 'Whether God only foreknew them, or also predestinated them, I did not at that time think it necessary to enquire or to discuss' (*De Praed. Sanct.* ix.17). Now he takes things a little further. He looks at the relationship between predestination and foreknowledge. Predestination cannot exist without foreknowledge, but foreknowledge may exist without predestination. There are things which God foresees, but which he himself does not intend to bring about (*De Praed. Sanct.* ix.19). Thus a man's future sins are seen clearly by God, but God does not make him commit them. He asks, too, what is the relationship between predestination and grace. 'Predestination', he concludes, 'is a preparation for grace'; that is, by choosing a man, God isolates him as a suitable recipient of grace. Grace is, in this sense, an effect of predestination.

This, then, is the picture we have so far: God knows in advance everything that will happen, for he is omniscient, and he is eternal; the future is present to him already. Within the complex of future events there are some that he will himself bring about, the events he predestines. Among them are the bringing of certain human souls to perfection. God brings them by the operation of grace, which thus acts as an instrument for putting his intentions into effect, but each of those human souls remains free. Providence simply exploits divine foreknowledge of what they will freely choose to do, in order to bring about their salvation.

The sequence of events in time is important in all this, not in relation to God, for God himself is outside time, but in relation to man. God calls men in two ways: some are called like those who were invited to the wedding, but did not come; others are called in such a way that they do come. These are called, not because they have believed, but in order that they may believe (*De Praed. Sanct.* xvi.32–xvii.34). If they had believed before they were called, they would have chosen God, and not God the believer (John 15.16). God chose the righteous not because he knew that they would become righteous of themselves, but because it was his intention to make them so (*De Praed. Sanct.* xviii.35). This is why the sequence is important. The Pelagians reverse it when they say that we are made holy of ourselves and by our own efforts, by the free choice of our own wills, and that God merely foresees that we shall do so, but takes no positive action in the matter. Augustine insists that God foreknew, not only our actions, but his own work, and that means he predestinated the elect to be holy and immaculate. He not only saw it coming about in the future; he made it happen, and because grace is an effect of predestination, he gave grace to those he had predestinated.

So much for the complex of foreknowledge, predestination and grace. Augustine's view of their interrelationship is now becoming clear, but what of the working of the human will, which we know co-operates with grace? How can it work together with predestination and remain free? How can free will operate under conditions of necessity? To understand this we must try to grasp the notion of freedom which was developing in Augustine's mind in the works of the 420s. If a man does what he wants to do, he acts freely; he is not forced to act, because he has chosen to act. If it so happens that what he chooses to do is what grace would have compelled him to do in any case, that does not diminish the freedom of his choice. The truly free will is the will that has regained its pristine freedom to choose the good and not only the evil. The free will of the elect is therefore, paradoxical as it may seem, more free than the will of the unregenerate man upon whom grace does not act with compelling force. The secret of true freedom is to give up the freedom to do evil which cannot be called a freedom, because it presents only one alternative. The good man regains his freedom to do good and at the same time loses the tendency to choose evil, with the aid of a truly liberating grace.

5 Neither a Pelagian nor a Manichee

Julian of Eclanum, son of a bishop in southern Italy, was an adherent of the Pelagians as a young man. When the movement was condemned, he refused to change his opinions, and he brought together a group of sympathetic Italian bishops to resist the condemnation. As a result he was obliged to go into exile, and in 419 he went to the East, where he took refuge first with Rufus, Bishop of Thessalonia, then with Theodore of Mopsuestia in Cilicia, and finally with Nestorius in Constantinople. His last years appear to have been spent in the island of Lérins and as a schoolmaster in a small town in Sicily, where he died some time before 455. He and Celestius remained friends, and Julian worked fiercely for his cause. He was widely-read in both Greek and Latin, in Pagan and in Christian writings. From 419 he composed a stream of letters and books, several volumes directed specifically against Augustine. Of his twelve uncontested works, several portions are preserved in Augustine's replies.

The interest of Augustine's response does not lie in the novelty of what he has to say; he had already said much of what he now had to say again against Julian; he is chiefly concerned to reassure Christians who were disturbed by the sheer volume and energy of Julian's outpourings, and for whom it was important that he, Augustine, should be seen to have the last word. The task of rebutting Julian had, however, a new colour in one respect, and an important one for Augustine himself. Julian had accused Augustine and the Catholics of being Manichees. He was not the first to say so, but he brought the accusation home hard.

In 421, in the second of his four books *Against Two Letters of the Pelagians* (II.ii), Augustine drew up a table of comparisons and contrasts in the hope of clarifying the differences between Pelagian and Catholic, Catholic and Manichee, Manichee and Pelagian. The Pelagians do not admit that God is the saviour of a fallen mankind; the Manichees do not admit that God is the Creator of all natures; the Catholic cannot associate himself with either position, for both these views diminish the Deity. The Pelagians regard the lust of the flesh as a natural good; the Manichees think that it has been an evil thing from all eternity; the Catholics date the evil in it from the fall of

Adam. The Pelagians say that even a wicked man can do good by his own free will; the Manichees deny that it is from a man's free will that evil takes its beginning; the Catholics maintain that each man is the source of his own evil (in his will) and that no-one can do good of himself. The Pelagians say that the soul is without sin, because man's nature is wholly good; the Manichees say that the soul is a particle of God, made sinful by the admixture of an evil nature; the Catholics deny that the soul is a particle of God, but they do not agree with the Pelagians that it is without sin in this life. Manichees and Pelagians agree in rejecting the notion that man's salvation depends upon the grace of Christ; they are alike in undervaluing baptism, the Manichees denying its usefulness to anyone, the Pelagians its usefulness to infants, who are without sin. They agree in doing dishonour to the flesh of Christ, the Manichees by their blasphemies concerning his birth, and the Pelagians by considering the flesh of those he redeemed equal to his own, in its freedom from original sin. As a statement of current positions on these issues of common concern, as Augustine saw them, this list is of considerable importance, but it hints at something else: a sense of incipient confusion in the minds of others, if not in his own mind, which made it necessary for him to take stock. He speaks later in the treatise (*Against Two Letters* III.vii.24) of the 'clouds' of extraneous questions the Pelagians use to confound the issues, the mistaken emphases which cause the Pelagians to value the right things (created natures, marriage, law, free will, the saints) but for the wrong reasons, that is, without a due sense of God's excellence and man's shortcomings: in marriage, for example, we must distinguish the evil of shameful lust from the excellence of marriage (*Against Two Letters* IV.i.1).

He was already aware that the Pelagians were calling the Catholics 'Manichees' (*Against Two Letters* IV.i.1), but the accusation had not yet struck home. This stock-taking exercise reviews Catholic, Pelagian and Manichean positions with a magisterial command of their similarities and differences. Augustine is anxious for the peace of mind of his Catholic readers, but he is not troubled on his own account. Julian of Eclanum was to make him think again, to force him to take stock of his own position to open up a question far larger than any he envisages here: was there indeed any truth in the notion that he who was not a Pelagian was by implication in some sense a Manichee, that there was no intermediate position such as Augustine allocates to the Catholics in his table?

It has been suggested that when Julian of Eclanum accused Augustine of 'being a Manichee' and of 'preaching fatalism', these were merely 'conventional bogeys'.[1] It certainly seems that in some circles 'Manichee' and 'Pelagian' had become general terms of abuse by the second or third decade of the fifth century. Yet Julian was pointing to a recognised antithesis between the 'Pelagian' and the 'Manichean' standpoints upon a complex of fundamental philosophical and theological issues. In this sense, Julian had presented Augustine with no empty challenge, and he succeeded in making him take stock of his position in the light of the idea that in taking up a position opposed to that of the Pelagians Catholic Christians had somehow identified themselves with the Manichees.

Julian calls Augustine a Manichee, not because he believes him to be still a follower of the sect, nor because he believes him to be consistent in his Manichean views on every point, but because, as he argues, the tendency of Augustine's thought is 'Manichean'. This is Manicheism by implication, not by conscious commitment, a Manicheism into which a man may slide unawares, and above all a discreditable decline. Neither 'Manichee' nor 'Pelagian' could have been used as an epithet so loosely twenty years earlier.

In the case of 'Pelagian' some distance had first to be travelled before the term had currency at all, before it could be broadened and debased. Writing in 415, Jerome had encouraged a tendency to identify 'Pelagianism' with other views in which he saw a departure from orthodoxy which especially troubled him: he held that the Pelagians were Origenists, or followers of Jovinian, but Augustine did not yet see clearly that any such thing as 'Pelagianism' existed three years earlier when he found himself 'compelled' to write against the teaching of Pelagius. In 427, when he looked back upon the episode in compiling his *Retractationes*, he was able to put a name to the movement and call it a heresy (*Retr.* II.lviii), but, as Robert F. Evans has pointed out, in the treatise *On the Merits and Forgiveness of Sins* to which Augustine refers, there is remarkably little direct reference even to Pelagius himself, let alone to a school of thought which may be called by his name. The treatise was written for the tribune Flavius Marcellinus who had run into difficulties in conversations with Catholics troubled by some matters which had been raised at the synod of Carthage of the previous year. There, Celestius, who brought the Pelagian problem to Africa as a live issue, had been questioned on his opinions. African Christians were disquieted by the implications of his views for the belief that it is necessary to baptise infants. Augustine mentions neither Pelagius nor Celestius in the first two books. Pelagius' name appears in Book III because Augustine had been reading Pelagius' Commentary on the Pauline Epistles, and had discovered there some points he now wanted to discuss. Robert F. Evans has shown convincingly that Augustine did not come to group the elements of the 'Pelagian' heresy together, or begin to think 'Pelagian' an appropriate name for the heresy, for some time.[2]

The same difficulty did not arise in the case of the term 'Manichee'. The sect was established; indeed Augustine had aspired to call himself a Manichee for several years as a young man. The innovation of the first quarter of the new century was to loosen and broaden the sense of the term until it was possible to speak as Julian does of Augustine the 'Manichee', despite the considerable body of his anti-Manichean writings, and his known hostility to all things Manichean.

How, then, did 'Pelagian' come to be opposed to 'Manichee' in the slanging-match Julian of Eclanum provoked by his attacks on Augustine? Was the sense of both terms so vague by then that we can dismiss these as 'conventional bogeys' and nothing more? It seems not. Augustine, at least, tried to redefine the terms, to give them a precision they had begun to lose, and Julian, too, rested his case partly upon accuracy of definition. Augustine found there was a case to answer, although he was confident that Julian was misrepresenting the Catholic position.

An important contributing factor to this process of enlargement of the sense of the terms 'Pelagian' and 'Manichee' was the growing contemporary awareness that there was a common ground of subject-matter on which both schools of thought touched. Augustine sent his anti-Manichean works to Paulinus of Nola,[3] no doubt so that he could make them available to any members of the local Manichean community in Rome who might be persuaded to study them. There is every probability that Pelagius read them in Paulinus' library.[4] Julian of Eclanum, too, certainly knew Paulinus. Paulinus wrote him a wedding-song.[5] Julian was well-born; Pelagius something of a *parvenu*. Nevertheless, Pelagius was well thought of by the best families in Rome.[6] Indeed, the Pelagians in Rome seem to have been something of an elitist group, and close-knit. If Julian of Eclanum was not 'protected' as Pelagius had been by an unconscious alliance of influential Roman families,[7] the social standing of the movement created a freemasonry which supported him, too, indirectly. Pelagius was not, then, an isolated figure, a Martin Luther who could do no other, standing against society. The world, at its most worldly and powerful, was not against him. He and his followers saw themselves as *integri Christiani*.[8]

Julian took up a cause which had been entirely respectable until Augustine began to write against Pelagius and the African bishops questioned the orthodoxy of Celestius, and he wrote, as Pelagius had done, with every means of access to Augustine's early writings, with a knowledge of the Manichean position, and, no doubt, recollecting many conversations in which these issues had been discussed. Pelagianism was, to a greater extent than Augustine perhaps realised, the product of a community's way of life, the united effort of a group of like-minded and articulate people, and it grew up at a time and in a place where Manicheism provided stimulating contrasts, for members of the Manichean sect in and near Rome were sufficiently numerous for Augustine to see the need to provide Paulinus with missionary textbooks. Ironically, Augustine's own writings, lodged with Paulinus, may have provided a further impetus for discussion, and so helped along the process of clarification of similarities and differences which encouraged Julian to feel that he stood on solid ground when he called Augustine a Manichee.

Pelagius himself can have been only partly responsible for these developments. His mind was not naturally of a speculative cast. There is some evidence that he drew on the texts available to him in Latin in writing his Pauline commentaries: 'Ambrosiaster' (c. 375), Augustine himself, on Romans, Rufinus' rendering of Origen (c. 405).[9] He takes from 'Ambrosiaster', for example, a number of thoughts on law and grace in which, perhaps, lay the seeds of future developments of his thinking.[10] Even his use of the questionable Origen does not seem to have caused him disquiet. He simply wanted to provide a practical Bible-study aid for his circle. His comments are brief and common-sensical.

Even when he was actively engaged in polemic, he does not appear to have given the Manichean threat as prominent a place as Julian does. The anti-Manichean current is there, but heretics of another kind concern him most. In some fragments which survive of his writings against the Apollinarians he takes issue with heretics who have been raising Christological questions. There can be no doubt that Pelagius saw himself as a defender of the faith, exactly as Augustine did. Indeed, he adopts much the same attitude as Augustine to unorthodoxy, and accuses the heretics of practices which Augustine points to in the teaching of the Manichees. The Apollinarians, says Pelagius, bring together Scriptural testimonies to defend their error. Their arguments are shrouded in the darkness of obscurity.[11] It may even be that Pelagius modelled his style as a polemicist upon Augustine's early works.

It was not until Julian took up the cause that further implications became clear. Both Pelagians and Catholic Christians distinguished themselves from heretics, and especially from the Manichean heretics, but they understood very well the nature of the common ground of interest between them. It is to be supposed that the Manichees were equally familiar with these matters, but they are not our immediate concern here; their presence is of interest for our purposes because they acted as a catalyst, sharpening and intensifying the contest between Julian and Augustine when it began, and giving Julian a convenient epithet of opprobrium to apply to Augustine.

The realities of the Pelagian position, in outline and in details, quickly became submerged in the controversy. Augustine defined Pelagius' terms for him. (One of the difficulties in determining what Pelagius thought Pelagianism meant is that the Augustinian material far outweighs the Pelagian in quantity.) It is not Julian's business to speak for Pelagius, so much as to destroy the credibility of Augustine's position by showing him to be a Manichee unawares. We are dealing, in the controversy between Julian and Augustine, not with 'Manichee' and 'Pelagian' worn proudly as badges, but with 'Manichee' and 'Pelagian' used as terms of abuse. It is to these secondary usages that we must now turn, but enough has been said, perhaps, to indicate that Pelagius thought of himself not only as orthodox, but as a protagonist for orthodoxy;[12] at the same time, as Bohlin has suggested, there was, perhaps, a current of anti-Manichean thinking in Pelagius all along.[13] There was some foundation for Julian's claim that if Augustine was opposed to Pelagius, he must be identifying himself with an old enemy of Pelagius' circle: the Manichee.[14] The roots of the problem lay in Rome, and Augustine in

Africa certainly did not perceive as he took up his pen against 'the Pelagian heresy' that in the minds of some of his Roman readers he was in danger of falling back into Manicheism. It was Julian of Eclanum who brought the fact forcefully to his notice.

Julian of Eclanum's polemic has the style of a man who sees the issues involved largely, as well as in detail. He saw the implications as neither Augustine nor a puzzled and defensive Pelagius had done at the beginning of the affair. Not only did Julian accuse Augustine of being a Manichee, a challenge which was bound to bring him up short, especially if he saw a grain of truth in the accusation, but Julian also accused Augustine of muddled thinking, in very much the terms Augustine had used against the Manichees. His view had always been that they could not think clearly because their minds were cluttered with 'bodily images'; that is, because they thought in material terms, they were incapable of conceiving of spiritual truths as requiring a different mode of thought. In Julian's eyes, Augustine's defence of original sin showed exactly this blindness. 'It is improbable; it is untrue; it is unjust', says Julian, of the very notion that God would allow a flaw to remain in the nature of man as a result of Adam's sin (*Contra Julianum* II.x.37). So a second accusation, of technical and intellectual inadequacy, is added to the first. Augustine's methods as a polemicist are turned back upon him in a manner beyond the powers of the less sophisticated Pelagius. Julian was a natural dialectician, with a bent for speculative thought that Pelagius did not possess.

To take the first of these challenges first: What, then, did 'Manichean' mean for Julian? What are the 'Manichean' aspects of Augustine's thought to which he points? The principal problem, perhaps, lay in the notion of fatalism. Robert F. Evans picks out 'the combating of Manichean fatalism' as 'one of the chief theological interests of contemporary Christians'.[15] Augustine's writings against Pelagius had certainly brought him some way towards a 'fatalism' which lent itself to identification with the Manichean view. Again, in defending the value of virginity, Augustine might be said to have moved towards a Manichean position on marriage; here, the position was less clear-cut, for in his treatises on marriage Augustine clearly takes a stand against the Manicheans in maintaining that marriage is a good. (This is the ground of the Jovinian arguments, against which Jerome took such vigorous exception in writing his two books

Adversus Jovinianum. Jovinian had argued that the Catholics were Manichees in their preference for celibacy.)

Augustine's attention was drawn to the problem by Count Valerius. He had heard that the Pelagians were saying that Augustine and the Christians of his persuasion condemned marriage. Augustine wrote him the *De Nuptiis et Concupiscentia.* 'In that work', he says, 'I distinguished, as far as I could, the good of marriage from the evil of fleshly desire' (*Op. Imp.* Preface). This was the key to Augustine's solution of the difficulty. Marriage itself is a good. He wrote at length on its benefits in the *De Bono Conjugali,* describing the perfect friendship of two souls looking to the same heavenly end. But he regarded the desire for sexual union in another light. It lay beyond the control of reason, and that, to Augustine, and to the mind of any contemporary Platonist, showed it to be, not a good, but intrinsically an evil thing, sanctified only within marriage, and for the procreation of children (where there was a reason for it) (*De Nupt.* I.iii.2). That is not to say that a natural appetite is an evil thing necessarily. The desire to have children and care for them and educate them is surely, says Augustine, an appetite not of the lust (*libido*), but of the reason (*De Nupt.* II.vii.17). It is the mode of begetting which has been infiltrated by evil, as a result of the sin of Adam. If Adam had not sinned, he would have begotten his children not by lust but by rational decision (*De Nupt.* II.vii.18).

The *De Nuptiis* did not entirely satisfy Valerius. He sent him a list of 'some passages taken from the work of Julian the Pelagian heretic'. Augustine wrote him another book, the *Contra Julianum.* Against this Julian wrote again, 'another eight books with much loquacity' (*Op. Imp.* Preface). The *Opus Imperfectum contra Julianum* is Augustine's reply, taking Julian book by book, up to the sixth. The first book deals with three of Julian's contentions on free will: if God is just he cannot impute sin to infants; since sin is nothing but ill-will, infants cannot sin, for the use of the will cannot be found in them; freedom of will, by which God emancipates man, must consist in the possibility of allowing onself to sin, or of abstaining from sin. The second book is directed against Julian's contention that the text 'through one man sin entered the world' (Romans 5.12) is to be understood, not in terms of a direct entailment, but as involving deliberate imitation on the part of the children of Adam. The last four books are all concerned with the arguments Julian had put forward on concupiscence.

It is easy to see, then, how closely the problem of marriage was linked in contemporary thinking with the question of the nature of evil, and here we are on Augustinian ground indeed. The connection is made early in the *Contra Julianum*; Jovinian had brought a charge of Manicheism against the Catholics on the grounds that their doctrine that Mary remained a virgin after giving birth to Christ implied that Christ was a phantasm, and not a real man with a material body. In marriage and procreation bodies are inescapably involved, and to take the view that marriage is an evil, or that it was impossible that Christ should have had a real physical body, was entirely in keeping with the Manichean view that matter is evil. The doctrine of original sin seemed to Julian to involve the acceptance of the idea that human nature is intrinsically sinful, and the concomitant view that sinfulness lies in the material nature of man, that the body is evil because it is a material thing (*C. Jul.* I.ii.4; I.vi.12).

All this smacks of Manichean thinking sufficiently strongly to encourage Julian to feel that he has solid grounds for his accusation. Equally, however, these arguments are so vague that Augustine is confident they can be used to show that it is Julian, not Augustine, who is the crypto-Manichee, the Manichee by implication. 'You say that any connection with the Manichees would overcome you', he says to Julian, ' but you have so strengthened them that you and they stand or fall together' (*C. Jul.* VI.xxvi.83).

Thus the two fall into an exchange of definition and counter-definition. Julian defines a Pelagian like this:

If anyone says that there is free will in men, or that God is the Creator of those who have merely been born [that is, not 'reborn'] he is called a Pelagian or Celestian.

Augustine defines a Pelagian differently:

A Pelagian or Celestian is he who does not attribute to the grace of God the freedom to which we have been called, and who denies that Christ is the deliverer of infants (*C. Jul. Prologue*).

It was clear to Augustine that what was required was an orderly redefinition of the issues; if this very serious charge against the Catholics was to be shown to be without substance he must make it plain to his readers that these were vague accusations, not exact and specific, and that any resemblance between Manichean and Catholic teachings on these points was illusory. Accordingly, he adopts an orderly approach in his preface. He proposes first to show how many 'great doctors of the Catholic Church' – men from whom Julian would not wish to dissociate himself – have taken up the positions Augustine himself has adopted. He will make it clear to Julian that if Augustine is a Manichee, so are many of the Fathers. Secondly, he proposes to show that the vagueness of Julian's accusations is such that Julian himself can be shown so to 'support the damnably and abominably impious error of the Manicheans that they cannot find such a defender even among their own adherents'. Thirdly, he intends to refute Julian's arguments point by point by adducing the authority of the Fathers. Fourthly, he will show by argument that it is the Pelagians, not the Catholics, who have slipped unawares into Manicheism. He intends, in other words, to bring these increasingly large and capacious terms within bounds, to show methodically what are the points of irreconcilable difference between Catholic and Manichee, Catholic and Pelagian, and to counter Julian's tendency to heap all together under a loose heading.

The Manichees 'teach that there are two natures, one of good and the other of evil, coming from two different, mutually hostile and co-eternal principles' (C. Jul. I.viii.36). In opposition to this, the Catholic faith teaches that the nature of God is the only nature without a beginning. Augustine's approach is along the lines of that of the books *Against Two Letters of the Pelagians*. These are the five arguments, says Augustine, by which Julian imputes Manicheism to him: he argues that by asserting the existence of original sin, Augustine is saying that the Devil is the creator of all men born, for he implies that all men are born of the wound the Devil inflicted on human nature when it was first created. Augustine is said to condemn marriage, for it generates something damnable in producing children born in a state of sin. Augustine denies that in baptism all sins are forgiven, for he holds that there remains in baptised parents the evil by which their children are born in original sin. Augustine convicts God of injustice, for how can it be just to condemn new-born infants. Augustine makes men despair of perfection, for they can never eradicate their inborn fault.

Something further is now required. Julian, like Berengar of Tours when he challenged Lanfranc, or Roscelin of Compiègne when he challenged Anselm in the eleventh century, had tried to make out a case for the ineptitude of his enemy in rational argument. Accordingly, Augustine attacks Julian for his failings as a dialectician, just as he had done with the Manichees. Augustine was a dialectician, too, at least sufficiently skilled to point out technical faults in his enemies' arguments, as we saw when he attacked Faustus and the Manichees for their logical ineptitude.

To be attacked in the same terms by Julian was evidently galling to Augustine's pride. He rounds on his attacker, matching insult to insult. Julian insults his reader as well as Augustine when he 'tries to teach how dialecticians construct syllogisms, a question no-one has asked'. Moreover, his renderings of Augustine's arguments bear no resemblance to the arguments Augustine has actually put forward: 'You pretend that I say what I do not say, that I conclude what I do not conclude, concede what I do not concede, and you draw conclusions which I reject' (*C. Jul.* III.vii.14).

Julian's dialectical weapons are like leaden darts, says Augustine. He is confident of his skill, and yet he makes no sense at all. 'You see how logically you have said nothing'; 'You do not see that what you have called a necessary argument does not follow' (*C. Jul.* III.vii.16). 'Since you cannot refute' my view, says Augustine, 'you try to create confusion for the unskilled by means of dialectic, claiming that you do not know in what system of logic I could have found the "convertibility of all contraries"' (*C. Jul.* VI.xix.60). The mark of Julian's dialectic is its 'incautious use' of such procedures as division and definition (*C. Jul.* VI.xviii.54). The level of Julian's technical skill seems to have been much the same as Augustine's. They knew the same range of elementary technical terms and they were probably well enough matched. Augustine has to resort to mockery often enough to show that he could not always prove Julian an incompetent dialectician by argument alone.

It may be that Julian had put his finger on a tendency of which Augustine had not been aware, and that Augustine had really been moving back towards a position on certain issues close to that which he had occupied as a Manichee. It may be that arguments put forward by Augustine in his anti-Pelagian writings had not shown the same attention to dialectical technicalities as the works of an earlier period, when Augustine had been closer to his own days as a philosopher, and when he had been addressing himself to a readership which prided itself on its command of reason. The anti-Pelagian writings had a more general readership in view. Yet in the *Contra Julianum* Augustine seems if anything more sure of his ground, more trenchant, less open to self-doubt and given to exploratory digressions than ever before. The interest of the terms in which the exchange took place perhaps lies elsewhere, in what it reveals of the interconnectedness of the whole complex of 'Manichean' and 'Pelagian' issues in the minds of many contemporaries. Because there was recognised to be so much common ground of subject-matter here, the developments of the first quarter of the century in enlarging the reference of 'Pelagian' and 'Manichee' are of more importance than we give them if we gloss over the epithets as 'conventional bogeys'.

The controversy with Julian did something more. It brought Augustine full circle. He looked afresh at the problem of evil as he had first conceived of it in the light of the Manichean teachings, and he was able to set these early reflections in the larger context of sin and redemption with which he had been concerned of late.

We have seen how, when he came to reconsider his writings in the *Retractationes* in the light of this controversy, Augustine devoted a good deal of space to the *De Libero Arbitrio*. He is more conscious of developments in his thinking since he wrote it than perhaps of any other work of his middle age, because he wrote *On Freedom of Choice* before he had realised the implications of Pelagius' teaching. Pelagius made him rethink his assumptions as perhaps no-one else could have done. He presented him with a new perspective on the problem of evil. When he wrote the *De Libero Arbitrio* Augustine was still concentrating on distancing himself from the Manichees. (He notes that, by denying that evil begins in the human will, they say that there is an independent source of evil.) (*Retr.* I.ix.2.) In the *Retractationes* he surveys the many knots he could not then untie, or had not space for (*quas vel enodare non poteram*) because they needed longer treatment. His perspectives have now changed, and he quotes various passages of the *De Libero Arbitrio* which he suspects may give the Pelagians grounds for calling him a Pelagian – mainly because he did not allow for grace, for that was not then under discussion (*de qua tunc non agebatur*).

Looking back, he can see that the beginning of his work against the Pelagians marked a turning-point in his thinking about the problem of evil: 'It is one thing to ask where evil comes from; it is another to ask how we may return to the former good, or come to a greater good' (*Retr.* I.viii). In the last years of his life it became increasingly clear to Augustine that the way to the Highest Good he had sought from his boyhood was not to be trodden by human effort, but only by the soul which allowed itself to be led by grace.

The problem of evil lay before him at last in its entirety, but it no longer made him anxious. Paradoxically, the problem of evil had shrunk from him as his perception of its ramifications grew, because he had come to recognise more fully the size and power of the Good, its ready and vigorous activity against evil. He had found in his idea of an overwhelming divine grace a principle which so diminished evil that it had come to seem to him, not insignificant, but ineffably ridiculous. Where first he had been aware of its perverseness and emptiness, its huge darkness, its hopelessly entangled knottiness, now at last perhaps he had come to feel its essential triviality in comparison with the light and power of the Good. In identifying evil as nothing, Augustine had taken a supremely optimistic view of the problem of evil.

VI · BECOMING AND BEING GOOD

1 The Happy Man

When Cicero wrote *De Finibus Bonorum et Malorum* on the purpose of human life, he chose a subject which was still fashionable among pagan philosophers in Augustine's day. Augustine comments on the large number of thinkers who have tried to determine man's proper end (*De Civ. Dei* XIX.1). Neither he nor the philosophers he had once followed had any quarrel with the idea that the pursuit of goodness is also the pursuit of truth and wisdom and happiness. It is agreed by common consent that the good man is a happy man. In the discussion at Cassiciacum out of which Augustine wrote the dialogue *On the Happy Life* (*De Beata Vita*) in 386, he and his friends looked at this assumption in the light of their beliefs as Christians. They found no need to question it.

When they came to examine some of the commonly-held ideas about the way in which it is possible for a man to be happy, however, they found them unsatisfactory. It seems obvious enough that the happy man must be free of the threat of his happiness being taken from him. He cannot be perfectly happy if he is anxious. The man who is happy because he is prosperous is therefore at risk of being made unhappy, because the pendulum of fortune may swing against him, and he may lose all his worldly goods. Even if it were possible for that threat to be removed, so that the prosperous man was *securus*, he could not be perfectly happy, because worldly goods cannot be fully satisfying (*talibus satiari non poterit*). Such a man would be wretched because there would still be something lacking to him (*De Beata Vita* II.11). If he is in fact content and feels no lack he may be happy, but then his happiness would really lie, not in the goods he enjoys (for we have agreed that they cannot satisfy him), but in his own moderation (*animi sui moderatione beatus est*). The true happiness he enjoys lies within him; it is independent of changes in outward circumstances, for as Seneca explains (*On Tranquillity*) it is

150

important to have confidence in one's happiness, and not to fear that anything that happens may disturb it.

In fact our happy man-of-the-world has kept the Stoic rule that no-one is happy who does not have what he wishes (*De Beata Vita* II.14) (*qui quod vult non habet*). He has conformed his desires to what he has. This is the advice Terence gives 'Since what you wish cannot be done, wish what you can do' (*Andria* 305, cf. *De Beata Vita* IV.25; *De Trin.* XIII.vii.10). This seems a practical enough recipe for happiness. It gives the happy man security and takes away his sense of loss or lack. It is entirely in keeping with the teaching of Epictetus, who encourages his readers in his *Manual* to distinguish between those things that are in their power (desire, aversion, opinion, movement towards a thing, their own acts), and those things that are outside their control (body, property, reputation, the holding of offices). If they concentrate upon training their wills to conform with the way things are, avoiding the temptation to wish that anything should happen, and wishing the things that happen to be exactly as they are, they will have a tranquil life; they will be happy. Only if the will consents to its being so can anything that can happen in the world be harmful. Lameness affects the body and impedes walking, but it does not affect the will. 'You can be invincible', Epictetus promises, 'if you do not enter into any contest in which it is not in your power to be victorious.'

This is not the Christian recipe for happiness, however. It involves a compromise with a world that is full of evil. The Stoic makes himself invulnerable to mental and spiritual pain, but he does not desire with passion to raise himself towards the highest good, or discover where truth lies. He has no need of God. As Seneca puts it (*Quaestiones Naturales* II.35), prayer becomes a mere device for soothing the sick mind. Urgent prayers, prayers expressing longing for something beyond his present experience, have no place. The Stoic takes the view that the fates govern human existence, and they cannot be moved by prayer. In any case, he does not allow himself to think that things might be better in case he should be discomforted by the desire that they should be so. The Stoic is a happy man in a cage, a man who dare not look up, in case he sees a possibility of happiness beyond his present imagining. Augustine and the Christians look for a higher happiness.

2 Man as He Ought to Be

One of the questions of Celestius with which Augustine deals in the *De Perfectione Justitiae Hominis* is whether or not man ought to be without sin. Clearly he ought; but if he ought, he can, argues Celestius. If he cannot, it would scarcely be just of God to require it of him, and if God did not require man to be without sin, that would mean that man ought to be with sin; that would be nonsense, for it is, by definition, not a sin to be as one ought.

The notion of 'ought' which is in Augustine's mind here has a sense of obligation-to-become, which is central to his thinking about human perfection in this life and in the life to come. When we say that man ought to be without sin we imply that men are not yet all in a sinless state. 'Ought', as Augustine is employing it here, measures that which 'ought' against an ideal to which it 'ought' to conform. 'Ought' has this particular meaning only when there is evil in the world, making things fail to conform to God's intention for them.

In an image oddly reminiscent of Epictetus' example of the lame man, Augustine points out that if we say that a limping foot ought not to limp, we imply that we have a clear picture of the way the foot ought to behave. We speak of 'curing' the foot. We use medicine, and ask the help of a doctor to prescribe it (*De Per. Just. Hom.* III.v). Similarly, in the case of the sick soul, we look for the medicine of grace and the help of the divine Physician. Healing, of body or soul, is a process, at the end of which body or soul will be as it ought to be. The word 'ought' will then become redundant. Body or soul will be as it is. 'Ought' is a directive, leading us to a perfection in which lies unassailable happiness. That 'oughtness' leads, as Epictetus also saw, to piety. He who takes care to desire as he ought and to avoid as he ought is systematically making himself holy.

To what, then, 'ought' a man to aspire? What will make him happy and good? As a young man, Augustine had made the mistake of looking for his satisfactions in the terms the philosophers suggested to him; in places where he might in fact have found them, he discovered only mediocre and ultimately unsatisfactory substitutes, which he later regarded as mockeries of reality. In his youth he sought for glory in the schools; the glory he wanted then was that of popular acclaim (*Conf.* x.xxxviii.62). This he came to see as a 'vain' glory (*vana gloria*) (*Conf.* IV.i.1), because it consisted in being held in esteem by others (*De Civ. Dei* v.12). The same error leads men to value military glory – the glory of Rome triumphant in battle.

Glory might have been a source of true happiness says Augustine, if he had then understood as he later came to do, the nature of the real glory of the martyr who witnesses to the truth and dies for his faith, of the Christian who fights the lusts of his body and his evil desires, and above all, of Christ himself, who won a victory over death and sin incomparably greater than the victory of the general over his enemy.

Glory is to be measured by God's approbation, not by the approval of men, and it is not to be had in its fullness in this life. These two principles became fundamental to Augustine's view of happiness. He learned to measure it against a divine, not a human measure, and not to expect to enjoy it fully this side of heaven. When he was 'converted' to philosophy he was filled with intellectual excitement (*De Beata Vita* 1.4). He wanted wisdom all at once; he wanted the praise of men, congratulations upon his cleverness. He learned slowly that the wisdom he sought was not immediately within his grasp; the happiness it would give him was of another order altogether from the febrile intellectual excitement of his youth; the approbation which would really satisfy him was God's. Just as a man cannot be happy for eternity unless he pleases God (and that is *gloria*), so he cannot be happy for eternity in ignorance of God (and that is *sapientia*).

Once he has understood what is needed to make him happy, he can seek wisdom rightly. The unhappy mind, as we have seen, is the mind which lacks something. A lack in the mind is nothing but *stultitia*, a 'foolishness' as contrary to wisdom as death is to life (*De Beata Vita* IV.28). The whole argument of the *De Beata Vita* can be summed up in a series of equipollent propositions; to be happy is to have no 'lack' in the mind. To be happy is to be free of 'foolishness'. To be happy is to be wise. To be happy is to seek wisdom. To be happy is to seek truth. To be happy is to seek Christ. (For wisdom is truth and Truth is Christ.)

This is where the Stoics have made a mistake. They have not set the standard of happiness high enough. They have not looked up and tried to conform their wills, not to things as they are, but to things as they ought to be.

If man was what he ought to be there would be no need for change in him. There is no movement or change in the Highest Good, and although created things differ from God in their goodness in being capable of change, it is a property of good to be static, and it is a property of evil to be in a perpetual state of change. Only when evil works upon created things do they change, and such change must be for the worse, because evil is stealing its very existence from the good; only by making good things like itself can it exist at all. It has a borrowed existence, by inhering in something which exists; its effect upon its host is to diminish its existence, and to push it further and further in the direction of non-existence. It is impossible for absolute evil to exist at all, for if it has entirely deprived its host of goodness it will have no existence left; host and parasite will disappear together.

Evil, then, is continually driving things in the opposite direction from the good and making them what they ought not to be (*Enchiridion* xii). That is why men are not good, as God intended. They are not as they ought to be. They are not wholly bad, but they are not good, either. (Seneca, in his treatise *On Tranquillity*, speaks of the muddle of human existence, the indecision which keeps men in suspense between two opinions, turning resolutely neither to the good nor to the bad.) What, then, is required to make men perfect? Clearly, they must reverse the process, drive out evil, and become wholly good, until they are as they ought to be.

THE PILGRIM'S PROGRESS

Augustine was sure that this could not be achieved all at once, for the slow, creeping effect of evil had to be progressively reversed, but was it possible at all? The reflections of the *De Peccatorum Meritis* had raised four questions in Augustine's mind. Can a man be without sin in this life? Is there in fact any example of a man who has achieved perfection in this life? If not, why not? Is it possible for there to be a man who does not sin at all in the course of this life, as distinct from a reformed sinner?

The first can be answered readily enough. If it were impossible for a man to be without sin, that would mean God's grace and truth and the free will he gave man were inadequate, and to believe that would be an insult to the Creator. But the theoretical possibility is one thing and the practical reality another. The Bible indicates that there is in fact no such thing as a perfect man. 'In thy sight shall no man living be justified' (*De Pec. Mer*. II.vii.8). Perfection will come after death, when the body is resurrected to join the perfected soul; in the meantime we have, after baptism, the first fruits of the Spirit (*De Pec. Mer.* II.viii.10). Perfection may be achieved in some specific respect, Augustine thinks – a man may be perfect as a scholar but not as a teacher of wisdom, perhaps, but full perfection is, in practice, not attained in this life (*De Pec. Mer.* II.xv.22).

Augustine believed that we must look for a reason in terms of the ignorance which continues to cloud our minds while we are still striving for perfection and the full illumination which it will bring with it, and in terms of the tendency to misuse the will which remains in us even when the penalty for original sin has been wiped out. We are hampered, in other words, by the remnants of those handicaps which made it impossible for us to make any real progress at all before baptism: darkness and concupiscence (*De Pec. Mer.* II.xvii.26–8).

The divine aid which grace gives certainly could make all men perfect, but we must remember that no-one deserves God's grace. God would be behaving with perfect justice if he helped no-one at all, since men turn away from him by their own choice. All gifts of grace are therefore acts of divine mercy (*De Pec. Mer.* II.xviii.31). There is no reason why God should bring anyone all the way to perfection in this life unless he chose, and it seems that he has not chosen to do so.

As for the fourth question, it is clear that no-one but Christ could live a life entirely without sin from the beginning, because only he was born without original sin. Every other man was once a sinner.

When Marcellinus received the three volumes of the *De Peccatorum Meritis*, he raised a query. He did not like Augustine's assertion that it was possible for perfection to be achieved, even though no-one had yet achieved it. He could see that it was an important point, but he did not see how it could be proved unless an example could be found. Augustine wrote him another treatise, which he came to regard as his best anti-Pelagian piece, the *De Spiritu et Littera*, to clarify the point (*Retr.* II.xliii). In so doing he began to open up new ground for himself, as he asked what constitutes the element of 'deserving' in perfection, what makes a man approved or accepted by God, 'justified' in God's sight.

If a man became perfect on earth, it would be only partly a human achievement, he is sure. There would have to be divine help. Pelagius is saying something very different, and highly dangerous, when he claims that perfection would be a human achievement alone, and that divine grace would not be needed (although it might assist); he is putting his trust in the efficacy of the law as a means of salvation. God, he holds, provided a straightforward set of rules, which would make a man righteous if he kept them (*De Sp. et Lit*. x.14). Augustine's objection to this is that Scripture states that law was not made for the righteous man (I Tim. 1.8) but to act as a warning for the unrighteous (*De Sp. et Lit*. x.16). Law creates offences by defining certain actions as breaches of the law. It thus makes sin 'abound' (*De Sp. et Lit*. vi.9). It is destructive; for it is the 'letter which kills' (*De Sp. et Lit*. xiv.23). Grace, on the other hand, is the gift of the Spirit; it makes goodness abound, and therefore it has the opposite effect to the law which makes sin abound. In putting their trust in obedience to the law, the Pelagians fall into the danger of self-glorification (*De Sp. et Lit*. xiii.21). We can see here the beginnings of that opposition of justification by faith and justification by works, which was to be read into the Pelagian controversy by generations of later thinkers.

Augustine prefers to see righteousness as a gift of God, not a reward for hard work and obedience to the law (*De Sp. et Lit*. xxix.50). He wants to make faith a gift of God, too, with the proviso that God supplies the power to believe, while the believer receives it by a free act of his own will (*De Sp. et Lit*. xxix.56). Faith is praiseworthy because it is held in love, but not where it goes under the law alone and is motivated by fear (*De Sp. et Lit*. xxxii.56). He makes the energetic striving for perfection of the Pelagians look very unattractive, as indeed he himself found it. It flouted one of the principles of his own faith – the need to begin by turning to God and asking for help, guidance, illumination. It denied the co-operative dependence on God which Augustine had discovered to be so delightfully necessary to his own spiritual progress. It had all the blindness and arrogance, to his mind, that the Manichees had shown in their own views of the road a man must follow to perfection.

'There is perfection and perfection', says Augustine (*Est ergo perfectio et perfectio*) (*Sermones Post Maurinos Reperti: Denis* xviii.3). He points out that Paul appears to contradict himself in the third chapter of Philippians, where he first says that he is not yet perfect (verse 12), and then speaks of himself and other believers as *perfecti* (verse 15). The first reference is, he explains, to the perfection which awaits the elect after death, when they will be perfectly good. Paul lays no claim to such perfection yet, but in some sense he regards himself as already perfect. This, says Augustine, is a reference to the *perfectus viator*, the man who 'travels well, walks well, keeps to the road' but is nevertheless a traveller, and has not yet arrived (*qui nondum perfectus est perventor*). His goodness cannot be said to be immovable yet, but in the future it will be possible to say of him: 'Now he has run the course and finished it, and he has stood firm.' Then he will be in a 'state' of perfection, while now he is in a 'process' of perfection, in which he is trying to arrive at the final state. The *perfectio viatoris* is 'to know that he has not yet arrived where he is going, to know how far he has come and how far he still has to go', 'Let us, then, know that we are not perfect, all we who are perfect, so that we may not remain imperfect', says Augustine, revelling in the paradox.

The perfect in this life, then, are those who are busy driving out evil. In the treatise on the perfect righteousness of men he describes how such men 'run perfectly' (*perfecte currunt*) (*De Per. Just. Hom.* VIII.xix). Their perfection consists not in their 'being' good, but in their 'becoming' good. The perfection lies in the 'running', not in the achieved state of perfection. To 'be' perfectly righteous, a man would have to be wholly without evil (*Enchiridion* xiii) and that is not possible to fallen man, this side of heaven. The good man is not yet perfect but he lives perfectly (*irreprehensibiliter currit*), by making sure that he is free of mortal sins and not neglecting to purify himself from venial sins by almsgiving (*De Per. Just. Hom.* IX.xx). He leads a life, in other words, of systematic rejection of evil, progressively becoming, with God's help, more and more what he ought to be. He is on a journey (*iter nostrum*) which is leading to perfection. His perfection consists in his 'running', not in his 'being'.

It was important for Augustine that he should be able to find a notion of perfection which did not concede ground either to the Manichees, or to the Pelagians. The Manichees revered the *perfecti* among their number in a way which had come to be repugnant to Augustine. The Pelagians held that a man might become perfect in this life by hard effort alone. The idea that human perfection consists in the 'running' of a 'course' rather than in any final attainment of a perfect state had the advantage of avoiding either of these positions. In addition, it made it possible to explain those Scriptural texts which exhort us to be perfect, and which the Pelagians were fond of adducing as evidence for their view that if God instructs us to be perfect it must be possible for us to be perfect, for he would not command us to do something which is beyond us. If we take such passages to mean that we must 'run' perfectly they present no difficulty (*De Per. Just. Hom.* IX.xx).

3 Becoming Good

Perfection in living was an ideal which attracted pagans as well as Christians. In his book *On Abstinence from Animal Food* Porphyry looks at the righteousness which is most beautiful when it takes the form of piety towards the gods, and which inevitably leads to justice towards men, too, for there can be no discord between the two (III.1). Cicero defines *iustitia* in the *De Inventione* (II.liii.159), as an attitude of mind (*animi habitus*) which accords with reason and with nature, and which is well-disposed towards the public good. Augustine discusses Cicero's definition (he says some of his friends have asked him for his comments), and although it is not strictly the definition he himself would give as a Christian, he finds nothing unacceptable in it (*De Div. Quaest.* Q.xxxi). There are, already in the pagan tradition, two aspects of righteousness which are fundamental to the Christian ideal, too. The perfect man must love both God and his neighbour.

Augustine is able to identify seven elements in human perfection, or rather, seven grades or steps towards perfection, which belong to the *perfectio currens* of this life. In his studies of The Sermon on the Mount he identifies each of these steps with its proper Beatitude. Those who 'fear' God are those who love him; the pious or holy are those who are 'meek', for they read Scripture in the right spirit of humble readiness to learn; those who have knowledge are the 'mourners', for they know how evil has affected them; those who have fortitude are those who 'hunger and thirst after righteousness', for they have wearied themselves with labouring to be perfect; those who have counsel are the 'merciful', for they are wise enough to see that in order to be forgiven they must be ready to forgive others; those who have understanding are the 'pure in heart', for they 'see' with the *oculus mentis*, the 'eye of the mind'; those who have wisdom are the peacemakers. We begin to run the perfect course, then, by loving God; through holiness we come to knowledge; by knowledge we come to fortitude; by fortitude we learn counsel; counsel leads us to understanding, and understanding to wisdom. Augustine later regretted that he had implied that all these grades of perfection can be reached in the present life (*Retr.* 1.18), but the scheme seemed to him to stand without need of correction. Perfection of living is progressive, bringing us steadily closer to perfection consummated, established for ever, the unchanging goodness out of which all evil has been purged.

It is, and here Augustine agrees with the *Manichean Psalm-Book*, not enough to love God; to live perfectly, a man must keep the commandments in wisdom and love; he must act perfectly towards others as well as becoming more perfect in his love of God. The *Manichean Psalm-Book* says that perfection consists in 'the commandments and wisdom and love' (*Manichean Psalm-Book* ccxxviii). 'All men of God are made perfect in this'. In the book *On the Christian Life* Augustine emphasises that there are many qualities the good man should possess, in order to be perfect before man and God: he must be just, pure, devoted, spotless, simple, gentle, dignified, prudent, devout, irreproachable, undefiled. He must avoid evil-doers and keep the commandments. In all these things he is perfect before men. He must fix his mind upon divine and heavenly subjects. Then he will be perfect before God. In this way he will love God and his neighbour perfectly (*De Vita Christiana* IX). These are the standards against which we must match ourselves ever more perfectly as we run. It is important that Augustine is speaking here, not of what is required to justify a man, but of the effects on him of gradually becoming more perfect.

The Bible, too, indicates that there is a route to follow as we 'run'. Job says that he has kept the Lord's ways: *vias enim eius custodivi et non declinavi a mandatis eius neque discedam* (Job 23.11, 12). This is partly a matter of keeping the law, if we are to take *mandata* at its face value, but Augustine prefers to put the emphasis upon the idea of a path to be followed, from which we must not turn aside. 'He keeps to the "ways" of God, who does not stray so that he leaves them, but makes progress by running along them.' Augustine found much to dislike in the law; it seemed to him to create stumbling-blocks for man; it certainly did nothing to help him to perfection. The road along which we must run will certainly not involve us in any breach of the law, and the law may show us where the road lies, but the important thing is that we should keep our destination in view, that we should run straight for the goal of perfection, and not turn aside from that line. We make progress by reducing our sins until we come to a point where we are without sin (*De Per. Just. Hom.* XI.xxvii). That can be done only by keeping to the road. The wicked man is the man who turns aside (*declinat, discedit*), for that is the mark of evil.

We shall inevitably begin from a state of sin. The first requirement is that we should 'turn aside from evil and do good', that is, get ourselves on to the right road. Pelagius had developed an explanation of the way this is to be done which Augustine found quite unacceptable. In the *De Gratia Christi et de Peccato Originali*, written about 418, he tried to explain why, and in so doing, he considerably developed his doctrine of a 'perfection of becoming'. Pelagius distinguished between possibility, will and action. Possibility is that by which a man is able to be righteous, will, that by which he wishes to be righteous, and action, that by which he is righteous (*De Grat. Chr.* I.iii.3–4). Possibility, says Pelagius, is a gift of God; it is part of our natures that it is possible for us to be good. (Augustine dismisses this narrow Pelagian conception of grace roundly in *De Grat. Chr.* I.xxv.26.) This *potestas* is not ours but God's; we have it whether we like it or not. The will to be righteous and the righteous act are ours alone, according to Pelagius. Because we have them we are able to turn from the evil and do good: *tam valentia ad declinandum a malo et faciendum bonum*.

Augustine points to Philippians 2.13; 'It is God who works in you both to will and to do' (*De Grat. Chr.* I.v.6). It seems plain enough to him that God does more than merely make it possible for us to be good; Scripture tells us that he assists both the willing and the doing. That is why we must look closely at what Pelagius is saying, or he will deceive the unwary and the simple, and even himself (*De Grat. Chr.* I.vi.7). Pelagius is prepared to concede that God 'helps' men to be good in many ways, by teaching, revelation, opening the eyes of the heart, showing what is to come, manifesting the tricks of the Devil – all the 'heavenly illumination which is a manifold and ineffable gift of grace' (*De Grat. Chr.* I.vii.8), but Pelagius maintains that in showing us these things, God is merely revealing to us what we ought to do. He is not pressing us to do it (*De Grat. Chr.* I.viii.9), and he is certainly not compelling us.

This is where Augustine would draw the line between law and grace. The law shows up what we ought to do, certainly, but it does not help us to do it. Augustine's idea of grace is that it is positively, indeed, forcefully, helpful. Pelagius makes grace merely a source of information, an aid to be used if we choose.

Pelagius and Augustine are agreed in regarding grace as a teacher, then, but they differ in their view of the results of the teaching. Augustine cites John 6.45: 'He who has heard and learned of my Father comes to Me.' If Pelagius is right, the passage should read 'He who has heard and learned of my Father may possibly come to Me' (*potest venire ad me*), for only the possibility of perfection would be a gift of grace, and nothing man could learn from God would directly affect his will or his actions (*De Grat. Chr.* I.xiv.15), but the mode of teaching Augustine recognises in grace (*docendi modus*) brings about an *incrementum* which is secret (*occultus*), because it is inward (*interius*), deeper than any change which can be brought about outwardly (*altius*) (*De Grat. Chr.* I.xiii.14). It is positive and forceful in its operation, drawing men on along the road, working upon their wills and their actions directly.

It does not transform a man all at once, however, the perfection is achieved gradually, *incrementum* by *incrementum*, and not evenly but piecemeal. If this is not so, what are we to make of II Corinthians 12.7–9, where Paul says that a goad of the flesh has been given him, so that he will not be puffed up by the greatness of the revelations which have been made to him? His mind is inflated, but we know that charity is not puffed up (I Cor. 13.4). Paul's *caritas* cannot have been equal to the strain which was being put upon it. He must still have been in process of being built up with *caritas*, and until he was solid in that respect, he needed a discipline of the flesh. He had 'not yet laid hold by arriving, upon that towards which he was running and making progress' (*De Grat. Chr.* I.xi.12). His charity was only partly perfect; he had not yet reached the *ultima et summa perfectio caritatis* (*De Grat. Chr.* I.xii.13).

So grace leads us through (*perducere*: I.xii.13). It is progressive in its effect. Indeed we can hardly be said to 'run' unless we make progress along the road (*De Per. Just. Hom.* xx.xliii). As we progress our spiritual health keeps pace, so that we may be said to keep up with ourselves. The 'running' may even be compared with the running of a sore, which is a sign that a wound is healing, but again Augustine emphasises that we must not expect to make progress so evenly that there are no setbacks, no times when one foot lags behind the other, no moments of depression. God loves a cheerful giver, but the cheerfulness will sometimes be obscured by *taedium* ' by which the gladness in which God loves the giver is dimmed', an obscurity the greater as each man makes less progress, less as he makes greater progress (*De Per. Just. Hom.* VIII.xviii).

Augustine becomes more and more emphatic that we must distinguish the process of becoming perfect from the state of perfection. It is one thing to depart from sin (that is, to be in process of leaving sin behind), another to have departed from sin (that is, to have left it behind once and for all) (*De Per. Just. Hom.* XIII.xxxi). With God, to 'be' and to 'be good' are the same thing. With man, that unity of being and goodness is something in prospect, not something in the present. It is possible to be upright in heart (*rectum corde*) in this life, for that means to be straining forward along the road, forgetting what is behind; it is possible to run a right course (*rectus cursus*) but a clean heart (*mundum cor*) is not possible in this life, for the man who is pure in heart is in a state of perfection. Uprightness of heart *in opere est*; purity of heart *in fine* (*De Per. Just. Hom.* XV.xxxvi). Uprightness is in the actions of this life, purity only to be reached in the end.

4 The Perfect Man

The Augustinian road to perfection, then, is full of pitfalls, and it is a road so long that he questions whether anyone comes to the end of it in this life. We must struggle for the rest of our lives with the will to evil which remains in us after baptism. The fact that wrong will remains is not in itself important. It is nothing to feel guilty about so long as we do not yield to it. In baptised infants it is of no account. When we do yield to it, as we are bound to do because of our fallen condition, we can, with the help of divine grace, purge our sins by repentance, and begin again. We shall arrive at perfection by a process of active co-operation with the grace of God. We are not stones to be moved about passively, but free rational beings who must exert our wills (*De Pec. Mer.* II.vi.6), when once God has made it possible for us to do so by the working of his grace upon us.

What are the implications of Augustine's system for practical Christianity? Augustine is often obliged to practise a subtlety which amounts almost to casuistry in his arguments, in order to flout none of the rules he regards as absolute. His is, paradoxically, both a flexible and a highly rigid system of thought. In the *De Doctrina Christiana*

(III.xii.18–20), for example, he distinguishes between those sayings and actions for which Christ or the saints were responsible, and which seem to many to be reprehensible in themselves, and sayings and actions which are truly blameworthy. It was not wrong for the men of the Old Testament times to have more than one wife, because it was necessary for them to beget numerous offspring, and they did it without lust. It would not be allowable now. Hosea kept company with a harlot (Hosea 1.2) because it was necessary to his prophetic task. Ordinarily, it would be a sin to do so, because it would be a sign of loose living. It ought to be regarded as a shameful thing to take off one's clothes at a banquet which has become a drunken orgy, but there is nothing wrong with nakedness at the baths. We must look, says Augustine, not to the things we do, but to our reason for doing them, interpreting the rules of conduct we find in Scripture in the light of the time, the place and the person to which they are intended to apply. Augustine lays a substantial foundation here for Abelard's view of the *Scito Teipsum* that the moral quality of an act depends on its intention, not on some objective quality in the act itself.

We must never fall into the error of thinking that there is no such thing as absolute right and wrong (*De Doct. Chr.* III.xiv.22), that all rules are appropriate to particular times and places, but the most important indication to be looked for is the presence of lust, cupidity, desire – the exercise of the unbridled will for evil. Anger may be defined as a lust for revenge; there is a lust for money which is called avarice, a lust for forcing one's opinion on others, a lust for applause (boasting), and other lusts, some of which have names of their own and others not (*De Civ. Dei* XIV.15). Lust rules out moderation – and nowhere, in Augustine's experience, so uncontrollably as in the case of sexual desire. Here he sees most graphically illustrated the runaway tendency of the will which has turned from the good. Sexual excitement takes possession of the body, and moves the whole man with a passion in which mental emotion is mingled with bodily appetite (*De Civ. Dei* XIV.15). No bounds restrain the will. It loses all sense of decency and order.

Augustine's pre-occupation with this particular perversion of intention, this diverting of the will from the good, which so clearly manifests itself in the body, reflects a common attitude among the philosophers. Porphyry speaks of the sexual abstinence of Egyptian priests, for instance, in Book IV.7 of his treatise *On Abstinence from*

Animal Food, but the body is frail and swept easily away by lusts only because of the sin of the soul; it is not in itself disposed to evil in its nature, as God made it (*En. Ps.* 142.18; 16.17). It is to the soul we must look for improvement, at whatever cost to the body's health and strength, because it was the soul, or more precisely, the will, where the trouble began. Accordingly, we must live our daily lives in the belief that perfection is to be attained in the soul, not in the body. We must treat the body hard, says St Paul, and Augustine agrees with him. The 'running' we have to do does not require us to nourish the body carefully, and oil it, and take care of the feet. The flesh should be subjugated even at the risk of damaging it. The whole course is run within.

In the *De Quantitate Animae* Augustine defines the 'upright' spirit (*rectus spiritus*) as a spirit which is seeking truth (*De Quant. An.* xxxiii.75); if it does so perfectly, it travels in a straight line; 'it cannot deviate or go astray'. We are on familiar ground here. The upright soul will see clearly with the eyes of an increasingly pure heart (*cor mundum*; *cor simplex*), straight into the truth. This is the 'heart' which is the seat of both feeling and thinking. It can become free of all desire for worldly things (*De Quant. An.* xxxiii.75) and it can make a rational decision to drive out error (*De Gen c. Man.* i.i.1). Then, its feeling and its reason free, it is energetic in pursuit of true delight (*delectatio*). For where the heart is, there is happiness or wretchedness, *beatitudo* or *miseria* (Matthew 6.21; *De Mus.* vi.xi.29). The upright soul is erect in its confidence that although it can be diminished or lowered by evil, it is impossible for evil to bring it to nothing (*De Im. An.* vii.12). As it stretches upwards and onwards to its goal it leaves evil behind.

There must be a bridge from 'becoming' to 'being', something in the process of becoming perfect which already foreshadows the stillness of achieved perfection. That, Augustine thinks, is the consistency of effort, the perseverance, which carries the perfect man through to the end of his life and brings him to his goal. *Perficere* was used in the pagan liturgies for 'making sacrifice' (Virgil *Aeneid* iv.638); a trace of the same usage is to be found in Ecclesiasticus 50.21 in the *Vetus Latina*, but it died out in Christian liturgies. There may, however, have been some such association of ideas in Augustine's mind when he thought about the ultimate realisation of perfection, to the point when a man, at his death, ceased to be in process of becoming perfect, and came to 'be' perfect. The words *perfruitio*; *perfruor*; *perducere*, are used by Augustine to refer to an enjoyment beyond that of this life, a leading of the dead resurrected into the Heavenly Jerusalem. *Per* suggested to him, it seems, something beyond the scope of the terms with which it is compounded. *Perseverantia* takes the perfect man through this life to the point beyond where it is swallowed up in a good which is itself *solidus*, which does not require 'sustaining'.

In the future the perfect man will stand still. He will be whole, full of *sanitas*, healthy and shining. He will be substantial, 'truly good substance', in which nothing will be lacking, for all need and deprivation, all the poverty of evil, will be driven out, and he will be wealthy (*De Per. Just. Hom.* XV.xxxv–xxxvi). Perfection will be consummated (*De Grat. Chr.* I.xiii.3).

VII · THE DIVINE IMPERATIVE

Augustine's idea of God remained, in its essentials, that of his philosophical days: he held firmly to the supreme goodness of God and he believed increasingly surely in his providential care for the world he had made. His conception of God had developed a majesty and a richness it had lacked before God became a person to him, someone with whom he could hold the conversation of which we hear one side in the *Confessions*. He was sure that ultimately nothing but good could come to the faithful soul; no threat or disturbance or trouble in this life could separate the Christian from the love of God (Romans 8.39).

But there was a darker side to his solution of the problem of evil. Not all of mankind were to enjoy eternal blessedness, but only those whom God had chosen. We have seen how Augustine came in the end to an extreme predestinarian view of man's destiny. This was a gradual development. He did not see at first where his thinking was leading him; but it was an inevitable conclusion if he followed his arguments through.

The logical sequence is set out most succinctly perhaps in the *Enchiridion*, the handbook he wrote for Laurentius in 423. Laurentius had asked him several questions, about man's end in life and the purpose of religion, the reasons which support faith (*Enchiridion* iv). Augustine answers him in technically exact terms, with references to the rules of logic. He explains that the supremely good Creator made everything good (x) and that evil in the universe is simply an absence of good (xi). Good creatures are not, however, perfectly good, because they are not like God himself, and so it is possible for them to be corrupted (xii). Augustine discusses the ways in which this may happen, and the roles of ignorance and lust (xxiv). When Satan and Adam sinned by their respective acts of wrong willing, God punished each of them. But man alone, because he had a body, was punished by being made mortal. God had threatened him with exactly this punishment if he sinned and so it was perfectly just that he should carry out his threat (Genesis 2.17; *Enchiridion* xxv).

The passing on of Adam's punishment to his posterity took place through a sexual act now tainted with lust, and a great trial to man on account of a tendency for sexual desire to run away with him and lead him into 'bodily imaginings'. The transformation of the sexual instinct into a form of bondage where the will is helpless to resist the tug of lust, has sometimes been given an importance in Augustine's thought out of proportion to its significance for Augustine himself. It was not an obsessive preoccupation with him, but simply an essential step in his logical progression from the sin of Adam to the predestination of the elect. Thus it was, he says, that, 'by one man sin entered into the world, and death by sin; and so death passed upon all men, because all have sinned' (Romans 5.12).

It followed that the whole mass of the human race was under condemnation, wallowing in misery, tossed about from one evil to another (xxvii). God judged it better to bring good out of evil than to wipe out evil and his flawed creation with it. So he preserved the fallen angels, and he fashions men daily as they are conceived and born and grow up into adults (xxvii). This saving work extends to the bringing back of the human will to its original balance, able freely to choose between good and evil. After the fall it was able to choose only evil (xxx). God saves men by an act of grace, which works by giving them faith (xxx). Faith is what makes them just; it enables them to return to full freedom and to good-willing and to good actions (xxxi–xxxii).

His method of doing so reflects the enormity of what was done when Adam sinned. So great was the offence and so towering God's 'just displeasure' (although we must not think of him as suffering 'feelings' of anger) that a Mediator was needed, someone who should offer a sacrifice in reparation (xxxiii). Augustine dwells at length, lovingly and with awe, upon this matter of the greatness of the work done to wipe out the offence – how the Redeemer could be no other than God himself (cviii) – and then upon sin in its full horror (xxxxiv–lii). He explains exactly where the act of redemption alters the human condition of sin, and where sin remains to be contended with (lxiv–lxxxiii). (The grace of regeneration washes away all past sin and all original guilt (cxix). Men go on sinning, but through divine grace their sins are not counted against them, provided a right will is there. Good works are valueless without the faith grace gives to prompt them, for therein consists their goodness.)

God does not save all men in this way, and in answer to the question why he does not, Augustine's answer is that to save anyone at all is an act of mercy on God's part. In strict justice, all men stand condemned. We should ask, not why God leaves some men to their doom, but why he preserves a few for heaven and blessedness (xcvii; xcviii). 'Who but a fool would think that God was unrighteous, either in inflicting penal justice on those who had earned it, or in extending mercy to the unworthy' (xcviii)? It is clear from this that no-one can reasonably glory in any merits of his own; the only rational response is one of humble gratitude for a free gift, which gives all the glory to God (xcviii).

This selective giving of the grace without which man is condemned is, then, entirely at God's will. God is immutable and omnipotent, and so his will cannot be thwarted. God was demonstrably able to take even an act of will against himself by Satan or by Adam, and turn it to his own purposes and make it work for good (c, cii). Indeed, he foresaw their rebellions and ordered his own purposes accordingly (civ). Augustine finds the internal coherence of his account of the matter growing tighter at every point, each principle supporting the next.

The pillars of the system were thus progressively thickened as the structure grew and they were required to carry more weight, and it is those pillars which give the whole its proportions and tell us where Augustine himself would place the emphasis. The first of these is undoubtedly the importance of the fall of Adam. That has consequences for everything which followed. Second in time and in importance comes the misdirection and misplacement of the sexual urge which was the instrument of the transmission of the flawed and mortal human nature of Adam. Over against these pillars stand the divine attributes, themselves immovable pillars: goodness (so that God cannot be the author of evil); justice (so that he is severe in his response to the great wrong which has been done); mercy (so that he freely forgives it and indeed takes action to put it right at incalculable cost to himself); omniscience (so that he knew before he created the world what would happen in it); omnipotence (so that his purposes for the world cannot be thwarted).

Given all these principles, self-evident to himself and to many of his contemporaries, Augustine could come to no other conclusion but that God must choose (without any possibility of changing his mind) some men to be saved; and that their salvation would be brought about by a free gift of grace, which would put right what had gone wrong in Adam and made him helpless.

Augustine's notion of election underwent a significant change about 397 between the first and second occasions on which he wrote in reply to questions sent him by Simplicianus. When he first answered Simplicianus, Augustine thought that man retained sufficient freedom of will to enable him to turn to God and ask his help (*De Div. Quaest. Simp.* I, Q.1.14). By the time he had composed his answer to Question Two, he had thought again about the passage in Romans (9.11) where Paul says that God loved Jacob and hated Esau before either was born. This led him to the view that God must make his choice before the individual is in a position to turn to God of his own volition. It follows that man is given two things by grace: first the power to will, and then the power to do what is willed (I. Q.2.10 and 12).

It has been argued that towards the end Augustine began to use the term 'predestination', not with the sense of determinism now usually associated with it, but to express 'the *definiteness* of the *plans* that are made'.[1] That is to say, Augustine was not perhaps going further towards a doctrine of divine compelling, but simply pointing out the absoluteness of God's arrangements, so that man should be seen, not as driven on by God, but as falling inevitably in with those plans as a free agent, God having seen clearly what he would freely do.

Whether or not this reading is right, there proved to be a good deal of room for manoeuvre in exactly this area of the relationship between human free will and divine grace and predestination among Augustine's readers and followers in the centuries to come.

EPILOGUE

1 Augustine and After

Augustine's solution of the problem of evil brought him in the end to an extreme position. Evil consists in the act of the free will of a rational creature which has turned away from the good. When Adam fell, the whole race of men who were to come from Adam was condemned with him; it became a *massa damnata*. Human nature itself was changed, so that the human will could not in practice choose the good any longer without assistance. Instead it developed a runaway tendency to will evil, with the result that willing became lusting and desires exceeded the bounds of reason. Sexual desire in particular seemed to have a life of its own, driving the body without reference to the rational soul's attempts to control it. Indeed it came to represent for Augustine the essence of what had gone wrong at the fall of Adam, and the way in which Adam's flawed nature was transmitted generation by generation.

As an act of mercy, God gratuitously chose a certain number from amongst mankind to be restored in the end to the state to which Adam would eventually have come if he had not sinned, and to enjoy eternity in the heavenly city with the angels. God made his choice in the beginning, before he created Adam, and it could not be altered. It follows that the rest of mankind is left to the consequences of Adam's sin, and thus to damnation.

A seeming-Christian can damn himself at any time. Augustine is most insistent on this point. (His doing so would simply show him not to have been one of the elect.) No-one can be sure that he is saved and no-one ought to regard himself as secure and free to live as sinfully as he wishes. But those who are truly elect cannot go astray. They persevere in goodness because God gives them the gift of perseverance. This again is a free gift, which cannot be earned, but a man may make himself more receptive to it by prayer. The sustaining grace which enables a man to be good must continue until the end of his life if he is to be saved. Thus Augustine accommodates within his system

170

the imperative that each Christian must make an effort to be good, even while he insists that he can do nothing by his own efforts, and even if he could, that they would be unavailing as a means of earning salvation.

Even in Augustine's own lifetime there were those who found some or all of this unpalatable, and tried to take up a moderate position, between the Augustinian and the Pelagian. These Semi-Pelagians accepted the need for baptism, and accepted that grace was given in baptism; but they rejected predestination and they said that grace was not – except in a few exceptional cases such as that of St Paul – an overwhelming force which governed a man's destiny with or without the consent of his will. Instead, they argued that grace is offered to everyone, and each man may accept or reject it freely by his own act of will. This view raised afresh a number of the difficulties which had led Augustine himself further and further into his predestinationist position against the Pelagians. But despite its inconsistencies it was more acceptable to many.

The controversy began about 425, in Augustine's lifetime. Cassian, in his monastery at Marseille, taught and wrote that the beginning of salvation lies with the individual, who must choose to turn to God.[1] He was displeased by Augustine's arguments in the *De Correptione et Gratia* that, on the contrary, the initiative always lies with God, and that grace overwhelms the individual will. Some of Augustine's supporters wrote indignantly to tell him of the errors into which Provençal Christians were falling (*Letters* 225, 226) and Augustine replied with his treatises *De Praedestinatione Sanctorum* and *De Dono Perseverantiae*.

Letter 225 is from Prosper of Aquitaine, who was to be instrumental in transmitting Augustine's doctrine of salvation. He explains what has been happening, and summarises for Augustine what the 'servants of Christ who live in the city of Marseille' believe. Their chief anxiety is over those lukewarm Christians who are so confident that they cannot lose their way to heaven that they make no effort to live good lives. They therefore teach that there is a possibility of voluntary consecration being an effective road to salvation – indeed, that all who are willing to believe and be baptised can be saved. Effort will be rewarded. God saw before the foundation of the world who would come to him in this way, and who would stand firm in the faith they had adopted: they were the men and women he predestined and upon whom he bestowed his grace. This explanation covers the case of infants, who are lost or saved when they die according to what God by divine knowledge foresees they would have become if they had lived. In this way the grace of God comes to seem a companion of human effort, not a forerunner (*Letter* 225.2–5). Prosper mentions by name two of the misguided in particular, Honoratus and Hilary, who had recently been made Bishops of Arles. His account is important not only for what it tells us of the extent and nature of the Semi-Pelagianism of the region, but also for the way in which he is able to put his finger upon those key issues which were to remain talking-points for centuries: the role of human effort and the notion of a compelling grace in particular.

The reaction against Augustine in Provence worked itself out during the course of the century after his death. Vincent, of the monastery at Lérins where Hilary, Bishop of Arles, had been a monk, remained an adversary of extreme Augustinianism in the middle of the fifth century. Faustus of Riez, a Breton, perhaps, by birth and himself once an abbot of Lérins, brought about the condemnation of Augustine's view at the Council of Arles of 473 and the Council of Lyons of 475. He wrote a treatise of his own, *De Gratia et Libero Arbitrio*, directed against Pelagianism, but emphasising the weakness of human will rather than its complete powerlessness. Man is, he says, like a glutton or a drunkard who has been in the grip of his bad habits for so long that he cannot easily summon the will to break them, and his recovery from his addiction is slow and painful as his will gathers strength and resolution.[2] By the time of the Council of Orange in 529, Caesarius of Arles was suggesting that perhaps Augustine's view had been more moderate than had been thought, and that he had been misunderstood.

Augustine came, indeed, to enjoy the support not only of his own African Christians, who had always accepted the correctness of his view, but also that of the Latin Fathers who came after him. Gregory the Great, for example, puts forward the view that 'our evils are all our own' while the good things we do are God's work as well as ours. God's grace goes before as a 'prevenient' grace to enable us to will rightly, and travels with us to help us so that we do not will in vain and can carry out what we will to do, as a 'subsequent grace'. He does not insist upon the irresistibility of grace, but, mildly expressed though it is, the position is Augustinian.[3]

2 The Carolingian Debate

The problem of the relationship between human free will and the foreknowledge, grace and predestination of God remained the principal point of controversy to arise from Augustine's teaching on evil for many centuries. It was not a controversial matter to all scholars during the centuries after the fall of the Roman Empire. Bede (c. 673–735) the great salvager of the secular and patristic learning of the ancient world, expounds the text 'Who comes to the Father but by me' in terms of a prevenient grace, by explaining that he who 'comes' is he 'before whom goes the grace of God': *ille venit, quem gratia Dei prevenit*.[4] In the early ninth century, the grammarian Smaragdus of Saint Mihiel on the river Meuse composed a *Diadema Monachorum* in which he explains the working of the grace of God in Augustinian terms. We can attempt some good works through the grace of God, but unless his grace helps us, we cannot carry them through. Our evils are solely our own, but the good we do is God's as well as our own. By prevenient grace and the good will which follows it, the gift of almighty God becomes our merit.[5]

Augustine's teaching became a subject of controversy again in the ninth century, when Godescalc, a monk of Orbais in the diocese of Soissons, began to teach 'new superstitions and a poisonous doctrine concerning the predestination of God. . . . saying that just as God's predestination works in the good, so it works in the evil', as his former schoolmaster Rabanus Maurus wrote to Bishop Hincmar of Reims in 848.[6] Hincmar was sufficiently perturbed by this to write a pastoral letter to try to ensure that the simple in his own diocese were not led astray. Godescalc's teaching caused offence to Rabanus because it constituted an extreme predestinarian view. Rabanus says that he 'dogmatises that the predestination of God so constrains every man that, even if someone wishes to be saved, . . . he labours in vain if he is not predestined to life'.[7] Amongst other leading scholars of the day, John Scottus Eriugena and Prudentius of Troyes were drawn in. Hincmar encouraged Eriugena to write his *De Predestinatione* and Prudentius replied to him in support of Godescalc. We owe much of our knowledge of the background to this debate to an eager letter-writer, Lupus of Ferrières (c. 805–62), who studied at the abbey of Fulda under Rabanus, and there met

Godescalc. He, too, was moved to contribute. His *Liber de Tribus Quaestionibus* takes a strong Augustinian line, but not so extreme a one as that of Godescalc.

Godescalc attracted attention from these considerable thinkers because he was raising fundamental questions about the nature and origin of evil, implying that perhaps after all God was responsible for it, if indeed he predestined good men to salvation and the wicked to damnation (what Eriugena calls a doctrine of ' two predestinations').[8] That would imply that God is the author of both good and evil. Godescalc was formally condemned at the Council of Quiercy-sur-Oise in 853, but the debate had brought a new vitality to the discussion.

3 The Logic of Evil

Like a number of eleventh-century monastic scholars, Otloh of St Emmeram was something of a logician. In particular, he possessed a logician's enthusiasm for resolving contradictions. He applied himself to the problem of evil in his *Dialogus de Tribus Quaestionibus*. As he saw it, the difficulty lay, not in accepting that sin and evil entered the world with the fall of Adam, nor in the view that the whole of mankind lay under a condemnation as a result, but in the untidiness of the present situation. If divine mercy fills the earth it is hard to understand how a man can be afflicted by so many evils, even when grace is working in him. Otloh suggests that it is God's will that men should not be stabilised in goodness by the action of grace, so that they may remain aware of the power of evil and the greatness of what God has done for them. The contrast is sustained throughout the treatise: God's just condemnation of the good angels is contrasted with his merciful redemption of man (who learns how great a matter his redemption is when he contemplates the state of the fallen angels). The contrasting examples of virtuous and vicious lives show men how to be good.[9]

The dialectician's approach to Augustine's resolution of the problem of evil also encouraged a renewed interest in the notion that evil is nothing: a return to the metaphysical and epistemological problems which had first concerned Augustine. One of the Carolingians, Fredegisus, Abbot of St Martin, Tours (died 834) wrote a brief *Epistola de Nihilo et Tenebris* in which he came to the conclusion that both 'nothing' and 'darkness' were really 'something', and that darkness was even to be regarded as a corporeal 'something'.[10] His reason for holding that 'nothing' is 'something' rests upon the principle discussed by Augustine in the *De Magistro*, that 'every finite noun signifies something' (*omne nomen finitum aliquid significat, ut homo, lapis, lignum*). It seemed impossible that there should be a word for 'nothing' unless it were really 'something'. Augustine and Adeodatus had discussed a line of Virgil word by word, to see whether this held true; the line contained the word 'nothing' and they found themselves in difficulties.[11] Augustine leaves the matter in the air, to await the attentions of these later logicians.

The problem presented itself in much the same form to Anselm of Bec two and a half centuries after Fredegisus. He tried to answer the question 'Why did Satan fall?' in the last of a series of short treatises designed to help his pupils read the Bible with an understanding of the way in which its language worked. His difficulty lay in the impossibility of discussing something (evil) which does not exist, and for which there can accordingly be no words, for no noun can signify what is not there to be signified. His solution was not so extreme as that of Fredegisus. He simply suggests that for purposes of discussion evil should be regarded as a 'sort-of-something (*quasi-aliquid*)'.[12]

The difficulty arose again many years later when he was writing on original sin (*De Conceptu Virginali*). He answers an objection which he knows is often made: that if evil and sin are nothing there seems little point in avoiding them, for wherein consists the fearsomeness of nothing?[13] Despite the Augustinian derivation of these discussions, the atmosphere in which they are conducted belongs to the eleventh century. Anselm was the first thinker since Augustine to take a comprehensive fresh look at the problem of evil. Unlike Augustine he did not begin from his own struggles with it; he took as given several of the principles Augustine had worked out with such difficulty. Nor does he discuss evil as a composite problem and as a whole in any single work. But he covers the subject thoroughly nevertheless.

In the *Cur Deus Homo* he makes, by implication, the point that the sacrifice of the Crucifixion was made for the salvation of all men. The reason why an angel could not have carried it out was precisely that he was not one of Adam's progeny, and therefore he could not put right what had gone wrong in Adam. Therefore, in becoming man,

God stood for the whole human race.[14] In the same way as the sin of Adam was transmitted to all, so the wiping out of sin was effective for all. But nevertheless, Anselm believes that only the elect are to be saved, a fixed number which God decided upon from eternity to make up, with the angels, the full complement of the inhabitants of the heavenly city. Yet if Anselm believes in predestination, he sees the doctrine of election as having only the most positive practical implications for the living of a good life; we must strive to be good, he urges, in numerous letters to his monks, for many are called but few are chosen.

This apparently contradictory advice is sensible enough in the light of Anselm's reconciliation of human freedom of choice with divine foresight, predestination and grace in the *De Concordia* which he composed at the end of his life. He begins by pointing to several Scriptural passages in which it is implied that grace alone is effective for salvation, and to others which seem to say that it is entirely a matter of the exercise of human will. He knows that many have tried to make themselves good by an exercise of will, and have found that they cannot do it.[15] His method of resolving the difficulty is to analyse the nature and function of the will. His terms are those of Augustine, at bottom. He distinguishes two wills, one for good and one for evil, from which whatever merit a man has derives.[16] He concludes that evil is done solely by man's will, while good is done by human will only in co-operation with a grace which he describes as both 'giving' and 'subsequent' (*dante et subsequente gratia*).[17]

The section of the treatise which deals with grace is the last; in the first and second parts Anselm had shown that human free will is not made less free by the fact of divine foreknowledge and predestination, but simply concurs with it.[18] This principle is now extended to the relationship between human will and divine grace. The result is an account of the matter subtly different from the notion that grace goes before or after the will, pressing it to work and sustaining it in its efforts. Anselm suggests that the will of a good man naturally coincides with the will of God. Grace does not override its freedom or compel it, because it is already inclined to go along with grace.[19] This resolution by harmony is typically Anselmian. It represents a new departure because it allowed for the possibility of setting aside the controversies of the Carolingian period and of Augustine's own day about the degree of compulsion involved in salvation. But it also preserved the spirit of the earlier attempts to keep grace and freedom in balance.

In the next generation there were some who took Anselm's line, in a modified way: Honorius Augustodunensis, an admirer who had met Anselm and heard him speak, and later in the twelfth century Frowin of Engelberg.[20] Alger of Liège wrote a *Little Book on Free Will* in which he considered what free will was before the fall of Adam and what it was afterwards, and suggested that predestination either for good or for ill has no compelling force. 'The predestination of God does not force us to good or to evil', he insists, although he holds to the Augustinian position that good comes only from grace, evil from our own willing.[21]

The great Cistercian Bernard of Clairvaux (1090–1153) did not always agree with Anselm, but he had certainly read him, and he was perhaps encouraged to attempt an analysis of the nature of liberty and the nature of will for the benefit of his monks. The occasion arose when he had been preaching fervently about the way he had found grace working within his own soul. One of his listeners asked him why, if grace is the source of all good human willing, there is any point in a man making an effort to be good.[22]

Bernard explains that both free will and grace are necessary for salvation. If free will is removed, there is nothing to be saved; if grace is taken away, there is no means of effecting salvation.[23] Free will is said to co-operate with grace when it consents to it, and that is what it does when it is saved.[24]

He proceeds to analyse 'consent' and the notion of 'voluntariness' and natural appetite. He concludes that freedom cannot be taken away from the will without its ceasing to be a will. It retains, indeed, three freedoms, that which a man has by nature, that which a man has by grace, and that which he will have in heaven.[25] He asks how freedom can still be present when all that is left to the human will is the power to will evil. He traces the interplay of grace and human free will in many of its Augustinian aspects, but with a twelfth century eye for definition and the technical logical underpinnings.

Like Anselm, Bernard wants to maintain both the indispensableness of grace and the inalienable freedom of the human will; and, like Anselm, he sees no difficulty in their being both present in the salvation of the individual. The 'merits' a man may be said to have are all the work of grace; they are, he says, like seeds of hope, hidden indications of predestination, presages of future happiness.[26]

The fact that Bernard was asked the question at all suggests that the old points of controversy were far from dead. Peter Abelard, the most famous and the most infamous of the Paris masters, was condemned at a trial at which Bernard himself was counsel for the prosecution, for holding a number of heretical views (not all of which are to be found expressed in his surviving writings): amongst them the opinion that human free will can, of itself, act for good; and the view that God can do no more for the man who is to be saved than for the man who is not, before he throws himself upon divine grace.[27]

But while the controversy continued, in its general structure and in its fundamentals the Augustinian explanation had become the accepted one, leaving, not the problem of evil as a whole, but a number of specific difficulties to be debated afresh in each generation. Hugh of St Victor, one of the first to try to put together a complete course in theology for his students, and Peter Lombard, whose *Sentences* became the most used theological textbook of the Middle Ages, thought that Adam's task was to acquire justice. His primitive state was neutral. He was the 'earth without form and void' of Genesis (1.2). They rejected Anselm's notion that Adam's principal task was to preserve the very positive state of justice in which he had been created. These specific difficulties were largely confined to the problem of the role of grace and predestination in their action upon human free will. Few authors explored the metaphysical implications as Anselm had done, and asked what evil might be.

Manicheism was persistent, however.[28] The twelfth and early thirteenth centuries saw the rise of many sects in the south of France and northern Spain and Italy and elsewhere who held the gnostic view that there were two principles, of good and evil. Alan of Lille, a Paris master who later taught in the south of France and preached against the heretics there at the end of the century, wrote a compound treatise against the 'unbelievers' of the day, Cathars, Waldensians, Jews and Moslems, in which he gives an account of the beliefs of the Cathars, drawing substantially upon Augustine's anti-Manichean writings.

4 Freedom of Action

Anselm and the scholars of the century after him were closer to Augustine in their view of the world than their thirteenth century successors and the later schoolmen. They were prepared to accept without question many of the assumptions upon which his thought rested as being self-evident. They shared his preoccupation with the mechanics of the effect of evil: the ways in which nothing might behave like a very powerful something; the paradox of a freedom of choice which, while remaining free, can now choose only the evil because it has lost its power to choose the good; the further paradox of the freedom which must co-exist with a divine foreknowledge incapable of making a mistake, so that it appears that every choice is predetermined, and every man's end is sealed by divine election. They understood clearly how one of Augustine's conclusions entailed another.

Their interest differed from that of Augustine chiefly in emphasis. They were far better logicians than he; they had the benefit of Boethius; and accordingly they were attracted to the problems of necessity and futurity with which he deals in his commentary on Aristotle's *De Inventione*. They had an interest in natural science, and so they asked by what process the effects of sin were transmitted from Adam to all his progeny (Anselm believed that some form of genetic change had taken place when Adam's system was poisoned by the apple). Above all, they enjoyed problem-solving, and the complex of Augustine's discussions of evil presented them with myriad technical difficulties: paradoxes and seeming contradictions of the sort which were the stuff of intellectual life to dialecticians who had newly discovered Aristotle's *Sophistici Elenchi* and learned how to identify fallacies of every sort.

Alongside this interest in the intellectual problems that evil poses if we see it in Augustinian terms, ran a renewed concern with the moral and personal aspects of the problem. The preachers of the twelfth century were drawn to the notion of a battle between the virtues and the vices such as Prudentius had portrayed in his fourth century poem the *Psychomachia*, and it became a common theme of their sermons. Preaching of this sort was something relatively new. Anselm of Canterbury was something of a pioneer in addressing his

179

community in his own words and making up new homilies for them, rather than having the homilies of Augustine or Gregory read aloud as was then usual in monastic houses. Bernard of Clairvaux made an astonishing impact upon his listeners by his preaching. In the first half of the twelfth century there were a number of successful preachers – Norbert of Xanten, for example, who founded the Order of Praemonstratensian Canons. But it was not until the latter half of the century that preaching began to develop into the formal rhetorical art it was to become in the thirteenth century, when Masters in the universities were to distinguish sermons designed for an audience of scholars and students, and dealing with technical points of exegesis and problems of speculative theology, from sermons given to ordinary people or to monks and nuns, and designed to encourage them to live better and holier lives.

In the first detailed instruction-book of the period on how to preach a sermon, Alan of Lille (died 1202) places great emphasis upon the preacher's duty to evoke in his listeners a lively sense of their own sinfulness, to encourage them to fight against the vices and strive to attain the virtues. The devotional writing of the later Middle Ages, as well as the preaching of sermons, was to follow his line energetically. An Augustinian sense of the essential uncleanness of bodily appetites, and especially of sexual desire, runs through Alan of Lille's imagery; he contrasts the beauty and purity of continence with the ugliness of giving way to desire. In most graphic terms he shows how original sin has altered human nature and flawed it.

These two developments, towards, on the one hand, the philosophical analysis of the problem of evil with the aid of improved logical methods, and, on the other, the evoking of a strong consciousness of sin in the individual, were to grow more pronounced during the thirteenth and fourteenth centuries. As they developed they took with them much that was Augustinian, but they incorporated new influences, too, so that the overall picture begins to change.

In the course of the twelfth century scholars had been travelling in Spain and the East in search first of the scientific works the Arabs had translated from the Greek, and then of the logical and metaphysical works of Aristotle. What they found and brought back took some time to find acceptance in the schools, and indeed there was painful controversy in the later thirteenth century over the acceptability of the new material to Christian scholars. The Dominican master of

Thomas Aquinas, Albert the Great, is the author of an enormous corpus in which he tried to set out the new learning in a manageable form. His account shows how different the study of man was becoming. The soul, Albert says, is the mover of the body. Within the soul the 'practical intellect' directs the will and the actions of each man by means of cognition and rational thought. Will is the natural appetite of a rational soul for the good as the intellect apprehends it. Free choice is found only in men. It consists in man's power to decide by 'arbitration' what is good and what is evil, according to the rule of reason. Once he has decided, he must act. Freedom consists either in yielding to the judgment of reason, or in turning from it. In that it is an arbitrating power, free choice belongs to reason; in that it is free, it belongs to will.[29] Albert's account of the freedom of the will is substantially different from that of Augustine (although it agrees with it at many points) because Albert is concerned in a new way with its operation or action.

Many thirteenth-century thinkers, it must be said, adhered to Augustinian principles, preferring them to the new Aristotelianism – Franciscan scholars such as the Englishman Alexander of Hales (c. 1186–1245), for instance, and St Bonaventure (1217–74). But the advent of Aristotle had made a difference. The new learning appealed to the would-be scientists of the universities. It encouraged the study of man within the framework of natural science, as an animal, if an animal with distinctive attributes. The 'Aristotelians' analysed the powers or faculties of the human soul which produced certain acts. This was not in itself a new approach. Gerbert of Aurillac had written a treatise on the difference between possessing reason and using reason, before he became Pope Sylvester II in 999. But the Aristotelians were interested in the specifically human powers which distinguish man from other animals. The Englishman Roger Bacon, one of the first experimental scientists (c. 1214–after 1292), draws from Augustine the doctrine that free choice is a matter of both reason and will. He applies to it the Aristotelian dictum that reason and will are different powers of the soul. It follows that free choice cannot be a distinct power of the soul, since it is clearly compounded of two others. Therefore, he concludes, it must be a power of the soul whose operations are diverse, but reciprocally ordered in their actions (Opus Maius III.299).

The reading of Aristotle also encouraged an interest in cause and effect, as bringing about human action. Aquinas lists the external and interior causes of sin in his *Summa Theologiae* II^i.Q.71–89. From Aristotle, too, came a habit of looking to the end or purpose of actions. Aquinas holds that every agent acts with an end in view, and that that end must be in conformity with his nature. He concludes that man's end, as a rational creature, must be to act 'according to reason'. On this basis he examines the end or purpose of human willing (*Summa Theologiae* II^i.Q.8–12). Augustine had considered the end of man, too, and he had written on blessedness; but his interest lay in the heavenly end, not the functional purpose of man. The thirteenth century saw the division of interest between the philosophically minded, who considered man in himself, according to his species, and the theologians, who continued to look at him in relation to God as his origin and end.

That is not to say that Aquinas left Augustine behind. On the contrary, he was anxious to create a synthesis in which Aristotle could be accommodated alongside Augustine. He quotes the *Soliloquies* in his discussion of *falsitas* in things, in sense-perception, in understanding (*Sol*. II.6; *Summa Theologiae* I. Q. 17), and Augustine remains one of his prime authorities. But there was a tendency for the method which Aquinas brought to perfection in the *Summa Theologiae* to result in an even presentation of all questions side by side, so that their relative importance is not apparent. Grace is shown as giving specific gifts, of prophecy, or tongues, or miracle-working (*Summa Theologiae* II^{ii}. Q. 171–8), and it becomes so subdivided as Aquinas takes the idea apart for analysis that it fails to emerge with the majesty of Augustine's conception. Whereas Augustine's free-ranging explorations of a question, his sometimes untidy and rambling digressions, had all been prompted by a powerful curiosity and a genuine uncertainty at times as to where the solution lay, Aquinas' purpose was to contain curiosity and to eliminate uncertainty, so as to present his pupils with a finished theology. 'We must now consider the good and evil of human acts,' he says, 'first how a human act is good or evil; secondly what results from the good or evil of a human act, whether merit or its opposite, sin or guilt. Under the first heading there will be three things to consider . . . Concerning the first of these there are eleven points of enquiry . . .' and so on (*Summa Theologiae* II^i. Q. 18).

It would not be fair to say that this diminishing was a result of the

influence of Aristotle, but the Aristotelian approach perhaps encouraged a certain mechanical quality which was already becoming
apparent in the late twelfth century. Speculative theology was
proving to be a matter of asking and answering with great formality
questions arranged in order so as to cover every possible aspect of
each subject. When Aquinas discusses goodness in actions, he
considers it under four aspects: generic, specific, circumstantial, and
deriving from the 'end' of the action. A good act belongs to the genus
of good things. It is specifically good if it has a proper object. It is good
according to the circumstances in which it is done; and it is good if it
has a good cause (*Summa Theologiae* II^i. Q. 18 a. 4).

It would be surprising if nothing new emerged from these
meticulous examinations, and in many points Aquinas' doctrine of
grace is his own. He added to Augustine's teaching a full-scale
enquiry into the working of human will before the Fall according to
human nature as God intended it to be; into the way the soul will
function in the state it finds itself in after death while it awaits
resurrection; and into the psychology of the angels. These are matters
to which Augustine had not been able to bring the benefits of a fully
Aristotelian education, and to Aquinas' eye they throw an altogether
fresh light upon the operation of grace. He is able to see grace not as
overwhelming human nature, but as bringing it to its intended
perfection as God designed it and to which he thus restores it.

Aquinas was perhaps the last major thinker before the Reformation
to propose much that was radically new in the attempt to resolve the
problem of evil. The sympathies of the thirteenth century Alexander
of Hales and Bonaventure, and the fourteenth century Duns Scotus,
lay with a view not unlike that which had been held by some of
Augustine's opponents in his own lifetime. They lacked that 'sense of
sin' so graphically described by J.B. Mozley: 'The doctrine of
original sin lies deep in the human heart, which has never truly and
earnestly perceived its guilt at all, without coupling with it the idea of
a mysterious alloy and taint antecedent to action, and coeval with its
own life.'[30] They preferred to think of original sin as no more than a
loss of those gifts of God which Adam had had before the fall; so that
some stretching or reaching towards goodness by any human being
brought its reward of a 'congruous' grace and led to at least a partial
recovery of what had been lost. Duns Scotus could not believe that
the will will not 'naturally tend' towards that which the understand-

ing rightly dictates (*Commentarius Oxoniensis in Sententias* III. dist. 27, q. 1, n. 13f); he thus rejected Augustine's principle that the effect of the fall was to strip man's will of its power to choose the good. The machinery of the Augustinian solution will not work with these modifications.

The sense of the importance of the fall and of the consequence of original sin, of the sheer scale of the damage to be repaired, returned with the sixteenth century. The reformers discovered Augustine anew, and discovered in him much that was to their taste. With Luther and Calvin especially, emphasis was placed afresh on the impotence of man, the efficacy of grace. The doctrine of justification by faith alone – and faith as the gift of God – was no mechanical speculation; it was the impassioned cry of men who, like Augustine, had agonised their way to a solution and whose attempts to impose order on experience kept the Augustinian dilemma alive to the modern world.

NOTES

Preface

1 H. de Lubac, *Augustinianism and Modern Theology* (London, 1969), p. 1.
2 Keats, *Letter* 123, April 1819, *Letters of John Keats*, ed. F. Page (Oxford, 1954), p. 266.

II · The Problem Presents Itself

1 W.H.C. Frend, 'The Gnostic–Manichean Tradition in Roman N. Africa', *Journal of Ecclesiastical History* 4 (1953), 13–26.
2 Zenobius (*De Ordine* and letter 2), Hermogenianus (Epistula 1), Manlius Theodorus (*De Beata Vita*). P. Courcelle first put this group together in *Les lettres grecs en occident de Macrobe à Cassiodore* (Paris, 1948), pp. 119–29.
3 For Augustine's references to *platonici* and Plotinus especially, see *Conf.* VII.xiii; VIII.iii; *C. Acad.* III.xli; *De Beata Vita* IV; *Sol.* I–IX; *Letter* 6.1.
4 Marius Victorinus, *Traités théologiques sur la Trinité*, ed. P. Hadot, Sources Chrétiennes 68 (1960), 7–76.
5 The Academy had gone through several stages since its foundation by Plato and the end of the fourth century B.C. Plato's followers at first held with their master that it was possible to attain intellectual knowledge. Arcesilaus, who died about 241/40 B.C., took a more sceptical view. He believed that knowledge was impossible and the change of direction he brought about was sufficiently marked for him to be regarded as the founder of the 'New', 'Second' or 'Middle' Academy. The 'Third' or 'New' Academy, which endured until Augustine's time was founded by Carneades (214/13 – 129/8 B.C.), who taught a method of arguing both for and against every question. Augustine learned the history of the Academy from Cicero's *Academica* (*C. Acad.* II.v–vi.5).
6 And Matthew 19.21.
7 See E. de la Peza, *El significado de 'cor' en san Agustin* (Paris, 1962), on the Augustinian notion of *cor* and on the Vision of Ostia, P. Henry, *La vision d'Ostie* (Paris, 1938).

III · Evil in the Mind

1 E. Gilson, *History of Christian Philosophy* (London, 1955), p. 70.

185

2 That is, intellect, being spiritual, has a mode of existence which resembles the Being or essence of Truth itself, in a way that the lowlier existence of material things cannot do. Corporeal things do not have so 'true' an existence.

3 P. Courcelle, *Recherches sur 'Les Confessions' de S. Augustin* (Paris, 1950), pp. 93–106.

4 See *The Cambridge History of Later Greek and Early Mediaeval Philosophy*, ed. A.H. Armstrong (Cambridge, 1970), pp. 15–16 for a summary history of the notion.

5 See R. Godel, 'Similitudines Rerum', *Museum Helveticum* 19 (1962), 190–3.

6 Sermon 81.8, cf. P. Brown, *Augustine of Hippo*, pp. 287–98.

7 A task that Bede attempted afresh in his *De Schematis et Tropis* and Peter the Chanter in the late twelfth century in his *De Tropis Loquendi*.

8 H. Chadwick, *Priscillian of Avila* (Oxford, 1976), p. 150 and pp. 206–8.

9 Anselm; *De Veritate*, ed. F.S. Schmitt, *Anselm; Opera Omnia*, vol. I (Rome, 1938), p. 177.

IV · Evil in the Universe

1 *De Conceptu Virginali* 5–6, ed. Schmitt, vol. II, pp. 146–7.

V · Neither a Pelagian nor a Manichee

1 P. Brown, *Religion and Society in the Age of St Augustine* (London, 1972), p. 202, and *Augustine of Hippo*, pp. 369–71.

2 On the process by which Augustine came to think of the heresy as 'Pelagian' see R.F. Evans, pp. 70–89. On Jerome, *ibid.*, p. 6.

3 Paulinus of Nola, *Letters* 4, 6, 45, 50, are to Augustine, *Letter* 3 to Alypius, Augustine's old friend, now Bishop of Thagaste. *Letter* 4 (v), of 395, mentions a gift of some of Augustine's works to Paulinus. These would seem likely to have been anti-Manichean pieces. Paulinus remarks (ii) that he has been provided 'with sufficient armour against the Manicheans'. In *Letter* 6 (ii), he says that he feels that he has come to know Augustine through his anti-Manichean writings.

4 P. Brown, *Religion and Society*, p. 212, suggests that Augustine may have wanted to make copies available to the Manichees of Rome and the Campania. In *Contra Secundinum* (xi), Augustine tells Secundinus the Manichee that he can read the *De Libero Arbitrio* in Paulinus' Library.

5 *Carmen* XXV, ed. G. de Hartel, Corpus Scriptorum Ecclesiasticorum Latinorum 30 (Vienna, 1894).

6 P. Brown, *Religion and Society*, p. 185.

7 *Ibid.*, p. 218.

8 *Ibid.*, p. 192.

9 A.J. Smith, 'The Latin Sources of the Commentary of Pelagius on the Epistle of St Paul to the Romans', *Journal of Theological Studies* 19 (1918), 162–230, compares Ambrosiaster and Pelagius at length, but his comparisons should be revised by comparing modern editions of the texts: H.I. Vogels' edition of *Ambrosiaster qui dicitur Commentarius in Epistulas Paulinas*, CSEL 81.1–3 (Vienna, 1966), and *Pelagius's Expositions of Thirteen Epistles of St Paul*, ed. A. Souter, Texts and Studies, IX.2 (Cambridge, 1923).

10 Ambrosiaster, *ed. cit.*, and Pelagius, *ed. cit.*, on Romans 1.7; 2.12; 2.15.

11 *Ambrosiaster, De Auctore, Operibus, Theologia*, ed. P.C. Martin (Rome, 1944), p. 207.

12 J. Rivière, 'Hétérodoxie des Pélagiens en fait de redemption', *Revue d'histoire ecclésiastique* 41 (1946), pp. 5–43, points out that Pelagius has some perfectly orthodox views, emphasising the death of Christ as an unmerited sacrificial offering for men's sins.

13 T. Bohlin, *Die Theologie des Pelagius und ihre Genesis* (Uppsala, 1957).

14 G.I. Bonner develops Bohlin's thesis, 'How Pelagian was Pelagius?', Studia Patristica, IX.iii (Berlin, 1966), ed. F.L. Cross, p. 353.

15 Evans, *op. cit.* p. 22.

VII · The Divine Imperative

1 E. Teselle, *Augustine the Theologian* (New York, 1970), p. 326.

Epilogue

1 Cassian, *Collationes* 13, *De Protectione Dei*, PL 49.897–954.

2 PL 58.783–836.

3 *In Ezek.* I, *Hom.* ix.2, PL 76.870D; cf. Cassiodorus, *De Inst. Div. Litt.* 20, PL 70.1146, and Isidore of Seville, *Sentences* II.5, PL 83.604B.

4 *In Ioan.* 6, PL 92.716, John 6.44.

5 PL 102.642, Chapter 45.

6 Godescalc d'Orbais, *Oeuvres*, ed. D.C. Lambot, Spicilegium Sacrum Lovaniense 20 (1945), Fragment.

7 PL 112.1554B, *Letter* 6.

8 John Scottus Eriugena, *De Praedestinatione*, PL 122.359.

9 PL 146.67B, 73D, 94B, etc. (59–136).

10 PL 105.756.

11 Augustine, *De Magistro* 2.iii; on the treatment of this topic by Fredegisus and Anselm, see D.P. Henry, *The Logic of St. Anselm* (Oxford, 1967), pp. 207–8.

12 *Anselmi Opera Omnia*, ed. F.S. Schmitt (6 vols., Rome/Edinburgh, 1938–68), I.246–51, *De Casu Diaboli* xi.

13 *Anselmi Opera Omnia* II.147, *De Conceptu* vi.

14 *Ibid*. II.52, *Cur Deus Homo* v.

15 *Ibid*. II.263.5–14, Question III.1.

16 *Ibid*. II.284.9–10, Question III.12.

17 *Ibid*. II.288.8–9.

18 *Ibid*. II.262.13–15.

19 Compare Anselm's discussion of the willingness with which Christ submitted himself to his Father's will that he should die for mankind, *Cur Deus Homo* I.ix, *Opera Omnia* II.61–4.

20 Honorius Augustodunensis, PL 172; Frowin of Engelberg, PL 179.1801–42.

21 PL 180.969–72.

22 *De Gratia et Libero Arbitrio Sancti Bernadi Opera Omnia*, ed. J. Leclercq and H. Rochais, vol. III (Rome, 1963), p. 165.

23 *Ibid*., p. 166.19–21.

24 *Ibid*., pp. 166.25–167.1.

25 *Ibid*., pp. 169 and 171.

26 *Ibid*., p. 203.15.

27 *Capitula Haeresum* VI and VII, ed. M. Buytaert, Corpus Christianorum Continuatio Medievalis (Turnhout, 1969), pp. 476–7.

28 S. Runciman, *The Mediaeval Manichee* (Cambridge, 1947) has traced the survival of the heresy into the Middle Ages.

29 *Alberti Magni Opera Omni*, ed. G. Borgnet, vol. XXXV, pp. 551–9.

30 J.B. Mozley, *A Treatise on the Augustinian Doctrine of Predestination* (London, 1883), p. 310.

BIBLIOGRAPHY

Editions of the Works of Augustine: collected works

Opera Omnia, Paris, 1679–1700, reprinted by J.P. Migne, Patrologiae Cursus Completus, Series Latina 32–47, Paris 1841–9.

Oeuvres de Saint Augustin, *Bibliothèque augustinienne*, Paris, 1947– .

Augustini Opera, Corpus Scriptorum Ecclesiasticorum Latinorum, Vienna, 1887– .

Augustini (*Aurelii*) *Opera*, Corpus Christianorum Series Latina, Turnhout, 1954– .

Obras de San Agustin, Biblioteca de Autores Cristianos, Madrid, 1946–67.

Opere de S. Agostino, Nuova Biblioteca Agostiniana, Rome, 1965.

For editions of individual works, see *Bibliographia Augustiniana*, ed. C. Andresen, Darmstadt, 1973, pp. 8–14.

English Translations

The Works of Aurelius Augustine, Bishop of Hippo, ed. M. Dods, 15 vols., Edinburgh, 1871–6.

The Fathers of the Church, Catholic University of America, Washington, 1947– . Vols. 2, 4, 5, 8, 11, 12, 14, 16, 18, 20, 21, 24, 27, 30, 32, 35, 38, 45, 56, 59, 60.

For translations into other languages, see Andresen, pp. 28–34.

Editions of Works of Ancient Authors Cited in the Text

Apuleius, *De Deo Socratis*, vol. III, ed. R. Helm, P. Thomas, 3 vols., Leipzig, 1908–59.

Athanasius, *Contra Gentes*, ed. R.W. Thomson, Oxford, 1971.

Boethius, *Theological Tractates*, ed. H.F. Stewart, E.K. Rand and S. Tester, repr. London, 1973.

   De Consolatione Philosophiae, ed. L. Bieler, Corpus Christianorum Series Latina 94, Turnhout, 1957.

Cassiodorus, *Institutiones*, ed. R.A.B. Mynors, Oxford, 1937.

Cicero, *Topica*, ed. H.M. Hubbell, London, 1968.

Epictetus, *Manual*, ed. W.A. Oldfather, 2 vols., repr. London, 1946–32.

Jerome, *Letters*, ed. I. Hilberg, Leipzig, 1910.

Justin Martyr, *Dialogues*, ed. I.C.T. Otto, Corpus Apologetarum Christianarum Seculi Secundi 1–5 (1876–81).

A Manichean Psalmbook (Part II), ed. C.R.C. Allberry, *Manichean Manuscripts*, in the Chester Beatty Collection, vol. II (1938).

Martianus Capella, *De Nuptiis Philologiae et Mercurii*, ed. A. Dick, Leipzig, 1965.

Pelagius, *Expositions of Thirteen Epistles of St Paul*, ed. A. Souter, Texts and Studies 9 (1923).

  De Natura, PL 48.599–606.

Plotinus, 'Enneads', *Plotini Opera*, ed. P. Henry and H. Schwyzer, 3 vols., Oxford, 1951–73, trs. S. Mackenna; 4th ed. revised by B.S. Page, London, 1969.

Porphyry, *On Abstinence from Animal Food*, vol. I, ed. J. Bouffartique, Paris, 1977– and tr. T. Taylor, London, 1965.

Proclus, *Elements*, ed. E.R. Dodds, Oxford, 1963.

Seneca, *Opera*, ed. E. Hermes, C. Hosius *et al.*, Leipzig, 1905–70.

Terence, *Andria*, ed. R. Kauer and W.M. Lindsay, Oxford, 1926.

Editions of Works of Mediaeval and Post-Mediaeval Authors Cited in the Epilogue

Abelard, Peter, *Opera Theologica*, ed. E.M. Buytaert, CCCM 11, 12, Turnhout, 1969.

Alan of Lille, *Opera*, PL 210.

Albertus Magnus, *Opera*, ed. A. Borgnet, 38 vols., Paris, 1890–9.

Alger of Liège, *Opera*, PL 180.

Anselm of Canterbury, *Anselmi Opera Omnia*, ed. F.S. Schmitt, 6 vols., Rome/Edinburgh, 1938–68.

Aquinas, Thomas, *Summa Theologiae*, ed. P. Caramello, 4 vols., Rome, 1948.

Bacon, Roger, *Opus Maius*, ed. J.H. Bridges, 3 vols., Oxford, 1897–1900.

Baius, Michel, *Opera*, Pontificia Universitas Gregoriana, Textus et Documenta, Series Theologica 24 (1938).

Bede, *Opera*, PL 90–95, CCSL (1955–).

Bernard of Clairvaux, *Opera*, ed. J. Leclercq and H. Rochais, Rome, 1957– .

Calvin, John, *Opera*, ed. H.W. Baum, E. Cunitz, E. Reuss, P. Lobstein and A. Erichson, Corpus Reformatorum, 29–77, 59 vols., Brunswick, 1863–1900.

Cassian, *Collationes*, ed. M. Petschenig, CSEL 13 (1886) and PL 49.

Chaucer, Geoffrey, *The Canterbury Tales*, ed. F.N. Robinson, Cambridge, Mass./London, 1933, 2nd ed., 1957.

Dionysius, Ps., *Opera*, PG 3–4.

Eriugena, John Scottus, *Opera*, PL 122.

Faustus of Riez, *Opera*, ed. A.G. Engelricht, CSEL 21 (1891). *De Gratia et Libero Arbitrio*, PL 58.783–836.

Fredegisus of Tours, *Opera*, PL 105.

Frowin of Engelberg, *Opera*, PL 179.

Godescalc of Orbais, *Oeuvres*, ed. D.C. Lambot, Spicilegium Sacrum Lovaniense 20 (1945).

Hincmar of Reims, *Opera*, PL 125–6.

Hobbes, Thomas, *Leviathan*, ed. M. Oakeshott, Oxford, 1955.

Honorius Augustodunensis, *Opera*, PL 172.

Hume, David, *Dialogues Concerning Natural Religion*, ed. N. Kemp-Smith, Edinburgh/London, 1947.

Jansen, Cornelius, 'Correspondence', ed. J. Orcibal, *Les origines du jansenisme*, Bibliothèque de la R.H.E. 25 (1947).

Lupus of Ferrières, *Opera*, PL 119.

Luther, Martin, *Werke*, ed. J.C.F. Knaake *et al.*, Weimar, 1883–   .

Otloh of St Emmeram, *Opera*, PL 146.

Prosper of Aquitaine, *Opera*, PL 51, English tr. by P. de Lether of works in defence of Augustine, Ancient Christian Writers 32 (1963).

Rabanus Maurus, *Opera*, PL 107–12.

Russell, Bertrand, *What I Believe*, New York, 1929, p. 29.

Smaragdus, *Opera*, PL 102.

Schopenhauer, F., *Collected Works*, ed. J. Frauenstädt, 6 vols., Leipzig, 1873–4.

Suggestions for Further Reading

I *General*

Andresen, C. *Bibliographia Augustiniana*, Darmstadt, 1973, contains a full bibliography.

Augustinus Magister, Congrès international augustinien, 3 vols., Paris, 1954.

Battenhouse, R. *A Companion to the Study of St. Augustine*, Oxford, 1955.

Bonner, G. *St. Augustine of Hippo: Life and Controversies*, London/Philadelphia, 1964.

Burnaby, J. *Amor Dei: A Study of the Religion of St. Augustine; The Hulsean Lectures for 1938*, London.

Huftier, M. *Le tragique de la condition chrétienne chez S. Augustin* (Tournai, 1964).

Portalié, E. 'Augustin', 'Augustinianisme', *Dictionnaire de théologie catholique*, vol. I (1903), *A Guide to the Thought of St. Augustine*, tr. R.J. Bastian, introduction by V.J. Bourke, Chicago, 1960.

Teselle, E. *Augustine the Theologian*, New York, 1970.

BIBLIOGRAPHY

II *Biography*

Possidius *Life of St. Augustine*, tr. M.M. Müller and R.J. Deferrari, New York, 1953.

Brown, P. *Augustine of Hippo*, London, 1967.

III *The Confessions*

Courcelle, P. *Recherches sur 'Les Confessions' de saint Augustin*, Paris, 1950.
  'Les Confessions' de saint Augustin dans la tradition littéraire; antécédents et posterité, Paris, 1963.

O'Connell, R.J. *St. Augustine's 'Confessions'*, Cambridge, Mass., 1969.

IV *Education*

Cochrane, C.N. *Christianity and Classical Culture*, London, 1944.

Finaert, J. *S. Augustin rhéteur*, Paris, 1939.
  'L'évolution littéraire de S. Augustin, Paris, 1939.

Marrou, H.I. *Augustin et la fin de la culture antique*, Paris, 1938.

V *Conversion*

Nock, A.D. *Conversion: the Old and the New in Religion from Alexander the Great to Augustine of Hippo*, Oxford, 1933.

VI *Neoplatonism and Christian Philosophy*

Alfaric, P. *L'évolution intellectuelle de Saint Augustin*, vol. I, Paris, 1918.

Armstrong, A.H. *St. Augustine and Christian Platonism*, Villanova, 1967.

Boyer, C. *Christianisme et néoplatonisme dans la formation de Saint Augustin*, Paris, 1920, repr., 1953.

Callahan, J. *Augustine and the Greek Philosophers*, Villanova, 1967.

Gilson, E. *Introduction à l'étude de S. Augustin*, Paris, 1929, tr. as *The Christian Philosophy of St. Augustine*, New York, 1960.

Hadot, P. *Porphyre et Victorinus*, 2 vols., Paris, 1968.

König, E. *Augustinus Philosophus: Christlicher Glaube und philosophisches Denken in den Frühschriften Augustins*, Munich, 1970 (= Studia et testimonia antiqua 11).

Markus, R.A. 'Marius Victorinus and Augustine', in *The Cambridge History of Later Greek and Early Mediaeval Thought*, ed. A.W. Armstrong, Cambridge, 1967.

O'Meara, J.J. *The Young Augustine: the Growth of St. Augustine's Mind up to his Conversion*, London/New York/Toronto, 1954.

Walis, R.T. *Neoplatonism*, London, 1972.

VII *Man's Knowledge of God*

Andersen, J.F. *St. Augustine on Being: a Metaphysical Essay*, The Hague, 1965.

Bourke, V.J. *Augustine's View of Reality*, Villanova, 1964.

Holte, R. *Béatitude et sagesse; S. Augustin et le problème de la fin de l'homme dans la philosophie ancienne*, Paris, 1962.

Nash, R.H. *The Light of the Mind: Augustine's Theory of Knowledge*, Kentucky, 1969.

O'Connell, R.J. *St. Augustine's Early Theory of Man, A.D. 386–91*, Cambridge, Mass., 1968.

Polman, A.D.R. *The Word of God according to St. Augustine*, London, 1961.

VIII *The City of God*

Barrow, R.H. *Introduction to St. Augustine: The City of God*, London, 1950.

IX *Pelagius*

Evans, R.F. *Pelagius: Inquiries and Reappraisals*, London/New York, 1968.

Ferguson, J. *Pelagius*, Cambridge, 1956.

Plinval, G. de *Pélage, ses écrits, sa vie et sa réforme*, Lausanne, 1943.

X *Free Will, Predestination and Grace*

Boyer, C. 'Le système de Saint Augustin sur la grâce', in *Essais sur la doctrine de Saint Augustin*, Paris, 1931.

Huftier, H. *Libre arbitre, liberté et péché chez S. Augustin*, Louvain, 1968 (Analecta Medievalia Namurcensia 4).

Rondet, H. *Gratia Christi*, Paris, 1948.

XI *Augustine and After*

Lubac, H. de *Augustinisme et théologie moderne*, Paris, 1965, tr. as *Augustinianism and Modern Theology*, London, 1969.

INDEX

absurdity 63
Academics, Academy 17, 18, 19, 72
Adeodatus 21, 25, 27, 54, 175
Adam 5, 82, 83, 84, 85, 117, 123, 124,
　125, 126, 128, 130, 132, 144, 166,
　167, 170, 174, 178
Alan of Lille 178, 180
Albert the Great 181
Alexander of Hales 181
Alger of Liège 177
Ambrose 15, 18, 19, 20, 21, 22, 60
Ambrosiaster 141
angels 83, 84, 94–5, 101, 102, 105, 106,
　167, 170
Anselm of Canterbury 51, 67, 98, 117,
　146, 175, 176, 177, 179; *Proslogion*
　51
Antichrist 106
Apuleius 102
Aristotle 32, 179; *Categories* 32, 33
Aquinas, Thomas 29, 182, 183
astrology 1, 15, 92
augurs 107
Augustine
　conversion 22, 32, 59
　the pear-tree episode 3
　works mentioned
　　C. Acad. 18, 24, 30
　　C. Jul. 145
　　Conf. 1, 2, 4, 23, 26, 29, 33, 45,
　　　51, 54, 58, 59, 64, 76, 121, 129
　　Contra Mendacium 66
　　De Beata Vita 24, 45, 150
　　De Bon. Conj. 144
　　De Civ. Dei 57, 100
　　De Doct. Chr. 53
　　De Gen. ad Litt. 45, 46, 47, 49, 60,
　　　81
　　De Gen. c. Man. 59
　　De Grat. Chr. 71
　　De Lib. Arb. 51, 60, 97, 112, 128,
　　　148
　　De Mag. 53, 54
　　De Mend. 65–6, 71

De Mor, Ecc. Cath. 74
De Nat. et Grat. 120, 133
De Nuptiis 144
De Ord. 91, 129
De Pec. Mer. 123, 133
De Per. Just. Hom. 152
De Trin. 58, 60, 61
De Ut. Cred. 74, 112
De Vid. Deo 61
Enchiridion 71, 166
Fund. Ep. 35
Retractiones 112, 122, 128, 139
Sol. 49, 52
authority 58–9

baptism 130–2
becoming 32
Bede 173
being 32, 34
Berengar of Tours 146
Bernard of Clairvaux 177
Bible 10, 11, 12, 14, 19–20, 59–61, 63,
　64, 65, 69, 75, 77, 78, 79, 84, 90, 93,
　100, 124, 154
'bodily images' *passim*
body 13, 14, 38, 41–7
Boethius 37, 39, 49, 94; *Consolation of
　Philosophy* 94
Bonaventure 181

Caecilianus 28
Caesarius of Arles 172
Carolingians 33
Carthage 4, 7, 10, 16, 18, 20, 27, 28,
　55, 122, 123
Carthage, Synod of 139
Cassian 171
Cassiciacum 23, 24, 25, 26, 27, 42, 49,
　53, 57, 58, 59, 60, 67, 91, 93, 112,
　113, 114
Cassiodorus 32
Categoriae Decem 33
Celestius 123, 139, 140, 145
Celsus 19–20

195